Escape from Cuba

Escape from Cuba

Personal Accounts of Those Who Fled Castro's Regime

Edited by ELOY L. NUÑEZ *and* ERNEST G. VENDRELL

McFarland & Company, Inc., Publishers
Jefferson, North Carolina

The editors of this book have pledged to donate 100 percent
of the royalties to the following charitable organizations:
Cuban Exile History Museum
Rotary International *PolioPlus* Campaign
St. Jude's Children Hospital
Wounded Warriors

ISBN (print) 978-1-4766-7604-3
ISBN (ebook) 978-1-4766-3656-6

LIBRARY OF CONGRESS AND BRITISH LIBRARY
CATALOGUING DATA ARE AVAILABLE

Library of Congress Control Number 2019053925

© 2020 Eloy L. Nuñez and Ernest G. Vandrell. All rights reserved

*No part of this book may be reproduced or transmitted in any form
or by any means, electronic or mechanical, including photocopying
or recording, or by any information storage and retrieval system,
without permission in writing from the publisher.*

Front cover image © 2020 Serge Geras/Shutterstock

Printed in the United States of America

McFarland & Company, Inc., Publishers
Box 611, Jefferson, North Carolina 28640
www.mcfarlandpub.com

Table of Contents

Preface
    Eloy L. Nuñez   1

Dream of a Free Cuba
    Luis O. Rodriguez   5

Facing the Possibility of Never Returning
    Ramón Luis Núñez   22

The Land of My Father
    Eloy L. Nuñez   36

Two Lives and Two Countries
    Diego Luis Mella   73

The Journey: Faith and Trust in a Time of Uncertainty
    Ernest G. Vendrell *and* David Ernesto Vendrell   90

My Pedro Pan Story
    Oscar Vigoa   114

A New City, a New Country, a New Life
    Mirta Solis Nuñez   138

Return to Playa Larga: The Story of Jesus Delgado
    Luis O. Rodriguez   153

Of Cuban Concentration Camps and the Struggle
    for Freedom: The Stories of Noel S. Varela, Henry Choren
    and Jorge Luis Brito
    Luis O. Rodriguez   164

Memories
    Corina Fernández-Máscaró   180

A Long Road to Freedom
    Francisco Pérez Sabatier   190

Epilogue
    Ernest G. Vendrell   210

About the Contributors   213

Glossary   216

Index   227

Preface

Eloy L. Nuñez

The darkness came over the island of Cuba on January 1, 1959. It is a darkness that persists to this day. It did not come suddenly or unexpectedly. As with all things evil, there were signs of what was to come. These signs were seen by a few, but were ignored by many others.

It should not have been a surprise to anyone. As with many calamities, events unfolded slowly at first, only to speed up at the end. Clearly, there were early signs—some would recognize the horrors to come but feared to acknowledge their suspicions publicly. Anger, disgust, a sense of euphoria, and a great deal of wishful thinking clouded the judgment of many.

It must have been the same in Russia in the years leading up to 1917, the year the Bolsheviks took power. Or in the years leading up to January 1933—when Adolf Hitler was appointed as Chancellor of Germany. In all these cases, the darkness crept in slowly—innocuously at first—and gathered momentum. Fidel Castro's rise to power—and Vladimir Lenin's, and Adolf Hitler's—all have much in common. All three historical events led to the death or misery of millions. All three started slowly and all three seemed unlikely to succeed. All three reached a critical point where history could have—and should have—changed forever, and the slaughter of millions of innocents may have been averted. But it was not.

The critical turning point for Lenin was when he returned from exile, years after being arrested for sedition in Czarist Russia. The critical point for Hitler came when he was pardoned and released from jail, after serving only nine months of a five-year prison term for attempting a coup d'état against the German government in 1923. Likewise, Fidel Castro's rise to power may have been averted had he not been released years early from a 15-year term by then Cuban president Fulgencio Batista. Like Hitler and Lenin, Castro had been jailed for attempting to overthrow the government. All three had been unsuccessful in their first attempts. Lenin for encouraging insurrection.

Hitler for his failed "Beer Hall Putsch," and Castro for his unsuccessful raid on the Moncada Barracks in 1952. Against all odds, all three of these men survived violent insurrections, imprisonment, and/or exile. Yet all three would come back with a sense of vengeance to topple the governments that had shown mercy to them.

The similarities in the stories of Lenin, Hitler, and Castro makes one wonder what could have happened if these men had not been released from prison prematurely or allowed to come back from exile. It also makes one wonder how many other potential tyrants have been unsuccessful because they were either killed or neutralized in such a way as to render them incapable of overthrowing a sitting government. One also has to wonder if it had not been for Lenin, Hitler, and Castro, perhaps a Leon Trotsky, or a Rudolf Hess, or a José Antonio Echeverría could have taken their places. The identities of any of these lesser-known men could have come to historical prominence, had it not been for their unfortunate missteps. It is quite disconcerting to believe that for every successful despot in human history, there could well have been a thousand unsuccessful ones that we will never know about, or that became mere footnotes in history.

History is replete with stories of false messiahs and despots who rose to power by a mixture of personality traits, including charisma, egomaniacal tendencies, and a sociopathic disregard for the basic human rights of others. Thugs typically capture peoples' admiration at first with charisma, and then hold their peoples' loyalties with fear and terror. And in the cases of Lenin, Hitler, Pol Pot, Mao, and Fidel Castro, a great deal of good fortune also had to occur for them to ascend to their positions. But none of these men, or the tens of thousands that would have ostensibly taken their places, would have been successful had it not been for a compliant population that allowed them to come to power. All of these men started with a minuscule group of devoted followers. In every one of these cases, the vast majority of the population either didn't pay attention, or didn't care because nothing was happening to them personally and directly. Ignorance, apathy, indifference, and lack of moral courage among the general population are the ingredients that allowed these men to come to power and to lead their people to eventual ruin.

This book is not a history book. It is not about Fidel Castro. It is about the personal stories of individuals and their families. The backdrop of mass movements of refugees and the mass extermination of the people involved serves only as an historical context for these stories. This book is *not* about "big history." It is about history at its most basic and granular level. It's about real people and how they survived and even thrived in the most difficult of situations.

This book tells the stories of the Cuban exile experience. It is told from the perspective of different writers. Some were young men and women at the time of the revolution. Others were just children. The stories take place in Cuba and in the United States. There are stories about those who risked everything and left their families and homes behind to seek freedom. There are also stories of those who stayed behind, with no other recourse but to adapt to the miseries of their new existence. There are stories about food rationing and forced labor camps as well as stories of false imprisonment and "show" trials whereby the guilt of the accused had been predetermined. There are stories about bearded thugs ransacking innocent peoples' homes for no other reason than because they could. The authors relate stories about the fear of having a child say something in public that could get them arrested by the secret police, in addition to experiences of firing squads, betrayals of trust and neighbors turning against other neighbors to settle grudges or to deflect suspicion from themselves. The authors also discuss randomness, and how the slightest smile or laughter, or a song at the wrong time or the wrong place, could be perceived as an affront to the revolution and result in a radical change of one's life.

Above all, these stories are about the courage of a few who dared to stand up and fight against tyranny. They exemplify the resolve and resourcefulness of a Cuban exile community that has adapted and thrived in the United States and elsewhere. The stories feature successful exiles who have become doctors, lawyers, police officers, teachers, actors, community leaders, and U.S. congressmen and senators. The final words of these stories have yet to be written. It should not surprise anyone who reads this book if a child or grandchild of a Cuban exile were to become the president of the United States someday.

The stories in this book show how the human spirit and desire to be free cannot ever be broken. A darkness has come over and enveloped a once beautiful country. These stories demonstrate that the light can never be extinguished.

Note to the Readers in Regard to Spanish Accents

Throughout this book, the reader will encounter apparent inconsistencies in the use of Spanish language accents. In coediting this work I've discovered the use of accents is not as standardized as one might expect. I had anticipated some variance based on geographic or cultural factors, but I had no idea that the inconsistencies would be so consistent. In the original manuscripts there were differences in the way that some families noted accents on their names. There were even some differences of opinion about the proper use of accents *within* families. In fact, within my family. I discovered my big brother Luis uses an accent over the letter "u" of our last name (as in Núñez). That was news to me. While this brought a brief moment of dissonance, I ascribed it to my artist brother's application of creative license.

    A great deal of effort was made to reconcile the variances in the use of accents throughout the text. Whenever I encountered a different accentuation, I usually went with the most conventional use. But as with the case of my brother's adoption of Núñez, when an inconsistency represents the author's perspective, I simply went with the preference of each particular writer.

    Eloy Nuñez (AKA Eloy Núñez)

Dream of a Free Cuba

Luis O. Rodriguez

My name is Luis O. Rodriguez and I am a representative of the over one million Cubans who, since 1959, have chosen exile rather than enslavement under a tyrannical communist regime. This story is based on my experience and that of my family while living in Cuba under Fidel Castro's oppressive, communist dictatorship and our later assimilation into American society.

I must sadly state that my account is one of thousands of similar life stories experienced by most Cuban families since 1959. Even today, only ninety miles away from Key West and just on the opposite side of the Gulf of Mexico, there live more than ten million Cuban citizens who have experienced similar abuses and, unlike my family and I, have been unable to escape from Castro's Cuba.

I believe that to understand what brought Cubans to the shores of the United States (U.S.), we must examine our past and identify the causes that led to such migration and exile. Earlier historical events, such as the exclusion of Cuban citizens from the discussions of the Paris Treaty that followed the Spanish American War, the subsequent occupation of Cuba by U.S. forces, the introduction of the Platt Amendment and the forced placement of Don Tomás Estrada Palma as Cuba's first president over more qualified Cuban war patriots, would be utilized by Castro as causes to fuel anti–American fervor in Cuban society and justify his Revolution. No matter how we deny it to ourselves, our republic always stood on unsteady grounds and the 1952 *coup d'état* by Fulgencio Batista sealed our fate. Yet, no single event, not even the repressive Spanish *Concentración* of the 1890s or the dictatorial *Machadato* of the early 1930s, has had a more devastating effect than Castro's Revolution. It is that infamous event and the destruction of Cuban society by a psychopath named Fidel Castro that opened the floodgates for our exodus.

My Exile Origins

My uncle, Luis Rodriguez, was our family patriarch. The son of an Asturian immigrant, he held the family together following the death of my grandfather in 1933. Through hard work and perseverance, my uncle saved enough money to establish a respectable hardware store in the central area of *Pinar del Río*. By 1961, the communist government had appropriated his hardware store and the future of the family appeared very bleak.

Our exile story began one night in 1961, as my uncle and his family gathered for dinner. The discussion of exile was set in motion by my 14-year-old cousin Miriam, when she engaged my uncle in conversation regarding her desire to migrate from Cuba to the U.S. Though very young at the time, Miriam had already experienced firsthand the callousness of the communist government at her school and she had an inner desire to live her life away from Cuba in a country where freedom of speech and religion are guaranteed civil rights.

Upon hearing of Miriam's desire to migrate to the U.S., my uncle became upset and told her that he would not permit her to depart from Cuba. I can only imagine what thoughts must have raced through my uncle's mind upon hearing such a request. On the one hand, my uncle understood that Cuba would never be the same again after Castro and, on the other, the thought of permitting his precious 14-year old daughter to migrate into the unknown must have horrified him and caused great pain.

In order to defuse the situation, my uncle asked Miriam to accompany him for a walk around the city's business district. As they walked side-by-side down the street that early evening, my cousin noticed a truck in the distance. Sitting on the open truck bed were a group of disheveled young girls. My

My uncle Macho and Irma's wedding in the late 1950s. My young cousin Miriam is standing on the left (Luis O. Rodriguez).

cousin quickly recognized them as girls who performed "volunteer work" in nearby farms for the new communist regime. Seizing the moment, Miriam pointed to the truck and she uttered to my uncle, "If you do not let me go, that will be my future very soon." Those words must have deeply hurt my uncle, but in hindsight, they were the right words to say at the time. It was at that exact moment that my uncle decided to allow my young cousin to migrate to the U.S. Upon returning home, my uncle told my cousin he would set the process in motion and he would send her abroad. The impending exile had just torn the fabric of our family.

My cousin Miriam would migrate from Cuba later that year as a member of the Catholic Church's Pedro Pan Operation. She lived at a camp in Florida City upon her arrival in the U.S., and subsequently also lived with foster parents in Miami. Eventually, she was flown to far away Wichita, Kansas, where she spent the next five years in a foster home, and later reunited with her parents and younger brother. My cousin would be apart from her family for her *quinces*, (a rite of passage for every young Cuban girl), and many other significant occasions. She would live a frugal life for several years and I'm sure, on many nights, she must have cried herself to sleep as she fought her loneliness. Yet, her strength never faltered and she survived it all. It is to her indomitable spirit and my uncle's love of family that I owe my freedom. Were

My cousin Iliana's birthday in 1964 (Luis O. Rodriguez).

it not for my cousin's courage and my uncle's resolve to send for us, my life would have been very different and just maybe not even worth living.

My Recollection

"*El hombre vence las dificultades*" (a man can defeat all adversities). This phrase was said to me by my 12-year-old friend as we partook in a friendly game of marbles and I complained out loud about my poor marble playing skills. It happened in 1969 at my old *barrio,* and I was barely six years old at the time.

That remark made me think that something was not right with my native country of Cuba. After all, why would a six-year-old child, such as I, need to act like a "man" or defeat any "adversities." All I cared about was playing marbles. Maybe, the phrase my friend uttered had something to do with those murals of gun-toting, bearded men I saw posted throughout my neighborhood, or those hour-long political speeches from a loud and boisterous man dressed in a green olive uniform that appeared every time I tuned in to a radio station or watched television. Several years would go by before I could comprehend that communist dogma was alive and well in Cuba. Castro's dictatorial tentacles of hate and destruction had extended even to a meaningless game of marbles played by children in a nondescript sandlot of my native city of Pinar del Río. It is from the age of six onward that the experiences I lived in Cuba became vivid in my mind.

My paternal grandfather, Tiburcio Rodriguez, was a *guajiro* (country person). He was a descendant of immigrants of the Canary Islands and he owned a small farm that he had purchased with the sweat of his brow several decades earlier, before Fidel Castro came to rule Cuba. My grandfather's farm was located in Ceja

My dear grandfather Tiburcio enjoying a good cigar at his farm (Luis O. Rodriguez).

del Negro, on the 12th kilometer of Viñales Road. The area is historically known as the place where in the 1890s, *mambí* General Antonio Maceo's army fought its bloodiest battle against the Spaniards.

My paternal grandfather could barely read or write and cared very little about politics, Castro's Revolution, or the changes that were occurring in Havana in 1959. His true loves were tending to his land, caring for his livestock and raising his 12 children. My grandfather's world was sent into turmoil in 1961 when Castro introduced his Agrarian Reform, an organized excuse by the communist regime to deprive citizens of their rightfully owned land and property.

Castro's Agrarian Reform, enforced at gunpoint, led to the seizure of a large segment of my grandfather's farm. My grandfather was left with a small piece of land for personal use and from that point forward, he was forced to sell the tobacco and produce he farmed to a government distributor at significantly reduced prices. The blatant theft of my grandfather's land turned my entire family into die hard anti-communists and though none of my family members resorted to violence against the regime, we were identified as second-class citizens for the remainder of our days in Cuba. In exchange for the theft of property, Castro promised *alfabetisación*, a thinly veiled government program disguised as an attempt to teach peasants how to read and write, but it was really intended to recruit government support and spread communist propaganda.

As I grew older, I learned from my mother that in 1965 my father was convinced that there was no future left for us in Cuba. He notified the local immigration office of his intention to travel to the U.S. My father's decision was viewed as an open act of defiance by the Cuban government, and he was immediately fired from his construction job and confined to a forced labor camp. In the eyes of the Cuban government, anyone who disagreed with its communist philosophy was a counter-revolutionary and a traitor to the homeland.

In Cuba, families identified as *counter-revolutionary* were constantly monitored by the government's Committees for the Defense of the Revolution (CDR). The CDRs are a government sponsored program that selected one residence and its occupants in every city block and empowered them as the "eyes and ears" of the government. The citizens selected to run the CDRs were the most ardent communists in the block. Those undesirable lackeys chosen for the task were bestowed with the authority to march through your home at any time of day or night and randomly conduct searches as they attempted to locate what they considered "anti-government propaganda" or "black market" products. The true intention of the program was to institute a constant state of terror in Cuban society. Many citizens were pushed to commit suicide or suffered from irreversible mental illness as a result of the continued harassment applied by government programs such as the CDRs.

By 1965, forced labor camps had become the norm for dissidents in Cuba. The camps were established by the government to house citizens who declared their intent to migrate from Cuba to the U.S. At these concentration camps, men were forced to work the fields "for the good of the revolution" in what amounted to no less than state authorized slavery. Even more draconian labor camps, such as the UMAP, were established and utilized by the government as "rehabilitating" centers for homosexuals and other individuals that the Cuban government labeled as deviant or "politically immoral." Entire families were removed from their neighborhoods, such as citizens of the Escambray region, and were resettled in similar camps. A particular camp in Sandino, Pinar del Río, was established and filled to capacity with such citizens with the sole intent to cleanse countryside areas of government dissent and armed opposition.

My mother and I would visit my father at those labor camps from time to time, and the conditions those men worked under were deplorable and not too far distant from what was experienced by Jewish victims during World War II or by Soviet citizens in the Siberian gulags. I will never forget seeing my father at a camp during the course of a visit. He was being forced to work in the fields cutting sugarcane while shoeless and wearing nothing but pants made from the cloth of a potato sack. That image haunts me to this day. I strongly believe the Cuban government would have exterminated its own dissidents were it not for international pressure.

As the years rolled by, I learned that in the late 1960s my older brother had been jailed at a prison by the Castro government for simply refusing to continue his obligatory military service in the Cuban army after his four-year stint expired. Years later, I would learn that in the 1970s my brother was "treated" with electro shocks at a government hospital named Guanito to "correct" his political leanings. The harm done by the Castro regime to my brother affected him to the day he passed away at the relatively young age of 62. He was an unaccounted victim of Castro's regime.

Also in the late 1960s, my sister was prohibited from practicing her profession as a schoolteacher due to the fact that she too had applied to migrate to the U.S. Other family members fared much worse. In the case of my cousin, *El Niño*, and his father, Eugenio, they were held in various detention facilities for months at a time for merely being suspected of "counter revolutionary activities." *El Niño* would tell the story of how, on more than one occasion, several guards transported him to a countryside field and pretended to prepare for his "execution" via firing squad. Just prior to his "execution" he would be asked to confess for crimes he had not committed and to provide information of other "crimes" committed by his "associates." Being innocent and having nothing to say, *El Niño* would prepare for death at the hands of the firing squad only to be laughed at by the guards as they yelled "fire" and pulled the triggers of empty rifles.

Another victim of the Cuban government was my young cousin Manolo. He was 17 years old when he was removed from his family in the town of Minas de Matahambre by the authorities and sent away to an UMAP camp. His mother, Nica, in her mid-forties, would not survive the pain and suffering of seeing her young son in a concentration camp and she succumbed to a heart attack. Her death was another unaccounted casualty of Castro's senseless tyranny.

As a child, I too dealt with the daily political barrage by the Cuban government. Every hour of the day I was reminded by teachers, sports coaches, neighborhood CDR officials, etc., that as a member of a family intent on migrating from Cuba to the land of the "enemy" (the U.S.), I amounted to a second-class citizen in my own country. The daily dose of hate spewed by government officials against non-sympathizers served to instill doubt and fear, even on a defenseless child.

I remember distinctively the epithets uttered against "our kind." We were referred to as *gusanos* (worms), *apátridas* (one lacking a nationality), or "mercenaries." As the years evolved, other dismissive words would be utilized against the later generations of dissidents. Insults such as *marielitos* (those who departed Cuba in 1980 from the port city of Mariel), *escoria* (human waste) or *balseros* (rafters) became part of the Cuban government lingo utilized to demean and offend anyone who challenged Castro's government authority. I too remember the constant lunacy of government officials preparing for "an imperialist attack" from the U.S. that most citizens longed for, but never came.

In 1971, after serving five years of confinement in forced labor camps, my father was permitted to migrate to Spain by the Cuban government, though the rest of the family was not permitted to travel with him. I must state that some of my father's friends who suffered the iniquities of those concentration camps would reveal to me years later that my father was punished repeatedly by the camp guards for speaking out against the injustices the laborers suffered at the hands of the guards. I was also informed that my father was accustomed to hard work and at times, when finished with his assigned field duties, he would help other sick, injured or simply heartbroken men to finish their tasks. For his courage and love of family, I will always be indebted to my father.

Later that year, as an eight-year-old, my mother and I received notice from the government that we had been granted permission to travel to the U.S. My mother and I then made our way to Varadero Beach, the location from where we were to depart. I distinctively remember seeing the airplane that was to transport us to freedom on the tarmac, and I remember the excitement of thinking that I would be riding in an airplane for the first time and that we would be one step closer to reuniting with my father. All of our hopes and dreams came suddenly crashing down when we were told prior to boarding that there was a missing document. We were told that we would not be able to travel to the U.S., and were ordered to return to our hometown. I remember pulling on my mother's dress and telling her to argue that "we have to travel so I can be with my father." It was not to be. No one heard our pleas nor did they care for our pain. We were ushered out of the airport and driven to a bus station. Much was said by the Cuban government about the Elian affair. No one knows our story.

Dropped off at the bus station, my mother and I were penniless, hungry, and with no means to return home. Luckily, the Lord watches over its most desperate servants and a bus station employee noticed us sitting on a bench in deep despair. I remember him asking us what had happened. Upon listening to our sad story, he walked over to the ticket counter and bought us return tickets for home. I will never know the name of that incredible soul who performed that act of kindness for my mother and I, but as long as I live I will remember that even in the darkest of hours, there are good people in this world and the sun will always rise the next day for the most destitute.

Soon after returning home, we were shocked to learn that the so-called "freedom flights" to the U.S. had been halted indefinitely and we would not be able to migrate from Cuba. Three long years would pass before my mother and I were finally permitted to travel to Spain to join my father. Those three years would be marked with hunger, anxiety, and the ever-present sense of loss. At times, we felt as though our family would never again be reunited.

In 1974, my mother and I were finally permitted to travel to Spain. We boarded an Iberia Airlines jet, and on a cold February morning we set off for Madrid. Left behind were my brother, sister, niece, and the rest of my family. They would remain at the mercy of an inconsiderate government that cared little about family reunification or the rights of its citizens. Left behind were also my childhood memories of running through the countryside, the song of the *tomeguin*, the spinning *trompos*, and the sweet smell of my grandmother Cuca's roses.

Our arrival in Madrid was a blessing for us. When my father had arrived in 1971, he had been unable to find employment. He had seen help wanted postings on a building that was under construction, and he went in the office to apply. He was then told *"hay trabajo, pero solo para los Españoles"* (there is work, but only for Spaniards). Distraught, he eventually stumbled into a Chinese restaurant named El Aguila de Oro in the Tirso de Molina neighborhood and was hired as a dishwasher.

By the time of our arrival in 1974, my father had proven his worth and was now in charge of the restaurant's kitchen. By then, he was an accomplished Chinese chef able to prepare 40 delicious entrees for satisfied customers. Leave it to a Cuban peasant to migrate to Madrid and find work in a Chinese restaurant! If there is a quality us Cubans are known for, it is our ability to adapt to any situation. My father certainly had that quality.

In Madrid, we lived in a spacious two-bedroom apartment near the Ventas bull-fighting arena. I remember walking down Alcala Street and tasting freedom for the first time in my life. I recall strolling past a theatre and seeing the James Bond movie *The Man with the Golden Gun* advertised on a poster. I saw toy stores and cafeterias that served anything you cared to eat. I remember walking into the department store El Corte Inglés and wondering if I was dreaming. Little did I know at the time that all those things and much more had been available in Cuba prior to Castro's arrival. It would take me years to fill in the holes left by the propaganda and disinformation of Castro's educational system.

It was easy to mingle with Spaniards. We shared the same heritage and last names with those citizens. Though my father worked most of the time to provide for my mother and me, it was there in Madrid that I began to notice the difference between a free society and the island prison that I had lived in for the previous 11 years of my life. Spain was a great layover, but the objective was always traveling to the U.S. That fact was never disputed or questioned.

My Dad and me in Madrid, at Ventas bull fighting ring (Luis O. Rodriguez).

After a three month stay in Spain, my parents and I traveled to the U.S., ready to begin our new life in the land of opportunity. My sister and niece would join us in 1976 and my brother, the last of our immediate family members to migrate to the U.S., would arrive in Key West, Florida, in 1980, through the Mariel exodus. Left behind would be grandparents, aunts, uncles and cousins, most never to be seen again. Our experience was by no means an isolated incident. The majority of Cuban families of the time suffered similar or worse fates. No one was spared by the ruthlessness of Castro's government and the puppet citizens that enforced its deeds.

Life in the U.S.

In May 1974, we traveled to the U.S. and my first sight of this country were the blue airstrip lights at Miami International Airport (MIA). I believe those lights pointed the way to freedom and a better life. Even to this day, I still rejoice when I am landing at MIA and see those blue lights. Present there that night to greet us was my cousin Miriam, the same 14-year old girl who had defied all odds back in 1961 and had chosen the road to freedom. Now 27, the mother of two children and one on the way, she was accompanied by her husband, Lee, an Anglo with a heart of gold, whose English language I could not yet understand, but whose kindness I would come to love and respect as an older brother later in life.

I remember that arrival night as though it was yesterday. Miriam and Lee drove us to Miami Beach, where we spent the night at The White House Hotel in South Beach. I recall thinking to myself that our journey to freedom had ended and our new life in America was about to begin. The following day we headed to Jacksonville, Florida to be reunited with my uncle Luis and other relatives.

My family settled in working class Hialeah, Florida. In 1974, Hialeah was still a quiet city in need of manual laborers to work in its factories. My father began to work in construction just days after our arrival. Needless to say, he was immediately employed based on his experience. From then on, my father attempted to pick up the pieces of our lives and restore our family to some sort of normality. My mother was hired at a local factory called La Campana that paid $65.00 a week. At the time, my parents were in their early fifties and never cared about being poor, but they were surely happy and thankful for the opportunity to become productive citizens in our new country.

My father rented an apartment on West 29 Street, across from Walker Park. It was at that park that I would learn to speak English, meet my new friends, play all sorts of sports, and evolve from being a Cuban exile into an American. At that park, I met kind employees who truly cared about children.

One older employee in particular, named Eddy Harris, was so committed to helping us that he even donated his own childhood sports trophies so that they could be reissued and awarded to children who played team sports at the park. Such kindness from Americans! Why then were some of my own countrymen in Cuba so cruel? Even to this day, some of my closest friends are those that grew up with me in Hialeah, and when asked about our origin, we proudly say, "I'm from Walker Park."

As I grew older and I attempted to adjust to my newly adopted country, I would often reflect on my earlier days in Cuba. Here in the U.S., I became a voracious reader and learned about the summary trials and the firing squads headed by Che Guevara in 1959 and the early 1960s at the Cabaña fortress. According to my mother, the horrific sound of the nightly firing squads also resonated from Cuartel Loma de Los Coches, in my hometown of Pinar del Río, as it silenced the lives of men and boys, some as young as 16 years of age. Patriotic men and boys who went to their deaths screaming *"Viva Cristo Rey!"* (Long live Christ our Lord) and *"Viva Cuba Libre!"* (Long live a free Cuba).

Here in the U.S. I learned that those young men who fought valiantly and spilled their blood in Bahía de Cochinos during the failed Bay of Pigs invasion in 1961 were not "mercenaries" as portrayed by the Castro regime, but rather patriotic Cuban men who tried to return Cuba's freedom. Here, I also learned how in 1962, Castro's Soviet folly placed the world at the brink of a nuclear Armageddon. I also learned about Castro's draconian Isle of Pines political prison and the torture of its prisoners. Sadly, it was also here in exile that I learned about the mid–1970s decision by the Cuban government to flood thousands of acres of land encompassing what little remained of my grandfather's small farm in Ceja del Negro to create a tourist game preserve. My grandfather, an 87-year-old a man by this time, was forcibly relocated

Me (Luis) in Pinar del Río, eight years old. Photograph dedicated to my exiled father (Luis O. Rodriguez).

to a small nearby town prior to the area being flooded to make way for "progress." Grandfather Tiburcio would survive this last affront for a period of six months before passing away. We believe sadness and despair played a role in his death. He was known to say "a man without land amounts to nothing."

Throughout those early years of exile, we enjoyed the great opportunities offered by this land of milk and honey and we shared many happy occasions, though never forgetting those we had left behind or the inner turmoil of our country of origin. I remember trying to act as "American" as possible in school and all other activities. In my new world, there was no room for Celia Cruz, dominoes or *guayaberas*. In my view at the time, those were implements of a past that had to be cast aside. How wrong I was! That Cuban heritage nostalgia would hit me years later with the force of a freight train.

The 1970s in South Florida were violent times as well. In 1975, as I rode my bus to school, I heard the news on the radio that an exiled Batista henchman named Rolando "El Tigre" Masferrer had been blown up in his car as he drove in the vicinity of Kendall. Not long afterwards, I also learned about radio newscaster Emilio Milián's near fatal car bombing. Milián was an honorable man who spoke openly against anti–Castro violence on his show *Habla el Pueblo*. Bombings of Cuban exile owned businesses, the FBI office, a U.S. Post Office, as well as political assassinations of those perceived to be Cuban government collaborators became the norm in Miami in those days. Many exiles from my parents' generation, could not bring themselves to condemn such acts of sabotage or terrorism. As hard as they tried, as a wise, older FBI agent would later confide, those exiles "had a dog in the fight."

The most profound incident I remember from those early days was the 1976 bombing attack of a Cubana Airlines flight that resulted in the death of 73 Cuban citizens, including the entire Cuban fencing team that had just won gold medals in the Central American Caribbean Championships. The incident is believed by many to this day to have been perpetrated by Cuban exiles. The incident made me wonder if those young men and women who perished on that fateful flight cared at all for Castro's Revolution and whether their deaths were as callous as those of the young men who were executed by Castro's firing squads. This was exile, and along with the good experiences, came the grudges of old.

I believe those acts of violence (allegedly perpetrated by Cuban exile men) would later in life forge my resolve to enter the law enforcement field. The opinion I held at that time (and still uphold to this day) is that the disdain that we share as Cuban exiles for all things related to Castro must be restrained. There is no room in our newly adopted homeland for such disregard of the law. Resorting to violence to avenge violence is not the ethical or moral way.

Professional Life

In 1984, as a 21-year-old, I joined the Miami-Dade Police Department (MDPD) and in 1986, I married Orquidea, my wife and soul mate, and mother of our two children, Ryan and Kathy. In 1992, MDPD detached me to Miami's FBI Joint Terrorism Task Force. I would spend the next ten years of my career there as a detective focused on matters related to the Cuban government and its exiles. My work assignments covered the gamut, from paramilitary camps in west Miami-Dade and Immokalee, to bombings of freight forwarding agencies, aquatic drive by shootings of Cuban hotels, to the 1996 downing of the Brothers to the Rescue (BTTR) airplanes and the Elian Gonzalez crisis.

The investigations I participated in clarified many things for me. To this day, I am fully convinced that the Cuban intelligence service has played a major role in every significant incident related to Cuban exiles in our area and Latin America. Penetrating Cuban exile paramilitary and social groups and disseminating anti-exile propaganda throughout the world has been a highly regarded mission of the Cuban government.

I have also learned that the Cuban government is not a legitimate government in the true sense of the word. The Cuban government is in control of an island prison, headed by two organized crime figures known as Fidel and Raul Castro. The only difference between the Cuban government and traditional Cosa Nostra crime families is that the Castros have possessed a military system that numbers in the thousands at their disposal, and it has free reign and a limitless budget to operate worldwide without facing political or legal repercussions.

The Cuban government has also played a quiet role in establishing U.S. based criminal trends. It has profited from activities ranging from *bolita* gambling operations since the early 1960s, to trafficking in marijuana and cocaine in the 1970s, to cargo theft since the 1980s, to Medicare and credit card fraud schemes to present day. The Cuban government has siphoned billions of dollars from the U.S. through its government operatives. For the last six decades, the Cuban government has also created, trained, and financed every leftist guerrilla that operated in Latin America, Angola, the Congo, and even Vietnam. Those guerrillas are responsible for hundreds of thousands of deaths and much suffering.

The totality of the genocide committed by the Castro regime against its own citizens will never be known. From the summary trials and executions of 1959 and later years, to imprisonment in jails filled with *tapiada* cells, to widely reported events such as the sinking of the *Trece de Marzo* tugboat and the downing of two BTTR airplanes in international air space, the list of crimes committed by the Castro regime is almost infinite. If we add the number of victims who have perished on makeshift rafts in the Gulf of Mexico, the young Cubans sent abroad to fight wars in Angola, and those who have died from the stress of their daily lives or hunger, the number of Cubans who have perished under Castro could surpass a hundred thousand.[1]

In 1998, as the lead case agent of an FBI investigation into a rash of hotel bombings that were taking place in Havana and Varadero Beach, I, along with a delegation of U.S. law enforcement officials, was ordered to visit Cuba by the FBI. In Havana, during the course of government-to-government discussions, I had the opportunity to come face-to-face with the representatives of the repressive regime that years earlier had stolen my grandfather's land, interned my father in labor camps, jailed my relatives, and turned me into a second-class citizen in my own country. I welcomed that face-to-face encounter.

I viewed my official visit to Havana as very gratifying. It became obvious to me during the course of that visit that those representatives of tormentors of old could not comprehend how an immigrant Cuban child that was forced out of his own country, would grow up and return to Cuba to stare at them in their eyes as a representative of the most powerful nation in the world.

During the course of the visit to Havana, I remember engaging two Cuban military colonels in a sidebar conversation about the differences of our law enforcement missions. The colonels mentioned they had assisted U.S. authorities in the then recent past by providing information that helped convict a South Florida homicide subject. The colonels were incredulous and they wanted to know the reason why it had "taken so long to try and convict" the subject for the heinous crime he had committed.

The colonels reminded me that in Cuba, a similar case would have called for "swift action" by the government. By "swift action," I was led to believe the colonels meant a trial by military officials, with no defense attorneys or guarantees for the accused and a quick trip to the gallows. I remember listening to their complaint, drawing on my life experience and sternly informing them that in my country (the U.S.), we have a system of laws that protects even the worst offenders with trials led by jurors, private and public defenders, and sentence appeals. I also enlightened the colonels by informing them that in the U.S., the length of a trial or the "pressures" of our society are not factors that determine a criminal prosecution since in American society, we would rather allow 99 guilty defendants to walk free than have our government imprison one innocent man. I believe my response had a profound effect on the colonels, and for the first time in their military careers, they may have understood the difference between their oppressive style of government and the liberties upheld by our courts and enjoyed by every citizen in the U.S.

I am convinced that had I not happened to be present on that trip to Havana, the Cuban government officials would have attempted to pull the wool over the eyes of the visiting U.S. officials by blaming all of their troubles on the "Cuban Mafia" (their latest epithet for our kind). One regret I have about the visit to Havana was staring at the Cuban flag that flies over the Nacional Hotel and not possessing the means to rid Cuba of its ruling scourge and returning freedom to its citizens. That dream will have to wait a bit longer.

My other regret in life is not having invested time in a joint effort with other exiles to catalog and archive the crimes committed by Castro and his henchmen and to identify those responsible for criminal acts for future identification and prosecution. It pains me to know that many of those who willingly helped Castro commit his crimes now walk among us in South Florida with impunity as members of our exile. Sometime in their lives, the government they helped implement eventually turned on them as well, and they too became victims of Castro's communist regime and exiles. I know their consciences must carry a heavy burden for they were the willing tools of the system.

The events that led to a Hialeah-raised Cuban immigrant child, growing up to represent our government in such sensitive international affairs baffles me to this day. The only explanation I have for that experience is that wonderful things happen in the U.S. This greatest of nations, full of opportunities, is a beacon of light for even the most wretched of souls.

Adjusting to our new country has not been easy for Cuban exiles and there have been some bumps along the way. Through the years, a few misguided individuals have used prejudice as a tool to slight us and make us feel unwanted here; however, for the most part, the majority of Americans we have met have shown us only kindness and have welcomed us with open arms.

As I age, I see what has been accomplished by Cuban exiles in South Florida and around our nation. From constructing beautiful skyscrapers on Brickell Avenue, to museums, to businesses of all types, I see the involvement of hard working Cuban exiles. From professionals in every field, to the arts and other sciences, Cuban exiles have demonstrated that even though adversity dealt us a bad hand, we have not been defeated, and, in fact, we have enriched our adopted country with our presence.

In time, those Cuban culture staples I once cast aside were dusted off the shelf and now help strengthen the fabric of my life. I could not dream of a world without the sound of Benny More, nor could I go a day without a shot of Cuban coffee, the promise of a mojito, a good cigar, or the distant shuffling sound of domino pieces. Enjoying those Cuban traditions does not lessen our love for the U.S., but rather, it enriches local culture and reinforces the ideals that forged this great nation. As for Cuban exiles, I compare our experience to that of a royal palm tree under the duress of a hurricane. We have been bent, but we have never been broken and we are here to tell our tale.

20 Escape from Cuba

My cousin Miriam, her husband Lee, my wife Orquidea and myself at a Pedro Pan gathering in 2016 (Luis O. Rodriguez).

I often think of Cuba as well. What does the future hold for my country of old? Many exiles are convinced that someday soon, with the passing of the Castro brothers, the communist regime and its draconian government policies will crumble into history's rubbish pile. Recently, I even heard a good piece of news from Cuba. The waters that once covered my grandfather Tiburcio's farm have been receding for some time and several of those family members we left behind long ago have located the foundation and water well of my grandfather's old farm house. I hear even fruit trees and colorful birds are starting to return to the area. That is an omen for good things to come.

I strongly believe that the day liberty and free trade returns to Cuba, the island will once again become a vibrant place and Cuban citizens will lead productive lives. On that day, the surviving members of my family and I will journey to the vicinity of where my grandfather's farm once stood and we will reminisce about the strength of character of our ancestors. My true hope is that these past six decades of pain will not be forgotten, nor repeated by the new generations of Cubans, and that the names of those victims who suffered at the hands of Castro's repressive government will be remembered for their resistance and unwillingness to kneel down before a tyrant.

NOTE

1. Garvin, Glenn. "Red Ink: The High Human Cost of the Cuban Revolution." *Miami Herald*, December 1, 2016. Accessed April 04, 2018. http://www.miamiherald.com/news/nation-world/world/americas/cuba/article118282148.html.

Facing the Possibility of Never Returning

Ramón Luis Núñez

What might have been a celebratory time for most kids my age, graduating from high school in 1957 when I was seventeen, seemed problematic. So, it was then, upon graduation time, that there were no diplomas handed out, no parties to attend or congratulations to be had. The University of Havana was closed.

It was a troubling time in Cuba, a civil war was going on, a time full of uncertainties. With nothing else to do, I went to work at Servitec, a business that my father and a group of engineers had just started a couple of years before, which specialized in aerial photography, mapping, and surveying. While working with my dad at Servitec, I decided that I enjoyed the work and I wanted to study civil engineering and specialize in mapping and surveying. I wanted to be a Civil Engineer, a Cartographer. The problem was that there was no place to go. The upheaval created by Castro's budding revolution and his commie thugs, with their bombings and assassinations and other acts of terrorism, had forced the universities to close. So, for the time being, our plans for any future we dared to dream were put on hold.

Then it happened. January 1, 1959, a day that every Cuban who lived through that time would never forget. Fidel Castro took over the country, and little did we suspect at that time that his grip would endure for more than 56 years and still counting. But we didn't know that then. For the moment, we were just hoping to get by—day to day. We didn't know then that Fidel Castro and his communist thugs would, in a short time, create such a hostile political environment that we would be forced to leave our homes, and everything and everyone in our lives behind. It was not my doing, but like any 19-year old guy without a plan, I seemed to be running into trouble as I stood against Castro's oppressive revolution.

My father was an aerial photographer and had been a member of the Cuban Air Force up to then, but with Castro's imposition of power, my father—as well as the rest of the men in the Cuban Armed Forces—was considered *persona non grata*. He had to find another way to provide for our family, and I was going to help him.

When schools finally reopened early in 1959, I enrolled in the School of Engineering at the University of Havana, but the political atmosphere was toxic. To add to my worries, my father's involvement as an expert witness in a trial against the Air Force men he served with (the infamous *Juicio de los pilotos*) was extremely upsetting and distracting.

As they barged through, destroying and replacing government and people in their way, Castro and his henchmen decided that a group of 60 or so pilots, gunners, and mechanics from the previous regime's Cuban Air Force were to be tried for "crimes against the revolution and genocide." The communist accusers crudely—there was certainly no Photoshop at the time—doctored up some photographs and hastily put together a tribunal like many others that were instructed to condemn anyone who was put in front of them. The men, whose only crime had been to serve their country prior to the coup, faced the following sentences: The pilots faced death by firing squad at the wall, the infamous *paredón*. The gunners faced 30 years, and mechanics faced 20 years in Castro's prisons.

Fidel Castro himself handpicked the tribunal that was supposed to be judge, jury, and executioner. That was one of his very first mistakes. His mistake was to select three decent, honest, and honorable men. Comandante Félix Lutgerio Pena, ex leader of the Catholic Youth as president of the tribunal; Comandante Aviador Antonio Michel Yabor; and First Lieutenant Adalberto Parúas Toll.

Castro's second mistake: The "revolutionary" prosecutor decided to choose my father as the expert witness to validate their key photographic evidence. When he was called on to testify on what turned out to be the crudely altered and doctored photos presented as evidence, my dad testified that the photos were not genuine. Immediately the prosecutor yelled: "Arrest that man!" pointing at my dad. To which Comandante Pena responded, and I'm paraphrasing: "I'm the only one in this courtroom that can order anyone arrested and if you don't follow the established rules, I will have you arrested."

The tribunal unanimously absolved all the accused men. But their victory was short lived. The following day, Fidel Castro denounced their acquittals on public television and condemned them, handing out "reduced" sentences. To make things look "legal," he ordered another trial, this time making sure he appointed a tribunal that would obey his wishes. Of course, the punishment was still unwarranted and unjust, but the lives of the pilots were saved and this seemed as good a victory as any. In the end, the men spent several years withering away, receiving daily beatings and broken bones while confined in Castro's crowded and filthy prisons. Many were kept clothes-less, in tiny cells without running water or light.

Later I asked my father, "were you scared when that was going on?" He told me that he was never so scared in his life, but that he could never let fear interfere with truth, justice, and the lives of innocent men. He was ready to go in front of the firing squad with them. That is the kind of man he was.

Only about a week after Castro's brutal reversal, I was visiting a friend when I heard a gunshot. I looked out from the balcony and saw this man dressed in olive green (revolutionary army uniform), hurriedly walking away from the driver's side of a parked car near the Posta 2 guardhouse entrance to the Cuban Air Force headquarters—now the Fuerza Aérea Rebelde. I made my way downstairs and outside as the neighbors came out of their homes to see what the fuss was about. I quickly recognized Comandante Pena dead in the driver's seat of his car with a gunshot wound to the left side of his head, the gun on the passenger side of the car. The bastards had murdered him and tried to make it look like a suicide.

I remember one afternoon I was hanging around with my friend Luis "El Nene" O'Farrill on the beach in Marianao. As the sun started to set, we made our way home and stopped to get *un cafesito* while we continued to talk about nothing in particular—probably girls. A few minutes later, we finished our three-cent coffee and got back in the car to head home. We weren't in any hurry and, I suppose wrapped up in conversation, I had forgotten to turn the car headlights on. A block or so from the coffee stand, a car abruptly cut us off, its occupants rudely shined a large and bright light on us and hastily approached us with their gangster-style .45 caliber Thompson machine guns. One of the men shoved his gun into the car and pressed its barrel onto my nose, making a painful but temporary imprint. "*Oye primo, te me

Mirror image: Twin daughters Crissy and Betty (Ramón Luis Núñez).

hiciste sospechoso!" (I'll never forget those words) he said smugly. It doesn't translate that well, but basically he said, "Dude, you looked suspicious to me." They ordered us out of the car and to put our hands on our heads. I knew enough at the time that these two thugs were part of the military police (called DIER, *Departamento de Inteligencia Ejército Revolucionario*)—in other words, Castro's commie thugs. We did exactly as they demanded as they searched our car. When they had pushed us around enough and seemed satisfied that we had nothing to offer, they let us go.

Nene and I seemed to find trouble with discriminating ease, pretty much anywhere we went. One day, while on a bus ride on a route 28 bus headed to the center of Old Havana, the bus made a regular stop in front of the giant stone stairway of the University of Havana. A group of coeds eagerly jumped on the bus holding cans and asking for money. One of them put the can right up to Nene's chest while parroting, "Donate for arms and planes to fight against the imperialists!" Public outbursts against the revolution were not typically tolerated, and the young "Fidelista" girls were not prepared for Nene's crude reply as he pushed the can away. "I won't give a penny to that murdering SOB!" The girl's face turned as white as a sheet of paper (probably mine did too, as did everyone else's on the bus). She quickly turned and hurried off the bus while yelling at her friends at the front of the bus, *"Esta bien, aqui ya to' el mundo dio!"* (It's all good, everyone here has given!) The rest of the bus ride to La Habana Vieja was decidedly quiet. The passengers were shaken up and probably worried about who might have heard Nene and what their fate would be, simply by being on the same bus with the outspoken youth. Everyone was scared.

As Castro's army continued to dig itself in and further impose on our lives, we tried to carry on as normally as possible; as possible as one might when people are being thrown in prison left and right for no particular reason at all. My grandmother had asked me to drive her to visit her son, my uncle Luis Pinacho, and my cousin, Luis Delfin Buria, who were prisoners of the regime in the huge prison at Isla de Pinos, an island off the south coast of Cuba. Our trip would last a couple of days. We spent as much time as we could with them. That night we stayed in a hotel in Nueva Gerona and the following morning, before returning to the mainland, my grandmother asked me to stop at a friend's orange grove. Visiting was what we did back then. We didn't lock ourselves in our homes and watch television all weekend long. Besides, all you would see was Fidel's face and hear his repugnant voice; we spent time with the people we loved. Anyway, the grove owner gave us a box full of Isla de Pinos oranges (these were the best oranges in the world, they were so good that they were only used for export; most Cubans have never tasted them or knew of them). I drove home with my grandmother next to me and our delicious and practically priceless oranges in the trunk. We drove onto the ferry, which took us to the port of Batabanó on the mainland. I took my grandmother home and arrived at my own home early the next morning. Before I went into the house, I took the oranges out of the trunk and brought them in with me. A few hours later that morning, the DIER thugs practically knocked our door down and barged into the house with their machine guns. They waved their guns around a lot, they didn't seem to notice—or care—they were scaring my mom, sisters and my baby brother. They held me and my dad against the wall and told me that I had been "observed" the night before unloading arms and ammunitions from the trunk of my car. The freakin' oranges! I knew who she was too, the old hag who "ratted" me out. It was our next-door neighbor. Finding no arms and nothing they could hold against any of us, the thugs left empty-handed once again. That was the first time that the DIER searched our house, but it wasn't by any means the last. It seemed to be at least a weekly occurrence. Luckily, the bastards never found anything they were interested in.

It was March 1959 when the French freighter *La Coubre* exploded in the Havana harbor while workers unloaded 76 tons of munitions. Hundreds of people were injured and many others died; a dozen or so vaporized, their bodies never found. Castro accused the United States of "imperialist sabotage," but most of us knew the explosion was probably caused by the incompetence of the workers assigned to unload the ship. They didn't even know they were unloading dangerous cargo. Nonetheless, it was a huge explosion and it blew off hundreds of windows from many city buildings in Havana, as well as across the Almendares River in Marianao, where I lived. The next day, I went to class at the University of Havana, and before I could enter the engineering building, I ran into a mob of Fidel supporters who eagerly approached me and handed me a broom. "Come on! We're headed downtown to clean up the glass and debris left by the explosion," they told me. "Sure thing!" I heard myself agree. But my stomach turned at the thought of helping advance their "revolution," as they naively called it. As soon as I was able, I sneaked out through an alley and threw the broom into a dumpster. That was my last day as a student at the University of Havana.

On countless nights, I could hear my mother and father discussing my fate as I struggled to get sleep. They ultimately understood and decided that they had to get me out of the country, or I was going to end up dead or as a political prisoner in a communist jail.

After the revolution, my dad was given a job at the cartographic institute. He was sent to the United States to buy an airplane that would be suited for aerial photography and traveled to the U.S. a few times on this assignment. The political atmosphere continued to worsen and one day, my dad took me to get my own travel visa during one of his own renewal visits to the American Embassy.

The consul at the embassy somewhat asserted that we were planning on defecting once on American soil and sternly stipulated that my mom, sisters and little brother would never obtain visas without our return. That stipulation was like a kick in the gut, taking the breath out of me, with one swift stroke of the pen. Neither of us said a single word.

As my father prepared to travel to the U.S. again, he took me with him for what would be our final trip to America—the original and ultimate, "take your kid to work day." The thugs let me bring 90 dollars. My father got zip—that was all we had besides the clothes on our backs and a small suitcase.

The Beginning of a New Life O'er the Land of the Free

It was on July 11, 1960, that my devoted and devastated father and I boarded a ferry to Key West—just another island only a few miles from home, but in the relative safety of the United States of America. This is the day that marked the beginning of my adult life.

All those nights my parents had planned and plotted our exit led us to this one fateful day. My parents had arranged with one of my father's business associates, Valentin Diaz, to drive us to the ferry terminal. In exchange, he would keep our car and give my mother, who would stay behind with my siblings, a predetermined amount of money. My father decided on the ferry to Key West instead of a 30-minute airplane ride because he knew too many people would recognize him at the airport where he was well-known in aviation circles. The ferry took about four hours, but it seemed like forever. In Key West, we boarded a Greyhound bus for Miami. It was night time when we arrived in Miami, and we quickly got a room in a small motel on SW 6th Street and 13th Avenue and tried to get some sleep. "In the morning," my dad told me as we dozed off, "we'll head to the immigration office and request political asylum." When we awoke the next morning, that's exactly what we did.

It was 1960 and the immigration offices in Miami were very professional, yet somewhat simple by today's standards—think Don Draper wearing short sleeves and a tie, no jacket. We walked up to the immigration officer, handed him our passports, and told him of our need to apply for political asylum. He listened to us and simply and confidently scribbled the letter "A" and some numbers on a memo pad equivalent to today's sticky note, but without the sticky part on the back. The "A" turned out to be for "alien" number. He put a phone number on the back of the note and told us that if anyone (the police, border patrol, etc.) had any questions, they were to call the number on the yellow note. Then he informed us that we would be scheduled for a hearing before a judge. That meeting never happened, as immigration policy took an unexpected turn with respect to Cuban refugees. The United States would further streamline and revise provisions for what was to come.

The next day—there was no time to waste—we went to see a former contact at a company called Air International at Miami International Airport with whom my dad had prior business dealings. During this visit, my father was offered a part-time job as a draftsman. It paid enough to rent a one-room apartment with a murphy bed, a recliner, a tiny bathroom, and a tiny kitchen.

It seemed only days later an old friend, Manrique Alonso, came to see us at the apartment. Manrique had left his family in Cuba as well and had no one in the States. Upon his arrival, he came to visit my dad who told him he could stay with us. A few days later, another friend, Jose Preciado came to visit. Preciado was a police officer in Cuba, but worked with my dad as an artist making decals in his shop. Preciado moved in too. Manrique had claimed the recliner to sleep in and Preciado grabbed whatever blankets we could spare—I'm sure there weren't many—and cuddled up in a makeshift bed. After a while, we procured a couple of cots and we had a regular bachelor pad happening in our tiny apartment. Just kidding; it was pretty brutal.

Knowing my father would probably starve to death if left to his own culinary skills, my mother taught me a few cooking tricks before I left home. Thus, I became the designated cook. While I was happy with this assignment, I insisted to our new roommates that I didn't do dishes. Apparently, we had a deal. I was pretty good at improvising with whatever groceries we had at hand, but whenever they got hold of a couple of bucks, Preciado and Manrique would buy some groceries and I would improvise some dinner. One evening, Manrique came home with what he assumed was a great bargain. With my limited English at the time, I read the label in the package of what looked like some kind of ground beef and it said something like "not for human consumption." It turned out to be uncooked dog food. I did not cook it; I threw it in the garbage can while the guys were looking almost with tears in their eyes. We thought that we were going to have *picadillo* and rice that evening, but again we ended up with fried eggs and rice instead.

Every evening, the four of us would hang around in the tiny apartment, everyone avoiding looking in the direction of the sink full of dirty dishes from the night before. Eventually, someone would ask "Is there anything to eat tonight?" I would casually reply: "I'll be happy to cook some dinner if I had clean pots and pans to cook it with." Immediately, someone would jump in and start washing the dishes from the day before. Basically, the dishes only got done when they were hungry. The four of us lived in the apartment for a little while, but whenever an old friend came by, he would have at least a night's stay at our humble little space.

During this time, another friend, Benigno Diaz, Valentin's brother, arrived in the U.S. with his family. Benigno purchased an old Studebaker for about $120, which he allowed me to use. I would drive him to work and use the Studebaker to drive everyone else around and do whatever errand needed to be done, including driving myself and the others in search of work. It was definitely a team effort.

One morning, I answered an ad for a night shift embalmer helper-slash-security watchman at an old funeral home on Flagler Street. I stood in line for several hours with what seemed like more than 100 guys in front of me, all hungry for work. When I had reached a spot where I could see the door—I was about eighth in line—the owner of the funeral home came out and said we could leave because they had found someone to fill the position. Some of the guys couldn't understand what he had said so I turned to them and said, "*nos jodimos*"—we are out of luck—and we all left. As we were walking away, one of the guys that was in line with me said: "You know, after all, this job was not too appealing to me." "Neither was to me" I responded, "but any job that is legal and allows you to honorably earn a living is a good job, no matter how menial, dirty or disgusting it may be." He agreed. We wished each other good luck and went our separate ways.

Meanwhile, my dad and I tried to pull strings from our end—talking to anyone who would listen—to get my mother and siblings to join us. But my mother wasn't sitting around back home in Marianao waiting for anyone to save her. Shortly after my dad and I left Cuba, she promptly took matters into her own hands. Someone suggested to her to talk to Monsignor Eduardo Boza-Masvidal, Auxiliary Bishop of the Archdioceses of Havana, who was helping people who were being persecuted by the communist regime and working very hard to help reunite families separated by the communist persecution. And so, my mother sat with the Bishop one morning and recounted our story. There were no lines to make, or messages to take for another person for another day. At that very moment, the Bishop without hesitation picked up the telephone and called—presumably the U.S. Ambassador in Cuba—who

My daughter Suzy (Ramón Luis Núñez).

requested the names of the family members still in Cuba. After the short conversation with the American Embassy Official, the Bishop instructed my mother to bring the passports to the U.S. Embassy the next day at 2 in the afternoon, and my mother walked out of the U.S. Embassy that next afternoon with the four passports and their corresponding visas stamped on them.

NOTE: Bishop Boza-Masvidal was later expelled from Cuba by the communist regime in September 1962, together with hundreds of other clerics, Catholics, as well as of other denominations. He became another Cuban Exile. He never gave up the struggle for the freedom of Cuba until his passing on March 16, 2003, in Venezuela. A true Saint!

A few days later, three months after my dad and I left Cuba, my father and I took Benigno's Studebaker and picked up the rest of our family members at the Miami airport. The Cuban government had allowed my mom and sisters the usual $90. Between them they had $270—practically a fortune. With that, and the little we were able to save, my dad soon procured a green 1949 Mercury for $100; the guys called it *"el avispón verde"* (the big green hornet). I took my dad to work and would spend the day running errands and looking for work myself. In our small Cuban exile community in Miami, we were always helping each other out. I was always driving someone somewhere.

Two or three days before the rest of our family arrived, we rented a two-bedroom apartment nearby, and Manrique and Preciado kept the tiny apartment. I finally got a job as a gas station attendant. It paid 74 cents an hour. Yes, they took Social Security and Income tax deductions out of it. I worked there until I got a job at Air International as a janitor; good timing, at about that time my father's part time job there ran out.

Soon afterwards, I was promoted to accounting clerk when they found out that I knew how to work with a huge accounting machine they had (I have always been very good with complex machines). That was a significant increase in salary. I was bringing home a little over $50 a week. The thing is, there was pride in every job. We all had the sense to make something more of our lives, even if it was just temporary—we thought it was temporary.

Now, I had a car of my own. It was also an old Mercury, but a good-looking car, for a young man, after all. Months later, one day that the old Mercury was in the shop for an oil change or something like that, I was walking to the bus stop, heading home from work at Air International and I ran into a Venezuelan man carrying a small suitcase who was looking for the bus stop himself. I told him to walk with me as I was headed to the bus stop myself. On our way there, we were approached by a border patrol officer who, after a few questions, asked us for our "papers." The Venezuelan, who was a crew member left behind by the rest of his crew, quickly presented to the officer his immaculate repertoire, and I handed him my "no glue sticky note." The officer, at first, didn't know what to make of the note, but he must have believed my story because he never called the phone number on the back of the note (Well, there were no cell phones at the time).

Later, my family and I moved into an apartment building called the "Colonial" on NW 15th Avenue, half a block south of the Orange Bowl stadium. I was the only one working for a while, and I remember when I filed my tax return for the first time. I was claiming my entire family as dependents. Also, I could not afford paying anyone to do my tax return. So, I did it myself. As a consequence, I was promptly audited and instructed to schedule a meeting with an IRS office. The IRS employee turned out to be a sweet elderly lady who was very impressed that a young man like me was taking full care of his family. She carefully checked my work and determined that I had short-changed myself. I later received a few more dollars from Uncle Sam. So, that was good. It also proved my father's advice that "honesty always pays."

As we settled in, we were eventually all able to find work. My mother took a job sewing at a garments factory, my youngest sister and I both had jobs at Air International, and my dad obtained a position at Apex Photography, and later at Associated Photographers in Miami, where he was a color photo lab supervisor until he retired many years later. Together, we purchased a house in the West Miami/Flagami area. I was the co-signer for my family's home. My family was, and has always been, most important to me; I am very proud of that.

In the meantime, as we were beginning to get into our second year in exile, I seriously considered enlisting in what later came to be known as the failed Bay of Pigs invasion in the spring of 1961. When I told my dad what I was considering doing, he just told me: "You are an adult now and I can't tell you what to do or not to do anymore. However, I can tell you that I think it is not a good idea. You need to make your own decision." Then he proceeded to explain his points of view.

The original idea for the Bay of Pigs invasion was started by President Eisenhower in 1959, when the U.S. began recruitment of Cuban exiles, and whose policies President Kennedy somewhat adopted. Like many Americans, I don't think Kennedy's heart was "all in it" with Eisenhower's CIA campaign. As with all CIA operations, it was supposed to be a covert one; however, everyone and their brother knew every detail about it. Including the Castro regime.

When the whole thing was over, I'm not even sure if I felt relief that I hadn't gone, or disappointment that it was not successful. But, we were definitely devastated to learn that many of our friends had been killed and many others were imprisoned by Castro's regime.

Shortly afterwards, Kennedy began negotiations to bring the imprisoned Cubans back to the U.S., but the relationship between the U.S. and Cuba was not getting better. In fact, it got worse—much worse. Between the Bay of Pigs debacle and what we would later know as the October Missile Crisis of 1962, many Cuban young men like me decided to enlist in the U.S. Army. There was a lot of chatter in Cuban circles, and we believed we could get our country back. But this time, we would fight as the most respected army in the world. This time, we would fight as American soldiers.

And the Home of the Brave

Like any other parents of young men possibly headed to war, my mom and dad were concerned that I had enlisted. But, we all understood it was the right thing to do. The day I was to report for duty, my dad drove me to 4000 Aurora Street, in Coral Gables where other enlistees were also reporting. As I was stepping out of the car, he grabbed me by the arm and looking at me with moist eyes told me: "I am very proud of you." I gave him a big hug and a kiss, turned around and walked into the building.

We were given our physicals and later put on a Delta Airlines flight to Fort Knox, Kentucky. I remember thinking that I am part of the American Army now, and at some point, I was going to help liberate Cuba. I was on the second group of 240 men that enlisted and was assigned to Echo Company, 15th Battalion, 4th Training Brigade, but there were thousands of Cuban young men like me who followed. Kentucky was *really* cold!

On October 22nd, 1962, President Kennedy notified America during a national TV broadcast that the Russians, in collaboration with the Cuban government, had set up a series of nuclear-armed missiles just 90 or so miles off the coast of Florida. This was a clear threat to the United States. In response, Kennedy sent American warships to block the Russians from further hostile activity on the island. Tensions ran high for those next few weeks, and Americans prepared for disaster much like we do now for an approaching hurricane, hoarding canned goods, gasoline, and other goods. Somehow, we averted disaster. The Russians removed their missiles, and the U.S. agreed to leave Cuba alone. There were additional concessions made by the Americans, but the end result would be that there would be no invasion of Cuba.

During my service in the U.S. Army, it became increasingly clear that we weren't headed to Cuba to fight against Castro. It was obvious that the United States' plans had changed and we weren't going home. At one point, officials approached a select few of us trying to entice us with the idea to recruit us as mercenaries to fight against communist insurgents in the Congo or somewhere else in Africa. A very small handful signed up for it. They were never seen again. The immense majority, including myself, decided if we weren't fighting for a free Cuba, or for the U.S., our hearts were simply not in it. If we weren't fighting to go home, we didn't want to fight at all. When I completed my time in the service, I simply left.

When I returned to our home in West Miami and to my old job at Air International, if it wasn't clear before, it was crystal clear now; this was our new home and I had to come up with a new plan. Cuba was lost. I began working on my future in my new country. At the time, Dade County Junior College (presently, Miami-Dade College) was beginning operations in an old abandoned World War II airport, Master's Field. The registrar's office was in an old hangar full of debris and with broken windows everywhere. I registered to begin studies on a two-year Associate Degree in Civil Engineering Technology.

In the meantime, I met the girl I would one day marry. We had a lot in common; she too had left Cuba as a young girl, leaving her mother and father behind. We would embark on our journey in a new country side-by-side; all things new from the eyes of displaced foreigners. During our courtship and into our marriage, Mirta always encouraged me to continue my studies. We married in 1964 at Saint Dominic Catholic Church in the heart of Miami, and enjoyed our honeymoon with a drive to Cypress Gardens in my brand-new Dodge Dart. At Cypress Gardens, we saw the water ski shows and Mirta loved the beautiful gardens. I enjoyed taking photographs of my bride strolling through the lush gardens. After that, we made a stop at Saint Petersburg, Clearwater, and Tampa, and many other towns in Florida. This was really the first time that I had a chance to enjoy being here. Then it was back to work in Miami, but not before getting the bug for traveling, being on the road, and enjoying so many beautiful places.

Our twin daughters, Beatriz and Cristina, were born in 1966. All the while, Mirta continued to encourage me to continue my studies. It was not at all easy to work during the day and attend school at night, but I knew that I had to be persistent and stick with it. I always wanted to be a Civil Engineer. My last job in Cuba before I left was working among Civil Engineers and they all told me that to get a good start in that profession, you must start as a "chainman" in a survey crew, the lowest rung in the ladder. The problem was that at around that time, there were hardly any survey crew chainman jobs available in Miami. The very few you could find paid awfully bad, and I could not afford the cut in pay now that I had a pair of one-year-old babies at home.

Late one evening in November of 1967, after coming home from school, I was reading *The Miami News*, and just like that, came across a very short article where it talked about survey crew chainmen jobs. One of the things the article said is that there was only one company in all of Florida who paid decent salaries to chainmen. It was Florida Power & Light Co. A miracle? I was not sure then, but that article in *The Miami News* changed my life forever.

A couple of days later I went to the job interview with FPL. The interviewer asked me lots of questions, as a good interviewer should do. When it came to the kind of job I was applying for, he said that there was a problem. "We only have two survey crews in the Miami Area," he said, "therefore we only have two chainmen employed and they like their job so much that for you to get one of those two jobs, we may have to kill one of them."

As I was getting up to leave and searching for words to apologize for wasting his time, he said: "Son, please sit down. I said that I could not give you a job as a chainman, I didn't say that I wouldn't give you a job at all." He then went on to explain that he had other positions he was convinced I was very qualified for, one of them would be mine just for the picking, and told me that I was not leaving the room without a job. "Can you draw?" he asked me.

That is how I got a job with Florida Power & Light working as a draftsman. Less than seven months later, I was promoted to Engineering Technician Trainee. When I was told about the promotion, I didn't bother to ask anything about salary, I figured that it would be OK anyway, for sure, a little better than draftsman. When my first paycheck as an engineering technician trainee came in, I believed they had made a big mistake. It was double of what I made as a draftsman. I was totally stunned. Again, great timing; our third daughter, Susana, was already on her way.

A year or so later, finally, I received my Dade County Junior College, Associate Degree in Civil Engineering Technology. That meant another promotion at FPL. Now, I was a Senior Engineering Technician. This was great, but my dream was to be an Engineer, not a Technician. However, I was exhausted. Nevertheless, I decided to go for it despite the fact that it would take me a very long, long time to complete a "four-year" engineering degree attending classes only at night.

Then, another miracle (by now, I truly believe in miracles). There was a shortage of engineers from all disciplines nationwide at the same time that the University of Miami was considering closing the Department of Electrical Engineering for lack of enrollment. FPL was in urgent need of engineers so, they sort of made a deal. If UM offered the whole Electrical Engineering Curriculum at night, making it less difficult for students who had to work full time during the day, FPL would pay the full tuition of selected employees. Thus, UM Electrical Department would remain open while FPL would get their much-needed engineers. That is why I gave up Civil and adopted Electrical Engineering as my new career and was able to graduate in 1977. No regrets.

In the early nineties, I took an interest in art and—just for the heck of it—went back to school, this time just for fun. I earned a Bachelor's degree in Fine Arts from Florida International University and graduated *Summa Cum Laude* in 1993. After my retirement from the engineering world, I have dedicated my life to be a professional artist. I have been painting ever since my retirement as an engineer.

Some of my accomplishments as an artist was to be named by the Florida Governor as Florida's Hispanic Artist of the Year 2010, with simultaneous exhibitions at the Florida Capitol Rotunda and at the Florida Governor's Mansion, where the Florida Governor himself threw a reception in my honor. Before that in 2007, I was invited to a reception at the White House together with a group of artists who were commissioned to design ornaments for the Blue Room Christmas Tree to celebrate the approaching National Parks Centennial. Not too bad for a Cuban Exile.

And as my father used to tell me: "Honesty and hard work always pay." I was able to prove him right.

My mother Pilar Pinacho Nuñez (Ramón Luis Núñez).

As a last thought, I will never forget those guys, including my father, I used to cook for in that tiny apartment in the Southwest section of Miami back in 1960. Their dream, just like thousands of other Cuban Exiles, was to return to Cuba in freedom and dignity. They passed on without realizing that dream. Today, now that I believe in miracles, I am only waiting for one more: The day when that dream comes true, even if I can't live it myself.

• • •

The last paragraph above was written in the late evening hours of November 25, 2016. The following morning, I was awakened by a telephone call telling me that the tyrant had died the night before....

The Land of My Father

Eloy L. Nuñez

Much of my story is told through the eyes of a child. I was four years old when my family came to the United States. A lot of my memories are of images that I still can't tell for sure if they are real or imagined. As I started to write this essay, I had to constantly ask myself, "Are these things that I actually witnessed, or are they 'secondary elaborations' based on the stories that I heard others tell?" To make sure, I had to ask my brother and sisters if what I saw, I actually saw. After all, they were older than me, and they could make sense of things so much better than I could ... to the extent that anyone could make sense of what happened to us and to many other families like ours.

So much of what I remember seems like a dream ... a dream from a long time ago. Like many dreams, some of the images are in black and white, and grey tones, but others are in vivid color. As a four-year-old, one color that I remember vividly was the color yellow—a very bright and intense yellow. That was the color that my father painted my favorite toy car. It was one of those toy cars that you sit in and drive forward by peddling like a tricycle, except that it wasn't a tricycle, it was an Army jeep, like the ones the U.S. Army had in World War II, but a miniaturized version. One of my fondest memories was peddling that jeep on the sidewalk in front of our house in Havana. Before it was bright yellow, the jeep was painted in a drab olive green color. I didn't understand at the time why my father had painted the toy jeep yellow, but as with most kids, bright colors are so much more interesting, and I loved that yellow jeep. Sadly, I never got to ride it much after it was painted. Someone in my family, either my father or mother, decided to give it away to another family. Unknown to me, we were about to move to another country, and we would leave everything we owned behind. I didn't know it then, but I would never see my favorite yellow toy car again.

As with any four-year-old, it was difficult for me to understand why something that you cherish is taken away and given to someone else. It wasn't until many years later as a young man, that I came to think about that yellow toy jeep again. It was then that I understood why my favorite toy was given to someone else. I also came to understand why my father had painted it yellow. He did it to protect me and his family. For you see, anything that showed any hint that my father served in the pre–Castro Cuban military would be perceived as a

Eloy's yellow jeep, before it was painted yellow (Eloy L. Nuñez).

symbol of defiance, and a challenge to the authority of the new Castro regime. Any color ... any song ... any symbol ... any thought that could possibly be linked to the past, could put our entire family in danger. I didn't realize then how much danger we were in. Unbeknownst to me at the time, my father and my mother did everything humanly possible to save our family, even if it meant leaving everything behind and starting over in a foreign county.

My father and my mother are my heroes. I can also say that about my older brother and my two older sisters. My brother "Gordo" (Luis), and my sisters "Pili" (Pilar) and "Laly" (Gladys) were like extra fathers and mothers to me. That's because I was the baby of the family. I'm not sure if my birth was planned or just an accident on my parents' part. My siblings were 17, 15, and 13 years old, respectively, when I was born in 1956. I have no explanation for the 13-year gap between the youngest of my two sisters and me, and I certainly don't have a recollection of that day. Nor did I ever ask my parents if they intended to have

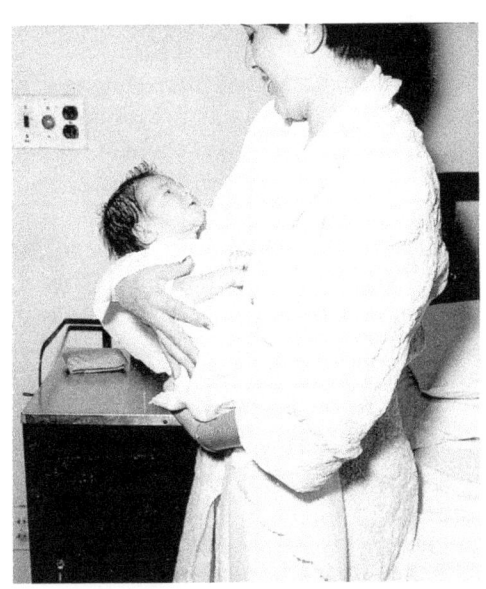

Eloy Jr. held by his mother Pilar on the day of his birth, September 15, 1956 (Eloy L. Nuñez).

me, or if my birth was just an afterthought. As far as I'm concerned, I didn't really care. I was just glad they did, and that I was born into this loving family.

I do know this—I came into the world during a tumultuous time in Cuba's history. It was a tumultuous time all over the world, for that matter, and Cuba seemed to be at the center of much of the Cold War maneuvering between the nuclear superpowers. Obviously, as a young child, I didn't know what was going on in the world around me. Like any four-year-old, my mind was undeveloped and I did not understand the economic and political upheaval going on around us. But young children can sense when things are not as they should be. Our family was about to be torn apart, and I did not understand why.

The End of the Dream

Before I tell about my memories of Cuba, I want to fast-forward to one of the most significant days of my life—the day that my father died. That was the day that my father's dream of returning to a free Cuba died. I remember that night very clearly. My father spent his last days in South Miami Hospital in February and March of 2000. I was a lieutenant of the Miami-Dade Police Department Bomb Squad at the time, and I had taken a couple of days off to be at my father's side at the hospital. Like most Cuban families, the four sons and daughters took turns staying with him at his bedside on a 24-hour basis. Leaving him alone in the care of nurses was unfathomable to us. My brother and sisters and I were there to support my mother, as much as we were there to support my father. Of course, my mother, Pilar, was at my father's side *all* the time—taking brief breaks to shower and eat, and then come back to be next to him. This arduous schedule went on for at least a month, in between two different hospitals, but my mother never wavered. She was at her husband's bedside all the way to the end. This was a love story.

It was my turn to stay at the hospital the night that my father died. Of course, my mother also stayed in the hospital room, curled up with a blanket and sleeping on a reclining chair next to my father. Even though it was my turn to stay, my sister Laly decided to stay as well. I think that she and I both sensed that this would be the last time we would see our father alive. Around 10:30 p.m., the room cleared out, as my brother Luis and his wife Mirta went home. My other sister, Pili, also went home. They all needed to get a good night's sleep, as their turn to stay the night would come in less than 24 hours. I recall that my *tio* (uncle) Luis, and my *tia* (aunt) Carmina had also visited the hospital that night, as well as my cousin Elizabeth. It was the typical Cuban gathering of family at a hospital—lots of joking and laughing—

even as my father laid in the hospital bed, struggling for every breath from a respirator tube inserted into his mouth. Everything that Cubans do seems to be excessive and funny and loud. We all joke about it, but despite the loudness and the inappropriate laughter in a hospital setting, it is truly comforting to be around the people that you love so much during such a difficult time. I think the joking is just a way of coping with the pain.

As the room cleared of the last visitors, we turned down the lights and my sister and I sat quietly in chairs next to my father's bedside. My mother quickly fell asleep on her reclining chair. She was clearly exhausted from this month-long ordeal. It was suddenly quiet in the room. All we could hear was my father's rapid and shallow breaths from the respirator. I could tell that he was really struggling at this point. I knew in my heart that this would be the night that my father would die, but I didn't say anything to anyone.

Just the night before, my brother, two sisters and I had met in the hospital lounge to discuss the next course of action for our father's medical treatment. He had been undergoing dialysis treatments for a couple of weeks; he would get worse, and then he would rebound and get noticeably better. The doctors had put a shunt into his neck where they would hook him into the dialysis machine. The dialysis seemed to help him a little bit at first, and that gave us all a sense of optimism, but over the previous two days, his condition had worsened. At this point, he could not speak or even smile as he always did. You know things are really bad when my father couldn't smile anymore. He had always found a reason to laugh and smile—often at the silliest things. During our conversation at the hospital lounge the night before, my father's doctor came in and told us that the prognosis was not a good one. He told us that my father was undergoing total organ failure—all his body systems were shutting down. He told us that there was nothing more that could be done. The doctor recommended that my father be taken to a hospice.

Despite the doctor's recommendation, my sister Laly was adamant about not giving up. I usually don't give up either, but this time I knew intuitively that the time was near. My brother and my sister Pili and I were in agreement. As difficult as it was, the three of us agreed that we would sign a "do not resuscitate" letter, and that we would ask the doctor to discontinue the dialysis treatments. Of course, if my mother had been part of the conversation, she would have sided with Laly, and would have wanted to fight until the end. In the end, we all came together and agreed to discontinue the treatments. But I don't think that my mother really understood what that meant. I think that part of her understood—her head, but her heart did not understand. I don't think she was ready for my father to die.

If you're reading this, you may think of a time in your life when you had to make a difficult decision that had to do with the life and death of a loved one. If you have, you know exactly what I am saying. There's no way to know for sure if you're doing the right thing. You don't know whether to keep trying despite the pain and discomfort to your loved one, or to hope that the suffering ends soon. Are we giving up too soon, or are we unnecessarily prolonging the suffering? Those were the questions that we asked ourselves, and since my father was no longer conscious, we could not ask him. Even though my instinct is to fight and never give up, I knew in my heart that the time had come.

Not more than fifteen minutes after most of the family left my father's hospital room and my mother had fallen asleep on the chair next to him, my sister Laly and I heard a horrible sound coming from my father. It was a sound that I had never heard before, nor have I ever heard thereafter. I would best describe it as a groan, but it wasn't quite like that. It was an unearthly sound. It was the sound of my father dying. My sister instinctively jumped up from her chair toward my father to help him, but I held her back. I didn't say a word. I didn't have to. She understood what was happening. A great man—our father—had just died.

My mother was still sleeping, and she had not heard the sound that my father made. The nurse came in to check on him, but she knew exactly what had happened. Nurses deal with death all the time. They recognize it when it happens. The nurse looked at my sister and me, and quietly backed away and left the room. I very much appreciated that act of kindness and respect on her part. She quietly closed the door behind her, and left my sister and me to be next to our father. I remember the two of us holding each other, while we sobbed quietly. I remember this like it was today. It was a very somber, but beautiful moment.

We waited about ten minutes before we woke our mother. My sister and I discussed how we would break the news to her. We decided to wake her and let her discover her husband's passing on her own. There is no good way to do this, but I think my sister's approach was the best way to do it. She had the wherewithal to tell my mother, *"Mami.... Papi te esta llamando"* (Papi is calling you). My mother dutifully got up from her recliner chair bed and went toward my father's hospital bed—as she had done thousands of times before. *"Eloy, que quieres?"* she asked him.

After getting no response from him, my mother realized that something was wrong. She yelled out to us, *"llama la enfermera!"* (call the nurse). That's when my sister and I came to her and told her, *"Mami.... Papi se murio"* (Father is dead). That was the moment that I heard a wail come out of my mother's chest that I had not heard before either. Like the sound that my father had just made as he died, the sound that came out of my mother was almost indescribable. It was the most gut-wrenching sound that I had ever heard. It wasn't very loud. It was the sound that a person makes when they realize that they have become permanently separated from their loved one

The Land of My Father (E. Nuñez) 41

My father (Eloy Nuñez, Sr.) and my mother (Pilar Pinacho Nuñez) (Eloy L. Nuñez).

"Till death do us part." My mother Pilar and father Eloy Sr. around 1940 (Eloy L. Nuñez).

after more than 60 years of marriage. As difficult as it was to watch our father die, it was much worse to see my mother grieving over his death. It was a grief that lasted for a very long time, and did not end until she died ten years later.

Within a few minutes, the room telephone rang. My sister answered. It was a call from my nephew Renny, all the way from Los Angeles. Renny asked Laly if my father was all right. He told her that he had sensed something had gone wrong. Could it have been that my mother's cry was heard by her grandson all the way from LA? Or maybe it was just a coincidence. I don't know enough to know anything anymore. Anything is possible, I guess.

We then called my brother and my other sister, Pili, and my wife Maria to give them the news. We didn't call the entire family until the next morning because we didn't want to wake anyone up. But somehow, many of them seemed to know what had happened, even before they were told. As is customary with Cuban families, almost everyone came to the hospital, either that night, or early in the morning.

Old Men and Their Stories

I don't remember much of what happened in the days immediately following my father's death. It's all a blur now. I can't even remember how I got home from the hospital that morning, or who took my mother home. I do remember making some phone calls for the funeral arrangements the next day. I didn't have to do much. As with everything they did, my parents had already planned ahead of time for their funerals. They did this because they never wanted to be a burden on their children. Both of my parents were class acts, and I can only hope that I can come close to being the class of person that they were. Everything that they did, they did it with care, and love, and with consideration for others.

Long before my father died, my parents had purchased three burial plots, side-by-side at a Miami Lakes cemetery. One plot was for my father, the other for my mother, and third one for my grandmother, Ramona—my mother's mother. My father and mother wanted to be buried beside each other, and I guess my father didn't mind that his mother in-law would be tagging along. It's not surprising. My father was always respectful to his mother in-law while she was living with them. In his mind, laying at rest for an eternity next to his mother in-law must have seemed like a small price to pay for having his wife and love of his life next to him forever.

My father's choices in death were no different than his choices in life. My father was the eternal idealist and dreamer. He was an artist and a master craftsman for many different things. When it came to drawing cartoons, and painting murals, and building miniature model cities, there was no one better. There were so many things that he could do well, but as with any person, there were some things that he did not do very well. One of the things that he didn't do well was to take practical, real-world matters into account when he planned for his funeral. That would explain why he chose a cemetery in Miami Lakes, and a funeral home 13 miles away on Bird Road and 82nd Avenue in the Westchester area where they lived. Thirteen miles may not seem like a long way in a small town like where I live right now, but a thirteen-mile funeral procession up through the Palmetto Expressway in the middle of a workday is quite a challenge. I am eternally grateful to the Motors Unit of the Miami-Dade Police Department for offering to escort the procession for that long and arduous trip.

Funeral services and burials are always difficult. My parents spared me from attending funerals when I was I child. They would take me to someone's house when I was younger, or leave me alone at home when I was a teenager, so I never got to attend a funeral until I became an adult. But now as I grow older, it seems that I'm more than making up for it. All funerals are difficult, but for me, the hardest were those of police officers and young people whose lives were taken much too early. Sadly, I have been to too many of those lately. As with all funerals, the grief is felt not so much for the person who has died, as it is for those family members who they left behind. The day of the funeral I didn't have much time to think about my father. I had to turn my attention to my grieving mother. That's what my brother and sisters did as well.

The thing that I remember most of that day were the short stories told to me by several old men whom I had never met before (nor have I ever spoken with them thereafter). In the central seating area of the funeral home, several old men—I can't remember the exact number—came up to me to pay their respects. One by one, they told me that my father had saved their lives. One by one, they told me that my father was the most courageous man they had ever known. They all told me their names and the branch of military that they served, but my mind was a blur that day, and right now as I write this, I cannot remember their names or even their faces. All I can remember was the reverence that they showed when they spoke about my father. Their words made me realize that the life and death of my father was meaningful to many people—not just to me and my family. It seems that my father had affected many peoples' lives.

The Quiet Heroes

Growing up in my parents' house, I had never heard my father talk about his military service in Cuba, or much of anything else for that matter.

Like most true heroes, my father never talked about himself. Instead, he focused on the "here and now" by working hard and doing all the things he loved the most, like painting, reading, travelling and listening to music. He and my mother loved to watch the Lawrence Welk Show, and since there was only one TV in my house in the early 60s, I had no choice but to watch it with them. I didn't like the Lawrence Welk Show very much—I thought it was corny—but some of my fondest memories are of watching *The Red Skelton Show*, Jackie Gleason's *Honeymooners*, and the *Flintstones* with my father. What I remember the most of those times is that my father and I would laugh at different things. The things that he found funny, I did not understand. The things that I laughed at, he didn't get. It was like alternating laugh tracks at home. Once in a while, we would laugh at the same thing, at the same time, and that was good. I miss the sound of his laughter.

My mother adored my father, and every once in a while, she would tell me how well respected he was among his peers. As a child growing up, I heard almost nothing from my father about his days in Cuba. Likewise, my mother didn't say much either—or maybe it was just that I wasn't paying attention as I should have been. I now look back to my childhood and realize that I missed many opportunities to ask my father and mother questions about Cuba, and how and why we came to the United States. At the time, I was preoccupied with the things that most children are preoccupied with—sports, games, and, later as a teenager, girls. In retrospect, I wish I had listened more to my mother's stories, and I wish I had asked more questions to my father. As it stands now, I have to rely on the stories of the old men who spoke to me at my father's funeral and my own recollections, most of which have faded. Reading my brother's story (in "Facing the Possibility of Never Returning") helped me to put the pieces of the puzzle together in my mind. His story provides the context that I needed to sort out the vague images in my mind, so that I can make some sense of things.

It was my brother's story that allowed me to understand what the old men at my father's funeral were talking about. These were some of the men whose lives my father had saved when he bravely stood his ground and testified the truth during the kangaroo trials in the early days of the Revolution. After hearing other peoples' accounts of the false trials and firing squad executions, I often wondered how my father's life had been spared. How can anyone be so courageous as to stand up against a system whereby the guilt of the accused has already been predetermined? How is it that my entire family was able to escape Cuba when many others did not? These are the questions that were partially answered in my brother's story. I find it somewhat strange that I had to *read* my brother's story after so many years of storytelling at family get-togethers. Why have I not heard this story before? Why did it take the writing of this book for me to find out that my two parents and my siblings were heroes?

I think the answer to that question has a lot to do with the personalities of my father and mother, and all my family members. Whenever we got together for a large family affair—which was often—we would tell stories about funny things that had happened to us. Nobody wants to dwell on stories of hardship. The stories that were told, and re-told, at these family outings usually had to do with our fishing adventures with Tio Alejandro and Tio Luis, and of course, the ultimate patient fisherman—my mother Pilar. Fishing was my mother's favorite thing in the whole world, and she would lean for hours on the railing of a bridge in the Florida Keys, holding her "yo yo" fishing line in her hand. When everyone else had given up because the fish had stopped biting and we were getting ready to pack up and leave the bridge to go back home, my mother would yell out that she just felt a nibble on her line, *"Aye! Una picada!"* After a while, we learned to stop listening to her. It was like the story about the boy who yelled "wolf!" But as the fates would have it, one time when we were packing our coolers and fishing rods to head back home, she yelled, *"Aye! Una picada!"* This time it turned out to be true. She hooked on to a 10-pound mutton snapper, and I had to run over to her and reel it in by hand. We were fishing off the top of the old abandoned Bahía Honda bridge in the Florida Keys, and we were at least 50 feet above the surface of the water. As I reeled in the huge mutton snapper, I got it within five feet of the railing. Unfortunately, the fish had one more fighting move left in it before I was able to get my hands on it, and it wriggled off the hook and fell 50 feet into the water. I doubt that it survived the impact, and surely it died in vain because we didn't get to eat it for dinner the following night. Undoubtedly, one of the big hammerheads that patrol the Bahia Honda pass would devour it and keep it from going to waste. That was one of the dozens of fishing stories that would be told and re-told at all our family gatherings. And every time it was told, my mother would mention how she never forgave me for losing that fish that night. Everyone at the family gathering would laugh at that—no matter if the story had been re-told a hundred times. It was this story, and many others that were told and retold at our family gatherings. That is why I never heard about our struggles in Cuba, and then later in Miami, during our early exile years. My family wanted to focus on the positive and funny stories—not on the sad ones. Reading my brother's story (in "Facing the Possibility of Never Returning") helped me sort things out in my mind. There are images that I thought may have been false memories because these things were never talked about at family gatherings. Now I know that what I remembered actually did happen.

Stay Quiet on the Bus!

My earliest recollections of Cuba have little to do with Castro or the Revolution. The most vivid memories are of my Tia Estrella (my father's sister) taking me to the Catholic convent and showing me off to the nuns. I remember panicking when the nuns surrounded me. They were merely showing their adoration for a cute four-year-old boy, but from my perspective, I must have thought that these ladies were going to harm me in some way. Now that I think of it, I feel bad for Tia Estrella. She was such a sweet lady, and I remember loving her a great deal. I feel bad that I was screaming like a banshee when she took me to the convent and introduced me to the nuns. I don't know why I reacted in such a way. I think it must have been their long black dresses—or habits as they are called. Being scared of the nuns didn't make much sense because these were nice ladies who meant no harm to me. But four-year-old children perceive the world in a visceral sense. These perceptions are based mostly on imagery and body language, and not so much on higher order logical processes.

Four-year-olds are mostly ignorant of the things that truly pose a danger to them. Often, they fear things that are not dangerous, and don't fear things that are. One dangerous situation that I had no idea of at the time, was when I said something out loud that could have easily landed any one of my family members in prison. I remember I was riding on the bus with some family member—I can't remember who. It might have been my mother or Tia Estrella—I'm not sure. In any regard, as the bus was moving, I looked out the window and saw some *milicianos* (Castro's militia soldiers) walking along the sidewalk. As an innocent four-year-old, I started to chant, *"uno ... dos ... tres ... quatro ... comiendo mierda y rompiendo zapato."* The literal English translation of this chant is: "one ... two ... three ... four ... eating feces and breaking shoes." That doesn't make a lot of sense in English, but I think that in Spanish, it was meant to mock the slipshod manner in which these *milicianos* marched. I don't know why I said that, or where I picked it up, but the people sitting around us on the bus were terrified. Kids repeat things that are said in the home. Surely, my family would be blamed for this simple transgression against the Revolution. No one dared to smile or say a word, out of fear that they may be branded as counter revolutionaries and taken away to prison. My mother (or Tia Estrella) had to be mortified. I now know that they must have thought that it was hilarious, but at the same time, they must have been mortified that a Castro sympathizer on the bus would turn them in. Fortunately for all of us, everyone on the bus kept quiet, as if nothing had happened.

I know that this incident happened because I remember it clearly. I also know because I have heard the story told at family gatherings many times. It's one of the few stories about Cuba ever told by my family. The reason that it was told is because it was funny. Imagine having to suppress an uncontrollable giggle in a public forum. But imagine that uncontrollable giggle fit causing you much more than embarrassment. In post–Revolution Cuba, something as innocent as that could cost you your life. As a four-year-old, I could not understand what the fuss was all about, but it was made very clear to me; never, ever say that chant again. Not even at home.

Bearded Soldiers in Our House

I don't have a clear recollection of what our home in Havana looked like. I do remember it resembling what I would call a townhouse, with a split floorplan. I remember that our front porch faced a main city street in Havana, and that there was a row of similar

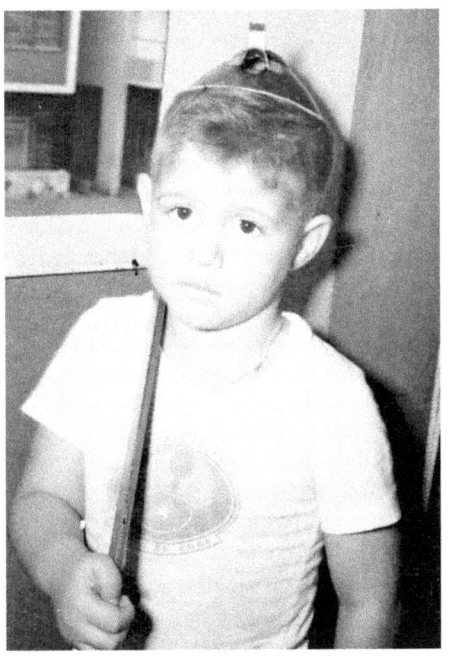

Eloy Jr., four years old (Eloy L. Nuñez).

houses, with a *bodega* (a food store) at the corner. I remember that bodega because I once hit a baseball with a bat all the way from the front of our house to the store. My cousin Pepe, who was pitching underhand to me that time, had to run down the street to shag the ball, as it kept rolling and rolling down the street. It must have been downhill because the ball just kept rolling and rolling.

I also remember being with my mother on the front porch of our house on another day and watching Castro's *milicianos* marching on our street from right to left. I can still see this image clearly. I remember my mother's face as she looked at me with a sense of anguish. I think I could read her mind at the time: "Please, don't say *"uno ... dos ... tres ... quatro ... comiendo mierda y rompiendo zapato* right now. Please keep your mouth shut." She didn't actually say that. Her eyes said it for her.

The sequence of these events is not clear to me, nor is it important that I tell them in chronological order. Another memory that I have of bearded men was when several of them forced entry into our house. There was a time when I didn't know if this memory was real or not. It wasn't until I read my brother's story that I was able to confirm that it did happen. That's because we had never talked about it in all the years since.

48   Escape from Cuba

I remember lying down on the floor, only a few feet away from the black and white television in our living room. I was watching cartoons—either Felix the Cat, or Popeye the Sailorman. I remember bearded men coming into our house. I remember my mother being very scared. I remember those men going through the entire house and ransacking it. I don't know what they were looking for, but I remember that they left a mess inside. I also remember one of the bearded men pushing my mother against a wall and hearing her protest. I don't remember my father being in the house that day, and I am not sure if this incident happened during the short time span that my mother, sisters, and I were by ourselves after my brother and father fled to Miami. All I know is that this memory has stayed with me all my life. It's a memory that I kept close to me in my years as a police officer in the Miami-Dade Police Department. I knew from my own personal experiences how terrifying it is for a family to have their homes invaded by armed, uniformed men. In the United States, we have strict constitutional protections to keep innocent people from experiencing what my family (and many other families) experienced on that day. Seeing this happening with my own eyes made me understand and respect the constitutional rights of others while I was doing my job as a law enforcement officer. This is something that stayed with me for my entire career. Even if someone inside the house being raided actually

Eloy Jr. turns on his television in Havana (Eloy L. Nuñez).

committed a crime, great care should be taken to protect the family members and other innocents who may happen to be in the house during the execution of a search warrant. Sadly, in post–Revolution Cuba, these armed bearded men could invade anyone's home, at any time, with or without cause. I have come to realize that the bearded men who entered and ransacked our home were probably not there to look for anything. They were there to intimidate us.

Taking a Ferry to Isla de Pinos

In preparation for writing my story, I started to read Armando Valladares' *Against All Hope*—an inspirational account of the travails of many of Cuba's political prisoners. I highly recommend this book for all to read. I would especially like for all the Castro apologists to read Armando's book. The story that Armando tells serves as a counterweight to those people who have allowed themselves to blindly and uncritically accept Fidel Castro's propaganda. Bending of the truth, and rewriting history is a hallmark of what Communists do. That's the only way that they can survive. Communism doesn't work as an economic system. That has been proven time and time again in Russia, China, East Germany, Cuba, and now in Venezuela. Communism disincentivizes peoples' motivation and leads nations to economic ruin. The totalitarian government that controls that economic system terrorizes its people and then lies to them. The government takes whatever property it covets and doles it out in the same manner that a pusher doles out drugs to his addicts. The people develop a lifelong dependence on the government. Communism survives because of dependence and fear. It is not because the people get free health care and education as the Castro regime claims. Communism would not survive where there is freedom.

Reading Armando's book reminded me of my family's trip to Isla de Pinos (Isle of Pines) to visit my uncle, *Tio* Luis (my mother's brother), and my cousin Delfin. Delfin was imprisoned at Isla de Pinos for no other reason than having been a captain and pilot of a B-26 bomber in the pre–Revolution Air Force. Delfin was sentenced to 30 years in prison for his offense of being a loyal military servant. That was his "crime."

Tio Luis was a sergeant crew chief on the same B-26 aircraft that my cousin Delfin piloted. As a lower ranked service member, he received a shorter prison sentence at Isla de Pinos. As it turned out later, Luis served only a couple of years of his sentence and Delfin was released some 15 years into his original sentence. Luis and his wife Carmina were allowed to leave Cuba, and arrived in Miami in the summer of 1962. I'm not sure exactly when Delfin was released and allowed to leave Cuba. I think it was some time in the early 1980s.

My mother Pilar and my sister Pili on a ferry ride in Havana harbor (Eloy L. Nuñez).

My uncle "Tio Luis" and his bride Carmina. Havana, Cuba, late 1950s before the Revolution (Eloy L. Nuñez).

Another family member who was imprisoned as a political prisoner was my brother in-law Renaldo Blanco Navarro. His "crime" was that he served his country as a captain in the pre–Revolution Cuban army. Renaldo served a few years of his prison sentence—I believe at La Cabaña prison in Havana. He was released in the early 1960s and was allowed to come to the United States, where he married my sister Pili and signed up for the U.S. Army. He was later commissioned as a captain in the U.S. Marines.

Later, when he arrived in Miami, I never spoke to Delfin about his long stay in prison. I sensed that he did not want to talk about it, and out of respect for him, I never asked. I did ask Tio Luis a little bit about it when I was in my early teens. Luis didn't want to talk about it much either, but he did tell me a little bit about how the prisoners were fed food with maggots in it, and how the guards would sometimes urinate in the prisoners' food. That account is corroborated by Armando Valladares in his book. I saw pictures of my uncle Luis before prison and he looked like a thin, but muscular man. When he came out of Castro's prison, he looked like a skeleton with skin. He stayed like that for the rest of his life. Tio Luis was a very gaunt man. He lived a good and honorable life in Miami. Luis and his wife Carmina had a daughter named Elizabeth, and three beautiful grandchildren. Luis passed away not too long ago (in the mid 2010's). He was my mother's favorite little brother, and one of the sweetest men I have ever known. Elizabeth was my younger cousin, but I loved her as if she was my little sister. I still do.

One common trait shared by my uncle Luis and my cousin Delfin was their unwavering love of life. Both of these men could have, and should have, been bitter about having some of their years taken away from them. But both of them always stayed positive. Always had a smile on their faces. Always did good things for others. Never complained. These men were great role models for me to emulate as a young man.

My brother in-law Renaldo didn't talk much about his stay in the prison either. The only time I recall him ever saying anything about it was during a "man only" work camping trip that he, his brother Nelson, and I took to Montura Ranch, close to Clewiston, Florida one weekend. I was 18 years old at the time, and I went there to help them fix up a trailer that he bought and set up on a plot of land that he owned. Our family had been camping at Montura Ranch in tents for many years, but I guess he wanted to upgrade to a trailer. I offered to help him because he was always kind to me. I thought spending an entire weekend to help him fix up the trailer was the right thing to do.

It was during that trip that he intimated to me some of the horrors in La Cabaña. Unlike my uncle Luis and my cousin Delfin, Renaldo was not a "sweet" man. I would describe him as a tough Marine. He was a very funny and charismatic man, but he was the prototypical Alpha male. I think that when I was younger, Renaldo perceived me as being a soft "mamma's boy" because I had a mother and two sisters doting over me all the time. I think I changed his perception of who I was on that camping weekend. I had now become a grown man, and I think that is why he opened up to me like he had never done before. Renaldo and I were never close, but that weekend, while working alongside him, I got to know him more. Yes, he was a tough guy. Nothing will ever change that. But that weekend I got to see the vulnerable side of him that I had never seen before. That's when I realized the mental scars that his stay at the brutal La Cabaña prison had caused.

I was only three or maybe four years old when my mother, my brother, and my two sisters travelled to Isla de Pinos to visit my uncle Luis and my cousin Delfin. I can't remember much, but I believe that this must have happened in 1959, or early 1960 because my brother was there, and he did not leave Cuba until the summer of that year. I remember boarding a ferry that took us across to the island. I remember vividly my brother boosting me up to a round porthole window that was only a few feet above the waterline. My brother said, *"mira ... un tiburon!"* (look ... a shark!). I can't honestly say that I saw the shark fin that he was pointing out to me. I just saw the waves of the sea. But that's about all I remember from that trip. Cuba is known for the very large sharks in its waters. The Hemingway classic, *Old Man and the Sea* comes to mind when I think of sharks and Cuba. I didn't see the shark that my brother pointed out to me that day, but the memory of it now makes me think of the hundreds of thousands of souls who crossed the Florida Straits on rafts to get to freedom. We know of those who made it across successfully, but we don't know of the many who did not make it. It makes me wonder how many of them had to fend off sharks like in the story *The Old Man and the Sea*. How many families perished in their attempt to gain freedom? Sometimes, we recover empty rafts at sea, or those that wash up onshore. It's impossible to know how many people have perished while attempting to cross the Florida Straits to their freedom, although there are estimates that between 25 and 50 percent of those who attempt to escape the island end up dying at sea. The memory of a shark sighting during our ferry crossing to Isla de Pinos also makes me think of my good friend Diego Mella and his heroic swim to freedom. But that's another story, and I'll let Diego tell that one.

I don't recall much of what happened when we arrived at Isla de Pinos. All I remember was spending time in a waiting area for a very long time. At some point, our family became separated, but I don't remember how or why that happened. In any case, we were eventually reunited and allowed to return home to Havana. I don't know if my mother ever got to see her little brother Luis, or whether we ever got to see my cousin Delfin. I never talked to my mother about this day, so my memory is very spotty. All I know is that our lives were suddenly upended, and we were forced to travel and to wait and to endure many hardships for no fault of our own. Two of our family members were being held in a prison where they were treated brutally by the guards. Like all the other political prisoners, the only reason that they were incarcerated was because they were on the losing side of the Revolution. Neither of these men had committed a crime. They were detained and convicted without the due process that we are accustomed to in our democratic constitutional republic. The basic rights that we take for granted in the U.S. and that Cubans took for granted before the Revolution had now disappeared.

In the preceding paragraphs, I have described my memories of Cuba the best I can recollect. I now turn the rest of my essay to my recollections of our early exile in the United States. My brother's story (in "Facing the Possibility of Never Returning") provides the dates and times of our arrival in America. I don't remember much of the trip from Cuba, other than my mother, two sisters and I boarded a plane in Havana. All I remember was when we arrived in Miami, we were greeted by my father and brother, who had come a couple of months earlier and had established a residence for the entire family in a brown brick or stone building directly across the street from the old Orange Bowl stadium. I remember that my father called the building "El Colonial." I don't know if that was its real name, or a name my father made up.

Final family portrait in Havana, 1960. Back row: brother Luis, mother Pilar, and father Eloy Sr. Bottom: sister Pilar (Pili), Eloy Jr., and sister Gladys (Laly).

The First Cuban Refugees in Miami

According to my brother Luis, he and my father arrived in the United States on July 11, 1960. They were among the first Cuban political refugees who came to Miami. As a four-year-old, I was mostly ignorant of the hardships that my father and brother had to endure in the months that preceded the arrival of the rest of us. It wasn't until I read my brother's story that I came to learn of all the challenges they had to endure. Nor was I aware of all the things my mother did to get her family reunited in the U.S. I have always admired my mother for her independence and tenacity, but after hearing my brother's account of my mother's exploits, I have even more respect for her. The woman was a lioness.

Despite all the hardships that my father and brother endured in those couple of months that preceded my arrival in Miami, they did a superhuman job of making everything seem as normal as it could be for me. I remember them showing me a really cool toy that they had bought to present to me on the day I arrived. It was a miniature surface-to-air missile battery that projected a light with the silhouette of jet planes on the ceiling of our apartment. These missiles looked like the Nike Ajax SAM missiles of that era. The object of the toy was to push a button to launch the little SAM missiles to try to hit the projected silhouettes. Now that I look back, I think it was pretty ironic that my first toy in Miami was a missile battery. From what I recall, the Cuban Missile crisis would come in a couple of years. I played with the missile toy for a while, but I think the one that really enjoyed playing with it was my brother. Even though he was already a young man, he still enjoyed building airplane models, and he was a kid at heart. He still is.

I remember that my father and brother had gone to great lengths to get the apartment at "El Colonial" ready for us, and fully stocked. I think it was a one bedroom, one bath apartment because I remember sleeping on a sofa bed in between my two sisters. I'm not sure where my father and mother and brother slept, but that little place held six of us for several months. It was a very old and ugly place, and I still remember the huge dead rats that my father would throw into the garbage can after extracting them from the mousetraps that he used to set. As I recall, there were many rats.

There was one incident at El Colonial that has remained in my memory. A young boy—probably around 7 to 8 years old—accidentally locked himself into a storage closet at the apartment. I think he must have been playing hide-and-go-seek with his friends. My older sister Pili and I heard the screams coming from the utility closet. We went over to the apartment manager's office to ask for help to unlock the door. My sister talked to an old man—I think it was the apartment manager—who had a key to the closet. After about 5 minutes, the old man came down and opened the closet door and let the boy out. I will never forget that boy's face when he walked out of the closet. His eyes had the look of terror in them. The boy had accidentally imprisoned himself in a small confined closet in total darkness. He may have been in there five, or ten minutes, or even longer. Since that day, I have had a fear of being locked up in a confined area in total darkness. That incident left a lifelong impression on me, and I'm sure that the boy that was locked in the closet never forgot it either.

El Colonial was ugly and rat infested, and we eventually moved to another larger apartment only a few months later. The only cool thing about El Colonial was that it was directly across the street from the Orange Bowl and on Saturday nights, we could see and hear all the commotion of the University of Miami games. I remember one time, my brother took me to a game and he snuck in after halftime through the open-ended east end zone. That was the first time I had ever seen a live football game, and I remember the colors and the bands playing, and the sense of excitement in the air. I became a fan of American football immediately, even if at four years of age, I didn't fully understand the rules of the game.

We would return to the Orange Bowl many times later in my life. The first time I went back was when President Kennedy addressed a large crowd after the Bay of Pigs debacle in 1962. I also have many fond memories of Dolphin and Hurricane games there later on. I know the Orange Bowl is no longer there, but I don't know if the old El Colonial still stands.

Another benefit of living across the street from the Orange Bowl is that there was a kid's park on the southeast corner of the property. My brother would take me to the playground there, and I would play on the swings and slides. As I look back, I'm not sure how my family was able to make my transition from Havana to Miami almost seamless. With all the hardships that they had to endure, it never affected their four-year-old boy. I was taken very good care of by my father and mother, and even more so by my brother and two sisters.

Since we left everything we owned back in Cuba, we arrived in Miami with little or no money. My mother once told me the story of how she had stashed $40 into her bra at the Havana airport so that we would have at least some money when we landed in Miami. But unfortunately, some *miliciano* at the Havana airport forcibly removed the money from my mother's bra and kept it for himself. That means that when we arrived in Miami, my mother was literally penniless.

We started life with nearly nothing, but somehow we survived. I remember my mother came home one day with a box filled with sugar, cooking oil, rice, beans, macaroni, and peanut butter. That box was a gift from the Catholic church. We were grateful for it because it helped us get through the first days. That box would be the only handout that my family would ever receive. My mother made sure to pay it back to the church many times over.

That means that my father, mother, brother, and sisters had to find jobs right away in order to survive. All but my sister Pili found work. Pili's job was to take care of her four-year-old brother at home. She preferred it that way. My sister Laly, on the other hand, preferred to go out and find some work. Both of them spoke English quite well, and both had been trained in Cuba to do secretarial work, so finding a job for either one was no problem. All my family members, like most Cubans, are very hard workers, and dependable too. My father possessed a lot of skills, and he easily landed a job first at Apex Photography, and soon thereafter at Associated Photographers, where he worked for many years until he retired. My father had mastered many technical skills in photography that made him a hot commodity.

My brother was also skilled in many technical areas and he was fluent in English. However, it was harder for him to find a good job at first, and I remember one day he came home with his face blistered and burned. He had opened an overheated car radiator and the hot water had splashed on his face. Back then, cars didn't have the safety features that they have now, and not knowing about the hot pressurized water upon removing the radiator cap, he burned his face badly. I felt so bad for him at the time. But the first degree burns that he sustained healed quickly and he was back to work soon thereafter.

My mother got a job in a frozen meat-cutting factory. She used to have to wear a jacket and wool cap on the job, even in the heat of the Miami summer. I remember that her job was to cut frozen chickens into quarters. One day she came home with a really deep cut on one of her fingers. She accidently almost cut her finger off while working there. I felt so sorry for her, but she never let anyone take pity on her. I was glad when she later found another job working as a "finisher" in a garment factory.

Within a few months, we moved from El Colonial to a larger apartment a few blocks away on 15th Avenue in Little Havana. I'm not sure if my memory is correct, but I believe the exact address of the place was 431 SW 15 Avenue. Why I remember that number after all these years is a mystery to me. I think we lived there about a year before we moved to our permanent house in Westchester. I have a few memories of life in that apartment. I remember the Goodyear blimp flying directly overhead several times. I thought that was the coolest thing I had ever seen. Of course, I had not yet seen a lot of things at that point of my life.

Life in "Little Havana"

It wasn't called "Little Havana" back then because there weren't many Cubans in Miami in 1960. The apartment on SW 15 Avenue was smack in the middle of what we now call Little Havana. We were halfway between Flagler Street and SW 8 Street, which was later called "Calle Ocho" and remains that way to this date. Not too far to our west was 17th Avenue. I'm not sure because it was a long time ago, but I think there was a Grand Union food store nearby, maybe on SW 8 Street, or maybe Flagler Street. That is where my parents would go shop for groceries. I also remember a phone booth on a sidewalk that many of the Cuban refugees like ourselves would use to call their family members in Cuba long distance. It was a small community back then, and everyone seemed to know everyone else. I remember my father and mother waiting in a short line for others to finish their long-distance conversations with their loved ones in Cuba. My parents had to take a lot of coins with them whenever they used this public phone booth to call home.

Soon after moving into the 15th Avenue apartment, we were able to afford a hardline telephone. I used the word "hardline" because I recognize that many of the readers of this book were born after the invention of cell phones and they may not realize how inaccessible and difficult it was back in the 1960s to make phone calls. The telephone was what was then called a "party line." That meant that many different households would share the same line. For example, you would pick up the phone and someone else from a different house location would be speaking. If you wanted to make a phone call, you would have to wait patiently until the other party ended their call. Sometimes you would have to pick up the phone receiver and check several times to hear if the other parties were still on the line. Fortunately, most conversations were fairly short—probably limited by the lack of privacy. But every once in a while, I remember my parents and sisters being frustrated at not being able to use the phone because the other parties on the line were still talking. One way to get on is to politely ask the other party to get off their conversation. That worked sometimes, but other times it did not. Sometimes, it infuriated the other party and that just made them talk longer out of spite. I suspect that having a Spanish accent in our voice may have had something to do with that.

Living in an apartment on SW 15 Avenue was not that much different than our home in Havana. The main difference was probably the size of the apartment. But in both cases, the building was a conventional square block structure with two floors. Whereas in Cuba, my family occupied the entire building—part of which was my parents' photo studio—in Little Havana, our apartment was just one of four. Shortly after we moved there, another family known to us moved into a separate apartment. Their names were Manolo and Mercedes Blanco-Navarro, their daughter Carmen, and their youngest son Jorge, who we called "Yoyi" for short. Manolo and Mercedes would later become my sister Pili's father and mother in-laws when she married their second oldest son, Renaldo.

The layout of the apartment building made it so that living was a bit cramped and therefore, there was very little privacy. There was no air conditioning, and on hot summer nights, it was not unusual for the occupants of all four apartments to gather on the front porch area of the building to cool down and to socialize after dinner. Fifteenth Avenue was not a very busy street, but it did have some light traffic. One evening, I remember a car with four men driving by very slowly on the Avenue in front of us. My family and several friends were sitting outside on lawn chairs when these men drove by. I saw three of them duck down so as not to be seen, and then the car sped off in a northbound direction. Someone on the porch said, "those are gangsters ... time to go inside ... let's go." My mother quickly grabbed me and we went inside the rest of the night. I have no idea who those "gangsters" were, but even as a four-year-old, I could sense that they were up to no good. That was the first time I had ever heard of the word "gangster," but it would not be the last.

Soon after our family moved into the apartment in Little Havana, my parents scraped up a little money to purchase an old black and white television. It had been several months since we had been able to watch any TV, but now with four out of six family members working full-time, we had sufficient income to afford the purchase. One of the first images that I remember seeing on that little TV was of the Brigade 2506 prisoners returning from their prisons in Cuba. There was live television coverage of the Brigade soldiers walking down the stairs from the airplanes onto the airport tarmac in Miami. Some of the soldiers walked down the stairs unaided by anyone, and seemed to be quite happy to be returning to their families in the United States. But the image that stuck in my mind the most was that of several men on crutches, missing one of their legs. That image left an impression on this four-year-old. I remember watching the live news coverage with my two sisters. I could sense their sadness. We were happy that these soldiers had returned to us, but we were sad that the mission had failed and that many of the soldiers would not be coming back. It was a very sad occasion for all of us.

President Kennedy and his wife Jaqueline came to the Orange Bowl shortly thereafter to give a speech to welcome the soldiers back and to get the Cuban people not to lose their hope. My family attended that event at the Orange Bowl, and at the time we felt grateful for the president to have come all the way to Miami to greet the soldiers and to address the small Cuban refugee community. But now that I am older, I realize that Kennedy's reason was not so much to re-inspire the Cuban exiles. This wasn't a pep rally. It was an attempt to do damage control after having made the catastrophic decision to abandon the soldiers on the beach of Bay of Pigs. Kennedy will always be remembered by Cuban Americans for being the president that promised much, but delivered nothing. He will always be considered by my generation of Cuban Americans as the president who betrayed the Cuban people. For me personally, it was not so much that he did it, but *when* he did it. I think Cuban Americans would have been more forgiving of Kennedy if he had changed his mind *before* the mission. Sending men to battle and then pulling out the promised support before the mission is complete and letting them die and be captured on the beach is more than incompetence. It is immoral. Sadly, this is a pattern that was repeated in later conflicts. Vietnam, Somalia, Iraq, and Afghanistan come to mind. In all these conflicts, presidents sent American or allied soldiers to war and then withdrew them before the mission was completed. The lesson that I have learned from these historical debacles is simple. Don't start something unless you're prepared to finish it.

For some Cuban exile fathers and mothers in Miami, the return of their sons from Cuban prisons was a joyous occasion. For others, there would be no joy. One evening that I will never forget, several families were sitting on the front porch area of the apartment building on 15th Avenue as had become the custom. My father and mother and my brother and sister were there, as were our future in-laws Manolo and Mercedes. Someone—I don't remember who—brought some bad news to Manolo and Mercedes. The news was that their oldest son Manolito had been executed by firing squad in Cuba. I then heard an ungodly scream come from Mercedes, followed by uncontrollable sobbing. Her oldest son was dead.

Those who were outside on the porch that night tried to console Mercedes, but there was nothing that could be said to her that made any sense. Some told her to keep in mind that her two other sons were still alive in Cuba, and that she should stay strong for them. Now that I think back at that, it was probably not the best thing to say to her. I think it was best just to pay one's respects, and then just leave her alone. Mercedes' second and third sons would survive. The second son, Renaldo, would later marry my sister Pili and have two sons.

For Cuban exile parents, the outcomes of which sons lived and which ones died seemed to be totally arbitrary. For my parents at least, they had all four of their children in Miami, so they did not need to worry as much as other parents. That of course would soon change when my brother Luis enlisted in the Army the following year. The Vietnam war was about to get started, and many sons of Cuban exiles decided to enlist and repay America for allowing us to live here. Some would not come back from that war either. Others would come back, but they would be severely maimed.

Our First House in Westchester

By 1962, with four out of six family members working full-time, my parents were able to save enough money to purchase their first house in the

Westchester area of Dade County. I remember that we went to see two houses—one just south of Coral Way around 73rd Avenue, and the other just three blocks north of Coral Way and 75th Avenue. The first house was OK, but when we got to the second one, I remember seeing the large grass area in the back yard and loving it. I started rolling around on the grass like a crazy boy. My parents laughed at me, but I think that was the main reason why they chose to buy that house instead of the other one. That was my family's house until my father and mother passed away in the years 2000 and 2012, respectively.

I started school shortly after we moved to our Westchester house. I missed kindergarten, so I had to start my schooling in first grade at Flagami Elementary School. The day that I started first grade, I did not speak a word of English. I felt so lost and embarrassed. Too embarrassed to even ask the teacher to use the bathroom. I must have been a pretty quick learner because by the time I got to sixth grade, I was chosen to be a school patrolman, a student librarian, and was elected as class president in the second semester. I also played the role of a policeman in the school play. I guess I was destined to be a policeman—even though I never really aspired to be one. The teachers must have seen something in me that I did not see in myself. That year I was also chosen by my teachers as the school's top student, and I was recognized by the American Legion. My parents of course were very proud of me for winning that award. To me, I was just glad not to do anything that would embarrass my family. That was my main motivator as a kid … and it still is. Never do anything that brings shame to your family. That is something that I have tried to live up to my entire life.

While my family moved to the Westchester area, Manolo and Mercedes and their family moved to Hialeah. Those two areas turned out to be the epicenters of Cuban American migration from Little Havana to the county's suburbs. Later, Cuban Americans would migrate to the Kendall area, and some to Broward County as well. But when I started first grade at Flagami Elementary in 1962, I was the only Cuban child in that school. I remember that all the teachers were very nice, and they were very patient with me. I was able to learn English very quickly, but I did not like Spanish class because at the time, there was no such thing as a "Spanish for Spanish speakers" class. I had to endure hours of, *"hola Isabel. Como esta usted?"* I never saw the sense of me having to endure those first grade Spanish classes, but there was no other place to put me. Everybody in the classroom had to take the same lessons. When the other kids found out that I spoke Spanish, they all wanted me to teach them the curse words. The problem was that my parents and brothers and sisters hardly ever cursed. The only bad words that I ever heard at home were *coño, carajo,* and *come mierda.* In fact, I learned most of the really nasty Spanish curse words from my English speaking American friends.

I'm not sure where they learned those words from, but I remember getting in trouble one day when I said one of those words in front of my mother at home. It's a bit ironic that I would learn most of my Spanish cuss words at a school where I was the only Spanish speaker at the time.

For at least a year, I was the only Cuban student at Flagami Elementary. I remember a little black Cuban girl that attended the school while I was in second grade. But this little girl didn't last long. I'm not sure what happened to her, or where she ended up. It was 1963, and I think schools were not yet racially desegregated. Another Cuban boy showed up in third grade, and another in fourth. By the time I left 6th grade, there were probably no more than a dozen Cuban children at that elementary school. By the time I started 7th grade at West Miami Junior (middle) High, a lot of Cuban kids had arrived in the U.S. I don't know the exact numbers, but by 1968, it seemed like about a third of the students at my middle school were of Cuban origin. That ratio would further increase by the time I got high school—first at Coral Park, and then at South Miami High.

Eloy Jr. and big brother Luis (Gordo), at their Westchester home, Miami, Florida, 1964 (Eloy L. Nuñez).

Our house in Westchester served as a temporary stop for many other family members who arrived after us. First came cousin Pepe in April 1962. Pepe was more like my second older brother than a cousin. I still think of him as a brother. Shortly after Pepe's arrival, my uncle Luis and his wife Carmina arrived in the summer of 1962. They spent several months at our house until they were financially stable enough to afford their own apartment. My grandmother (my mother's mother) Ramona and her oldest son, my uncle Alejandro, arrived in Miami in 1965. My other aunt Carmen came later. All of them stayed at our house for several months until they were able to afford their own places. All this caused some discomfort because our house at the time had three bedrooms, but only one bathroom. There were times where as many as eight or nine members of our family were sharing one bathroom. Now that I think of it, that may partially explain why my brother Luis enlisted for the Army.

We Are American Citizens

By 1964, my brother had gone away to basic training in the U.S. Army, and sister Pili had married Renaldo, the second son of Manolo and Mercedes. Renaldo had also enlisted in the U.S. Army, and later in the Marines as a commissioned officer of the rank of captain. Renaldo and Pili's wedding featured a line of military men in their Class-A uniforms from different branches of the military. I remember as the couple exited the church, they walked underneath a gauntlet of military men holding up their ceremonial sabers to form a tunnel. The wedding ceremony was very impressive, and my sister was the happiest she had ever been in her life. She was marrying the boy who she adored and loved back in Cuba. His life had been spared, but his brother's life had not. That sort of thing can mess up someone's mind, and perhaps that may be part of the reason why the marriage was not as successful as the wedding. Sadly, the two were divorced many years later.

In 1964, all that were left living at our house were my mother, father, my sister Gladys (Laly) and me. Of course, we had the many family members who stayed with us for a month or two, but now my brother had gone off to the Army, and my older sister Pili was married and living in Dallas, Texas with her military career husband. By this time, my father and mother had decided that we would apply to become U.S. citizens. To do that, we had to fly to Toronto, Canada, and then re-enter the United States. I'm not sure why we had to do that, but at the time, that must have been a condition for us applying for residency and later for citizenship. So, my father planned a trip to Toronto, via New York City. By this time, Renaldo and Pili had their first child—Manolito (Manny)—who was named after Renaldo's slain older brother. They ended up moving to Queens New York, and my father planned the trip so that we would visit them there before going to Toronto.

We took a plane from Miami International Airport to New York City (I can't remember if it was La Guardia or Kennedy). Onboard were my father, my mother, my sister Laly, and me. Back then, my father insisted that we all dress up when we flew on airlines. My father wore a coat and tie, and he made me dress up too. My mother and my sister wore long 1950s style dresses. We must have looked like something out of an Ozzie and Harriet episode. While we were there, we visited the New York World Fair, and the Statue of Liberty. The World Fair was fun and exciting, but the Statue of Liberty was beautiful and inspirational. Even though I was only 8 years old at the time, I fully sensed the significance of visiting the Statue on our way to getting our American citizenship. We ended our trip in Toronto, but not before we took a side tour to Niagara Falls. That was our first real vacation since we left Cuba. It was a memorable trip, and really showed us what it meant to be Americans.

Shortly after that, my brother finished his Army tour and came back home. I was so proud of him in his Army uniform. My big brother Luis has always been my role model and my hero. I have always called him "Gordo" but at the time, he was rail thin and muscular. "Gordo" was a name that he would gradually grow into later in his life. Gordo met a beautiful and classy lady named Mirta and they soon got married. They had three daughters: twins Cristina (Crissy) and Beatriz (Betty), and later Susana (Suzy).

Next it was my sister Laly's turn to marry. Laly met a wonderful man named Onuence Medina and they got married and had a son named Daniel (Danny). I don't consider Onuence to be my brother in-law. I con-

Sister Pili and husband Renaldo Blanco, flanked by their two sons Manolito (Manny) on the left, and Renaldito (Renny) on the right, Westchester neighborhood of Miami, 1969 (Eloy L. Nuñez).

sider him to be my brother. That's how much I love him, and how much I love my sister in-law Mirta. We have been blessed by having a wonderful extended family, where everyone is kind, everyone is respectful of each other, and everyone has a great sense of humor. There is nothing more fun and satisfying than having all these people gathered together for a family outing.

There are many more funny stories that I could tell, including the time that a City of Miami officer issued a $2 ticket to my mother for jaywalking across a Downtown street while trying to catch a bus that was leaving us behind. I will leave that story for another time because I want to wrap up this essay soon. All I can say is that my mother was not very happy with me after I took the officer's side, instead of her side. I guess that was another early indicator that I would grow up to be a policeman one day. And as my mother found out the hard way—I would become an incorruptible policeman when I grew up.

I will end this section with the story of our first true vacation since arriving in the United States. My parents took the family on a road trip to St. Augustine, Florida in 1966. Back then, an uninterrupted interstate I-95 did not exist, therefore, my father decided to take U.S. 1 all the way from Miami to St. Augustine. My grandmother Ramona came with us on the trip, along with my parents, my sister Laly, and me. After a long road trip, we arrived at the outskirts of St. Augustine, where my father saw a restaurant and decided to stop there for dinner before checking into a nearby motel. I remember walking in and the five of us being seated at a table far away from all the other patrons. At first, I didn't think anything of it, but it later became apparent that we were not welcomed at this restaurant. I say that because for about 20 minutes, no waitress came to ask us for drinks or anything else. They would walk right by us as if we didn't exist. Several other families came in after we did, and they were served right away. Eventually, my father got up and asked the waitress to attend to us, but the waitress walked away and did not speak with him. That's when my father decided to take us out of there. We ended up going to a Kentucky Fried Chicken instead.

I remember feeling so bad for my father and mother when this happened. Nobody deserves to be treated in such a manner, but especially these two people. They were both the sweetest and most loving human beings that I have ever known. All their lives, they helped anyone and everyone that needed help. I remember our house being a place where many people of all colors would be invited to come and eat dinner at our table. There were many stories of my mother helping others. She once saved a choking child at a grocery store. Whenever she was at a hospital, either as a patient or just visiting, my mother was like another nurse to the patients. My mother always acted quickly to help people in distress, even when others would freeze with inaction. Likewise, my father was always thinking of others. He was respectful of the environment. He's the one who taught me to respect animals and plants, and to never leave litter anywhere. These were two genuine and good people. They did not deserve to be ignored like they were. That incident gave me a little taste of what it must have been to be an African American in some parts of the U.S. during the 1960s. I can personally attest—it's not a good feeling to be ignored like that.

After finishing our dinner at KFC, we checked into a motel room. All five of us in the same room. The motel had a pool in the front, and my sister and I wanted to go swimming, but of course, there's the Cuban 3-hour rule about not swimming or showering after eating. So, we had to wait until the next day to go in the pool.

The next morning we went to visit the historical district of St. Augustine. My father purchased tram tickets for all of us so that we could ride around and see all the historical sites. I was so impressed with the beauty of that town—and I was especially impressed with the fort, Castillo de San Marcos.

I thought the moat around it was so cool. After finishing up a tour of the entire fort, my father decided that he wanted to visit the Fountain of Youth. So, we strolled over to the tram station in front of the fort and waited for the tram to take us to the Fountain. We waited and waited, and when a tram finally showed up, it turned out that it was not the one that was headed that way, so we had to wait some more. Meanwhile, I was looking at the little fold-up brochure map that the St. Augustine Chamber of Commerce provides to all its visitors. I told my father that the Fountain of Youth was only four blocks away, and I suggested that we walk there via a shortcut that I had seen on the map. Unfortunately for all of us, my father listened to my advice and decided to have us all walk to the Fountain. What I didn't realize was that the Chamber of Commerce brochure map was not drawn to scale, and only the main streets were pictured. Those four blocks turned out to be fourteen blocks, and about a twenty-minute walk. It was summertime, and it was very hot and humid. That twenty-minute walk was rough on all of us, but it was especially difficult for my grandmother.

When we finally arrived at the Fountain of Youth, we were all hot and sweaty and dehydrated. Our feet hurt too. Clearly, my father had made the cardinal mistake of basing his decision on the judgment of a nine-year-old. But despite being aggravated at himself for letting me sway his decision, he never said a word to me, and he never blamed me for it.

The humorous part of this story was when we arrived and purchased our tickets to enter the Fountain of Youth. As soon as we got inside, the first thing my sister did was take off her shoes and dip her bare feet into a small stream of cold running water. We waited for a couple of minutes for her to cool off her feet, and then we moved along into a building. That's when we noticed that the stream where my sister put her bare feet in to cool them down, was the same stream of water going into the building.

When we walked in, we were each offered a little tiny paper cup of Fountain spring water. That offering was intended to be a novelty as part of the Fountain of Youth experience. It was not meant to re-hydrate our dehydrated bodies. My mother, being a Lucille Ball clone—a naturally funny human being, without trying to be—kept asking the man who was giving out the little cups of water for more, and more. I remember drinking about ten of those little cups of water, and seeing all my family members doing the same. I looked around, and everybody was looking at us funny. They must have thought that we were a bunch of zealous foreign pilgrims who were there to drink the water in order to stay eternally youthful, as the legend has it. Never mind that we were probably drinking the same water where my sister had just soaked her feet. We didn't care. We were so tired and so thirsty that nothing else mattered to us. The rest of our stay at the Fountain, instead of paying attention to what the narrator of the guided tour was saying, we decided to go under a large shady tree and cool down. That was our last stop, and after finishing at the Fountain of Youth, we then went back to the motel, and my mother let my sister and me go in the pool the rest of the evening. We had had our fill of the magical Fountain of Youth water.

Working in the Darkness

As I grew older, my father would sometimes take me to work with him during the summer months when there was no school. I think he was trying to teach me his trade, and at the same time keep me out of trouble. I was a good kid, and all I ever did was play sports after school. But even good kids do stupid things once in a while. I was no exception. I was 13 years old when I arrived home from school one day, and I realized that I had left my house keys at home and therefore, I could not get in. The middle school lets out at 3:30 in the afternoon, so I would have to wait until around 6 o'clock for one of my parents to get home to let me in. So instead of waiting for them, what did I do? I did one of the stupidest things I ever did in my life. I decided to break into my own house. Worse—I decided to break the glass pane of the door with my fist, thereby cutting myself pretty bad. So … I broke in, and then put a paper towel on my fist to slow down the bleeding. Then I did something even more stupid. Instead of throwing the blood-soaked paper towel away, I decided it looked really cool and I kept it. This is something that Beavis and Butthead would have done, except that I did it about 25 years before they existed. I guess in that sense, I was ahead of the times.

If breaking into my own house and cutting my fist with the glass, and then saving the bloodstained paper towel wasn't stupid enough, I then did something even more stupid. I decided to go play baseball with my friends at the schoolyard. I covered my wound with an ace bandage and grabbed my baseball glove and bat, and left the house unattended, with a glass door broken, and blood on a paper towel and on the broken glass. I thought I would impress my friends with the blood that seeped through the Ace bandage. Never mind the possibility of dirt getting on the wound and developing an infection. Those things never occurred to me. But the worst part of all this was the distress I put my poor mother through.

You can imagine what must have gone through my mother's head when she got home and saw the broken glass and all the blood. I was nowhere to be found, and my mother got hysterical. She started calling all the neighbors and some of my friends' mothers to see if they knew where I was. Nobody knew. So then, my mother walked three blocks to West Miami Junior High School, where my friends and I would often play sports after school. I was up to bat in a sandlot pickup game when I saw my mother walking toward the field. She was a good four hundred yards away, but I recognized her from that distance. I had never seen her walk all the way to the school, so I figured something was wrong. I was so insensitive and clueless that I didn't realize that she was there because she was in a panic worrying about me. I walked toward her and met her halfway. It wasn't until I got close to her, that I realized that she was crying. That's when I realized what I had done. I made my mother worry about me for no good reason. I was such an idiot. To this day, I still feel remorse about that.

In any regard, I think my father thought that I would benefit by coming to work for him at his job at Associated Photographers. For the rest of the summer, I rode to work with my father every day, and came home with him every day. It was a straight shot on SW 8 Street, from 74 Avenue, all the way to South Miami Avenue on the edge of the Miami River. I did this for a few summers, and when I got my learner's permit driver's license, my father would let me drive back and forth. Thankfully, I never wrecked his car on all these commutes down crazy SW 8 Street.

My father was hired by Art Apple, the owner of Associated Photographers, back in 1961 or there about. Mr. Apple, as my father and I always called him, was a very nice man, and he loved and respected my father. The feeling was mutual. My father held Mr. Apple in very high regard.

I didn't realize it until just moments ago when I Googled the name "Associated Photographers" that I learned that Mr. Apple had once been in the U.S. Army Air Corps' Photo Reconnaissance Squadron collecting aerial imagery for intelligence purposes. This may explain why Mr. Apple hired my father so soon after we came from Cuba. My father was also in the photoreconnaissance section of the Cuban Air Force, where he served as a lieutenant, and often flew in the same B-26 airplane as my cousin Delfin and my uncle Luis. My father never told me this, but aerial photography was probably the common link that brought him to work at Associated Photographers. Now that I think of it, it is quite possible that the two men may have met in Denver, Colorado years earlier, when my father attended a training course there. Aerial photography is a very specialized field, and not too many are experts at it. That these two men shared the same background has to be more than just a coincidence.

At Associated Photographers, there were two labs—one for black and white photo development, and the other for color photo development. Back then, all photos and film had to be developed by hand. Machines that do the job on their own came later in the mid 1970s. Associated Photographers was a small company back then. I don't remember exactly how many employees, but I would estimate that there were no more than seven or eight, including the owner and the front desk secretary. Some of the employees were photographers who specialized in large mural photography. The company catered mostly to business advertising, billboards, and posters, sometimes for political campaigns. On occasion, they would do colorization of black and white portraits. That was one of the areas that my father specialized in. Back then, people would pay good money to have an expert craftsman colorize their black and white portraits. This was a very laborious and precise endeavor that would often take hours, if not days to complete. I used to watch my father do these colorizations. His visual focus and his hand control were remarkable. If it had been me doing it, the picture would have been a giant ugly smudge. My father was a very talented craftsman. He was also a master of free-hand calligraphy.

But the colorization of black and white portraits was not my father's main job. His main job was in the color laboratory. He was the only employee who had the training and technical expertise to do color work. That's because back then, color photography was a multi-step process that required highly specialized skills. Unlike black and white photography, which requires only three chemical steps, and is done in a lab with a soft red light, color photography is a multi-step process that must be done in total darkness. The difference between black and white film processing and color film processing is like the difference between a cook at a McDonald's and a chef at a five-star restaurant. It's not even close.

Nowadays, we use digital cameras, and our phones take photos that are as sharp as any expensive 35-millimeter cameras of the past. There is no longer any need to develop the film in a 16-step process like it was back then. In that process, the color lab technician has to work in total darkness to extract the film out of the camera, or out of its protective case

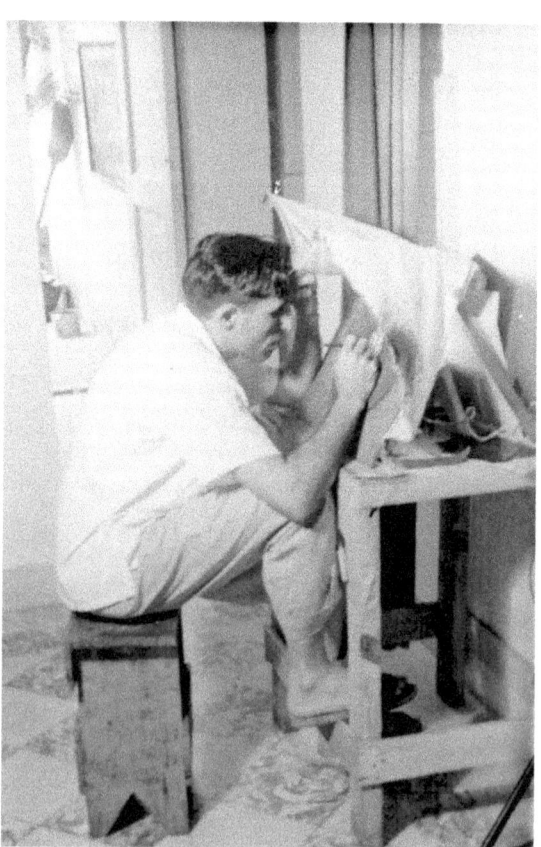

My father Eloy, the artist at work. Havana, Cuba. Unknown year (Eloy L. Nuñez).

so as not to ruin it by exposing it to light. When my father developed film in his color lab, he would have me sit in a chair in a corner out of his way. He would close the door and a sign outside the door would warn others not to open the door. If anyone opened the door to the lab during this process, all the film would be ruined. My father would develop 24 rolls at a time, by putting them on a specialized rectangular shaped metal cage basket with a handle on it, similar to the contraption that fast food restaurants use to cook French fries. He had to do this in total darkness—relying on tactile senses only. Each of the 16 steps required that the cage box with the 24 rolls of film be dipped into a different chemical. Each chemical had a different function, and these 16 steps had to be done in the exact order, and for a precise time period every time—otherwise, the film would be ruined. There was no margin of error. There was no way to recover film that was exposed to light, or left in the tray of chemicals for too long or too short a time.

Wall mural painted by my father Eloy. Unknown year (Eloy L. Nuñez).

At every step, my father would have to reset the alarm clock to the precise time that each of the 16 chemicals required. My father used two large black clocks that hung on the wall. The short and long hands on the clock had to be set by hand. The tips of both hands, and the 12 positions on the clock were marked with luminescent tape that glowed in the dark. This allowed my father to see them in the total darkness. I don't remember exactly the minutes that each step would take, but the entire 16-step process took about 30 minutes.

He would start by setting the clock a certain number of minutes, and then he would dip the basket with the 24 rolls into the first vat of chemicals.

A 1977 family gathering in our parents' house in Westchester. Standing from left to right: Eloy Jr. holding newborn son Eddie. Wife Maria Elena, sister-in-law Mirta and brother Luis, sister Pili, sister Gladys (Laly) and brother-in-law Onuence; nephew Manny. Sitting: twin nieces Crissy and Betty, mother Pilar, father Eloy Sr., niece Suzy, nephews Danny and Renny (Eloy L. Nuñez).

When the loud buzzer would go off, he would transfer the basket into the second vat and would reset the clock. He would work his way through 8 chemical vats on one side, and then make a U-turn for the next 8 vats on the other side. At every step, he would reset the clock for a precise amount of time. All this in total darkness. I can't say I saw him do all this while I was sitting in the chair in the corner because it was all done in total darkness. But I "observed" him doing it with my ears. I observed him doing this process so many times that I could tell what step he was at, and how long the next step would take. I must have observed him do this entire process about three or four times a day, for every workday during my three-month summer vacation. I sat and "watched" my father working in total darkness at least a hundred times. In the hundred times I was there, he never made an error. None of the other technicians could do what he did. Everyone else worked in the black and white lab. In fact, none of them ever entered the color lab. That color lab was my father's realm.

At the end of my father's career, shortly before he retired, a large machine was brought in to do the work that he used to do by hand. I remember the day that the machine was shipped to Associated Photographers. I helped unload it and wheel it in with pallet jacks into a room adjacent to my father's color lab. It was a very large and heavy piece of machinery, and it barely fit through the main hallway. All the employees helped to gently guide it into the small room, where it took up the entire space. That machine made color film processing by hand obsolete. A few years later, that machine would become obsolete as well.

Those many hours I spent sitting in a corner of my father's laboratory in total darkness allowed me to think a lot about things. Being in total darkness is a strange feeling. After a while, you start to see things that are not really there. I must admit, that at first, I was a bit scared. But after a while, I became so accustomed to the darkness that I no longer feared it. Even though I could not see him, I could hear him, and I knew that my father was always there with me. Many years later as a police officer, working the midnight shift, I was sometimes afraid of the darkness. But even when I rode alone as a one-man unit, I felt as though someone was always next to me. I don't know who that person was because I could not see him, but I knew he was there.

My father always said that he would love to go back to Cuba someday, once it was free again. Sadly, he and my mother both died before they realized their dream. A darkness has fallen over the land of my father. Someday, I hope to go back

Top: Sister Gladys (Laly) and her son Daniel (Danny). *Bottom:* My two sons, 1 year-old Richard (Ricky), and 8-year old Eduardo (Eddie), Miami, Florida, 1985 (Eloy L. Nuñez).

The family in Homestead mini-station grand opening, 1995. From left to right: Pili, Maria Elena, Eloy Jr., Eloy Sr., Luis, Pilar, Gladys (Laly) (Eloy L. Nuñez).

and see where our house used to be, and see if the market down the street is still there. I would like to go back to the convent where my aunt Estrella used to take me to meet the nuns. I would like to go back and watch a baseball game. Someday—when my father's land is free—I will go back and honor him and my mother for all their sacrifices. But that day is not today.

Two Lives and Two Countries

Diego Luis Mella

I was born in the City of Guantánamo in 1949 to a family of loving parents and an older brother who constantly watched over me, since I was what today they call hyperactive. I had a normal childhood I guess; my first memories are of a small house right across a train yard, with a railroad crossing nearby, a small creek with lots of trees and birds, and a few friends to play and fight with. Soon enough, my parents matriculated me in La Salle Catholic School for kindergarten. The school had the biggest yard I had ever seen—half of a city block—and it contained a basketball court, physical education corner, and other activities. I loved that school and have fond memories from it, but my time there did not last long. The year was 1954.

My father had a good job and owned a 1954 jeep that he bought from the American Naval Base; the jeep was a re-tread from War World Two, but worked great and he used it for work and to take the family around. My grandfather Diego had bought a nightclub just outside of town called Picolo's Club; it had no walls, but it was very accommodating and had great music, both Spanish and American. It also had a small parking lot, and across the street was an apartment building where American Officers lived with their families off base. I spent lots of time in the summers there for many reasons; a river behind the club, lots of freedom, and American kids to play with across the street. I saw them playing baseball in a makeshift field and I walked over just to see them play. After a while, they came over and gestured to me if I wanted play. I agreed to, and quickly joined them. Baseball is Cuba's favorite sport and despite the language barrier, they became my friends. I began to learn English from them and I taught them Spanish, and their parents would invite me to their homes to eat all the time. The grownups would visit the night club after work to have a few drinks and hold their parties. That was my first introduction to the American way of life; it was 1956.

First Life Change

I thought that my life was perfect; I played, went to grammar school where I excelled, had some great friends, and lived near a river. What else could a kid want? Then, my father took a new job as a representative for a subsidiary of Colgate/Palmolive in the City of Holguín, in Oriente, Cuba. My father told us that this was the job of his life. Initially, all was great. My father had a great salary, we had a great house, I attended another Catholic school, The Marist Brothers, and I became a Cub Scout; this was 1958 and I was eight years old.

Around that time, a bearded man named Fidel Castro was the conversation of the day. News of a killing of a high-ranking police officer in the corner of my school minutes after school let out was a shock to us, and it made the national news. My father did not like politics, but somehow he did not like these *rebeldes* (rebels), especially after a Spanish couple that was visiting a neighbor said that this Fidel was using the same tactics that the communists in Spain had used in the Spanish Civil War. How prophetic they were.

Second Life Change

After Castro's triumph in January 1959, my father started to conspire against the so-called Revolution, and joined a group called *23 de Noviembre*. Shortly after that, my father made my mother, my older brother and me move to Santiago de Cuba to get away from his activities. My mother was very unhappy and the arguments between them were loud and fierce. I did not understand what was occurring and my brother and I were full of trepidation. For a third time, I was changing schools and leaving friends behind to start anew in another city.

My mother placed us in another La Salle school in Santiago, and we were fortunate that the principal there used to be the principal in Guantánamo and knew us. In the meantime, my father would visit a couple of times a month, and sometimes he used me as a courier to deliver envelopes to some "friends." I learned years later that those friends were co-conspirators. At the time, my father was the military chief of his organization in the north of Oriente.

After a few months, my father stopped his visits and I kept asking where he was, but mother could not say. It was early in April of 1961 and something was happening, but we did not know what. The police were out arresting people, and there were tensions in the population. On April 16, 1961, we heard explosions and people screaming in the streets. We looked out the window (we lived on the second floor of an apartment building) and could see planes dive on the Santiago de Cuba airport and the smoke and explosions coming from the area. Everyone knew what it was! "La Invasion" (the American Invasion). People in the streets were jubilant and we could smell freedom in the air. The jubilation did not last long. In April 19, 1961, the invasion was defeated and the Brigade 2506 composed of Free Cubans had to surrender after they ran out of ammunition. The U.S. Government, led by President John F. Kennedy, abandoned them on the beaches of the Bay of Pigs.

We suspected that our father was involved because of his absences, and we worried about him. The communists were out in mass arresting people and a few months later, he was arrested in Holguín. When we received the news, we all cried and wondered about our fate. It was only us now; my mother, my 15-year-old brother and I, alone with no means of support.

My father faced a tribunal in Santiago de Cuba and we attended the trial. There was scant evidence against him; a lot of hearsay, but nothing else. Despite that, the prosecutor asked for the death sentence. The judge reduced it to 30 years in prison and eventually, on appeal and aided by a phone call from a cousin of my father who was Comandante Che Guevera's secretary, the sentence was changed to 20 years in prison.

When we got home, I was still 12 years old, but I was no longer a child. Something happened inside; I decided that I would do whatever I could to help my family, to fight injustice, to do what is right, and to face life as it comes. The year was 1962.

Third Life Change

While my father languished in Boniato prison and later in Isla de Pino prison, my mother took over. My mother was pregnant at the time my father was arrested, and she had very little money to support my little sister (she was born a few months after my father went to jail) and us. Our last hope was my grandfather Diego, the family patriarch. He came to Santiago and gave us some money and assured us that he would return to help us. As destiny had it, he passed away a couple of months later.

My grandmother Josefa took charge, moved in with one of her daughters, and gave us her house to live in. She also gave my mother her share of my grandfather's savings; this gave us a chance to forge ahead and survive for a little while. So, we moved back to Guantánamo where we started, six years later, but in truth, it felt like a lifetime for me. It also made me self-supporting, defiant, and resolute.

Fourth Life Change

It was immediately clear to me that my mother could not feed four mouths. My brother, who was now 18 years old, had found a job in the school system, in the arts department. The money was not great, but it helped. All the schools were now public since the regime confiscated all private schools in order to indoctrinate the children.

In a trip to Santiago, sometime in 1963, I ran into a priest I knew from my days as an altar boy and we chatted for a while. He was to me at the time a source of comfort, and the idea came into my mind that perhaps I could be a priest. In my return home, I went to speak with my Parish priest and told him about my idea. He was not convinced that I had a vocation and refused to endorse my idea. Father Pastor Gonzalez was a great religious figure and an activist against communism, and I went away sad and disappointed.

On further reflection later, I saw no other way out to help my family and also embark in a new direction that I thought I was good for. That decision made, I went to see another priest I knew in Santiago, Father Pedro Meurice, who was at the time the secretary to the Archbishop. After our talk, he said that he was going to recommend me for the next class at the Seminary San Basilio El Magno, in El Cobre, Oriente, under the administration of the Society of Jesus for a secondary education.

In my third year in the seminary, about the end of 1967, most of the seminarians were forced to join the Cuban Army work battalions. This was the way for the communist government to fight against the Catholic Church that was hurting for priests. Some very young seminarians were exempt, but I was not one of them. The government had just made a mistake and the Headmaster told me that they may come back for me, and he suggested that I leave the seminary until the repression eased up.

I arrived in Guantánamo with no idea what to do. As I could not be out of school or out of work in the communist system, it would be a matter of time until they found me. Then, I learned that the Superior School of Physical Education in Habana was looking for athletes to be instructors in different fields and there were slots open. I decided to apply and was accepted, since they were short of applicants. I thought that God actually created that position for me. A year later, I graduated as a Judo Instructor, with a Black Belt, First Dan, and assigned to the City of Guantánamo. I was eighteen years old.

Young Diego, third row, second from right (Diego Mella).

Inside the System

In January of 1969, my father's sentence was lifted and he came home. After that moment, I worked under duress and endured close scrutiny by communist elements in the Sports Department for obvious reasons.

One sunny afternoon, the Director of the G2 (Secret Police) of the Ministry of the Interior and his bodyguards showed up at my judo school while I was teaching a youth class and directed me to train his people and those of the Border Battalion surrounding the U.S. Naval Base in Guantánamo Bay. I refused the order and argued that Judo was a sport and not a self-defense method. He seemed very angry at this, and took out his small Makarov pistol and, pointing it at my chest, asked me to take it away.

My whole class behind me was whispering loudly about the pistol and I said to the Director, "*Compañero* (Comrade) my students are here and I am not qualified to do that; why don't you call the provincial commissioner and ask him?" He looked upset and said, "We'll see about that," and left in a huff. At that point, I knew that I was in trouble.

As I arrived home, I told my mother and my father, recently released from a seven-year prison sentence (he never knew why, probably his cousin again intervened) what transpired. Knowing that I could be imprisoned at any moment, they agreed that I should leave town immediately. After hiding in several cities in the homes of friends from my seminary days for about a month, I decided to return home and hide out until I had a plan for my escape from that hell.

In the meantime, my mother had spoken to a close friend who knew of a small group of youngsters that were getting ready for a quick escape via Guantánamo Bay. The leader of this group, who I did not know very well, grudgingly agreed to incorporate me in this venture.

The Escape

A few days later, early in the morning, I walked about 5 miles to an area just outside of the city limits, across the river Guaso, and approached a gas station/bus terminal that was usually full of people going to work or leaving for small towns. I quickly observed some guys I knew, mixed with other young guys I had never seen. I asked one of them why they were so many and he said that we were waiting for a large truck to take us to the appropriate place to begin our journey. The group of freedom seekers was over twenty, and in my mind, this was dangerous; too many youngsters together, mostly white and no adults, was too suspicious and might attract state security.

I walked away about 70 feet with two of my friends, including the leader, and waited. After an hour, the leader called his contact and was told that the truck driver changed his mind and was not coming. One of the kids in the group said that his father had a car, an old 57 Plymouth and, after calling him from a public phone, the father agreed to pick him up. When I heard the conversation, I was determined to shadow that kid wherever he went. I was not going to stay behind.

In about twenty minutes, I saw the Plymouth over the bridge and moved myself next to the kid and the group leader. When the door of the Plymouth swung open, six kids went in: the son, the group leader, and four of his close friends. As the door started to close, I jumped on the back, headfirst. Some of the kids wanted me out, but the father said, "Close the door and let him be, we are attracting attention." The door closed and I said my second prayer of the day.

The father let us out on a dirt road, near a sugar cane field. We were all dressed as sugar cane cutters; it was about 9:00 a.m. After a walk of about a mile, we entered the swamps that surround most of Guantánamo Bay, and after wading through the mosquito and Cayman filled swamps until dark because we got lost, we finally broke through and saw the Guantánamo Bay waters; it was about 7:00 p.m. We rested for a while, but the mosquitoes were fierce and in the hundreds, and we were really thirsty; nobody thought of bringing water.

I decided to get into the water to escape the mosquitoes and hide my face with my shirt, but they came through anyway. At this point, I made my decision; I was going to start swimming from that point; it was about 8:00 p.m. The leader argued that we were too far from the jump point and we should wait until we got there. I said, "It's dark and we don't know where we are; at least I can see some and know where to swim to." There was a heated conversation and most decided to go swimming. One of the kids refused, and we said our goodbyes and left him there.

We swam for a long time, until one kid got hit in the face by a flying fish. He started to scream so loud that the leader had to hit him to shut him up. Sounds travel far in open waters and there were patrol boats; we heard one far away earlier, so others could be around. We continued the swim, but the kid kept lagging behind. The leader went back twice to help him, and I did once, but we were getting very tired. After a short time, he disappeared from view and we thought that he drowned. Miraculously, we learned later he was able to find his friend ashore and went back to town. A few weeks later, he tried again, and that time he made it to freedom.

At about 6:00 a.m., we saw a real bright light shining towards us. The leader said that it should be the entrance canal where the Americans have a bunker called "The Patana" that means "small pier." As we got close, we were able to see a bunker atop a small hill, and it was like the American flag painted in the concrete was telling us: "This way, boys."

We were very worried in case it was a Cuban trick, but we had no choice. We were done physically, and there was a Cuban Guard Tower across the channel, about 30 feet tall. Dawn was coming fast and the Cuban tower would soon see us in the water and could open fire on us. I was blinded by a search light coming from the bunker area and that told me that the bunker had to be the U.S. Marine outpost.

We clung to the rocks and all of us were really tired. After a quiet and quick meeting, I volunteered to go up the rock hill and look around, never thinking what a skinny 18-year-old with a "Speedo" swim suit and painted black with motor oil looks like. Once up, I walked up to the bunker, under the searchlights, looking for a door; I could see the slits on the concrete but no light inside.

As soon as I turned the corner away from the tower, I observed some stairs leading inside what looked more and more like a pillbox, and saw a black door. I stopped to listen, but there was no sound from within, so I knocked on the steel door. After a couple of knocks, my knuckles hurt, so I pushed to see if it was open, and it was. The door opened to the inside without any noise.

I stood on the threshold of that door trying to peek inside, not realizing that, like a movie theater, someone inside could see me clearly, but I could not see until my eyes adjusted to the dark. After a few minutes that felt like hours, I took a couple of steps in and started to hear people snoring. Now, I

Escape from Cuba

Army Times article, November 4, 1970 (Diego Mella).

began to sweat when I saw the figure of a man sleeping on a cot with an olive green uniform similar to the ones the Cuban army wears. Well, there was no going back, so I shook the man once on his shoulder. He murmured something and kept sleeping, so I shook him again and he turned around and saw my silhouette. That's when all hell broke loose.

The man stood up, screamed something that sounded like intruder, and I began to hear rifle bolts chambering rounds. The lights came on and I was looking at more than 15 men pointing rifles at me. By this time, I had my hands behind my neck and was saying "refugee, refugee." I sincerely expected to be shot at any moment. Instead, a large soldier came to me and asked me "are you alone?" I had studied English in the seminary and had a rudimentary knowledge of it. I answered "No, more down" and pointed outside. A number of soldiers, that later said that they were U.S. Marines, rushed outside and I was told to sit on the ground against the wall. After a few minutes, they came back escorting my friends and they sat next to me.

When we realized that we were safe and had successfully arrived to our freedom, we began to laugh and pat each other for a while. We asked for Coca-Cola, but they only had water, so we drank the water and smoked Camel cigarettes that another Marine gave us.

It is hard to understand to this day how lucky we were that wonderful day. After a few hours of interrogation by Naval Intelligence, a bath, a meal, and a physical examination by a doctor, we were ready to roll. The next day, a Naval Aircraft took us, and 20 other refugees that were already on the base, to Miami where we were welcomed to our new land, the United States of America. This was August 21, 1969.

The New Life

Upon arrival in Miami, we were processed by Immigration and interviewed again by unknown American agents. After they were done with us, I contacted an aunt who came to pick me up. After two weeks, I found work in a factory that built emergency evacuation slides and rafts for airplanes and attended night classes at Miami High School to improve my English. I quickly realized that alone in a strange land, with very little money, and relatives that could only look after themselves, the future for this 18-year-old without means was very uncertain. After a couple of months, I moved to an apartment with a friend I met from the City of Baracoa, a city near Guantánamo. He had recently been discharged from the U.S. Army, and that planted a seed in my mind. After careful consideration and consulting with an older cousin, I made up my mind; I would enlist in the U.S. Army.

United States Army

In January of 1970, I volunteered for the draft and entered the United States Army. This decision was a monumental step and a fortuitous event in my life. To say that it was difficult may be an understatement. Basic Training is normally a very challenging enterprise, but when you add a lack of proficiency in the language, a foreign culture, no friends, and a freezing winter at Fort Jackson, South Carolina, one has to walk in my shoes to know what it was like.

One night, doing "Firewatch" (a fancy term for staying awake all night and making sure that the furnace was working) as penalty for not understanding what the Drill Sergeant had ordered me to do, I resolved to be the best soldier I could be, work harder than the rest, and study all I could in order to forge ahead and make a life for myself and give back to the country that welcomed me with open arms.

After graduating from Basic Training, with a promotion to Private 1 for helping other recruits pass the Bayonet Course, I was transferred to Fort Bliss, Texas, the U.S. Army Air Defense Center. In typical Army fashion, I was assigned as an Office Clerk in a Training Battalion. Imagine this Cuban refugee talking, typing, and filing documents in English. No matter; I asked the Non-Commissioned Officer in charge to let me go to school to better do my job. To my surprise, he agreed and sent me to Personnel Specialist School. With my new English vocabulary and my brand-new diploma, I was assigned to a HAWK missile company where I found a former teacher from New York working as the head clerk. He was my tutor and became my friend and taught me all I needed to comfortably do my job. I took this to be a great omen.

Aided by a Fourth Army Inspection that my Company passed with flying colors and a grueling background investigation when they found out that the one with the keys to all the secret documents on the missiles was a recently arrived Cuban refugee, I became probably the first Private First Class in the Army with a Top Secret Clearance. You may think it was humorous, but not to me at the time. They took me into custody, drove me to the Army Intelligence Office, and for three days made me go through my whole life until they knew it better than me. It was a good thing they were smiling when the final decision came from the Pentagon; "you can keep him," and gave me a commendation for a job well done for the work I did in the office before and during the inspection.

My Army times were the best a soldier could have. During this time, I won the U.S. Fourth Army Judo Championship in 64kg and was a member of the Ft. Bliss soccer team that beat a German Army Team and took third place in the Fourth Army Soccer Championship at Ft. Hood, Texas.

In 1971, already promoted to Specialist Four, my mother and young sister came from Cuba and came to live with me in El Paso, Texas. I then took an opportunity to take an early out and was honorably discharged from the U.S. Army. We moved to Union City, New Jersey, where my mother had a sister and looked ahead to my next challenge, confident that I was ready for my new life in the United States, a place I still did not know well outside of the Army walls.

The New Jersey Experience

As we arrived in Union City, New Jersey, in December of 1971, we shuddered in the cold and rainy weather and wondered if we made a mistake. The money I was able to save in the Army did not go far. The winter clothes, rental of a basement to live in, and used furniture took all the savings. Luckily, I was able to find a job really quickly in a financial company of a national clothing chain, working in the mailroom. There, I befriended a co-worker whose father worked for a New York Investment Company.

After speaking with my co-worker's father, I applied and went through an interview process; at the end, I was hired by Merrill Lynch, Pierce, Fenner, and Smith, a National Investment Firm in New York City, as an Internal Auditor. The job was well paid and important, but it was too boring for me and the trip to and from New Jersey was tough.

Another friend from Cuba, living in Elizabeth, New Jersey, told me about a good paying job as a Junior Accountant for a Financial Office of a food retailer. I decided to give it a go, but it was also a dull and boring job. After eighteen months of this, I realized that the good pay did not compensate for the feelings of going nowhere and became restless.

Not long after, I was walking by the police department in Union City, New Jersey, one quiet afternoon and I saw a sign that said "Policemen Wanted." I said to myself: "Well, if I could be seminarian, a judo instructor, a soldier, an internal auditor, and an accountant, then I could be a policeman." I went in and started the process with an application.

The next day, I drove to Newark, New Jersey, and started the naturalization process. God was still with me. The young agent that I was assigned to asked me if I was a veteran. It turns out he was an Army veteran also and had left the Army about the same time I did. He said that since I was a Vietnam-Era veteran, I was entitled to citizenship, so he started the paperwork.

The police process was quick and when the list came out, I was number one. Soon, I received a letter to appear for the final interview. The problem was I had not yet received my Naturalization Certificate. Guess what? I received it the day before the interview.

A Policeman's Life

In April of 1973, less than four years after I arrived in the United States, I was accepted in the Union City Police Department, a heavily Cuban populated city, and graduated from basic police training from the New Jersey State Police Academy at Sea Girt. At the time, I was sure that I would be in Union City, with my mother and sister for a long time. Well, this was not to be.

After a short time on foot patrol, I was ordered via radio to investigate a case involving a vehicle full of armed man in the vicinity of my area. As I arrived in the area, I saw a car resembling the description given by radio coming towards me, and behind the car was a police cruiser. I radioed the police car to stop the vehicle and he turned his red lights on. As I approached the vehicle on foot, I could see the right front passenger with a green blanket covering something; I drew my firearm and told the passengers not to move. When I removed the green blanket, there was a shotgun in plain view. All four passengers were armed and were arrested and taken to the station. Little did I know that the large man with the shotgun and a 38 caliber revolver in his pocket was a big organized crime capo by the name of Jose Miguel Battle. This revelation changed my life around. I was told at the police station that I could not charge him, but I could charge the others. This was strange and not the right thing to do, so I went upstairs and told the Desk Lieutenant that something was not right and he got it right away. I went back down to my desk and the Lieutenant came down a few minutes later and ordered all the prisoners to be charged.

Just before the preliminary hearing, I was called aside by the Deputy

Chief and told not to testify against Battle. I went and testified anyway and the case moved to the next step.

The following week I was again approached and told not to show up in County court, but I refused to comply. The next day, the owner of a chain of furniture stores, a Cuban American, who knew me and had many friends, called me and asked me to stop by his office. When I got there, he said that he was informed that a $50,000 contract has been placed on my head by organized crime, and asked me why this was so. I told him that it was probably because of my testimony against Jose Miguel Battle. He then said that he was going to talk to a friend that owns a chain of plumbing stores for some help, and in the meantime, to be careful. Talk about fortunate; I was walking the beat at that time and completely exposed at all times.

I left his office with a lot of trepidation; how can someone protect himself while walking the streets at night? Back at the station, I went to talk to the Chief of Detectives and he said that unless there was an attack on my person, they could not help. I realized then that this department was a corrupt organization. I did not know at the time that the Federal Bureau of Investigation had already opened an investigation into the Union City Police Department.

I still had to work my shift so I spoke to a friend from Guantánamo that I knew had a gun and, after I related my problem, he agreed to walk the streets with me until I heard from the furniture store owner. It did not take long before I got call from him and I went back to his office. He said to me, "Sam, the Plumber, said not to worry, the contract has been invalidated." Well, I did not know this man, but I really wish I knew because he had the power to save my life. Years later I learned who Sam the Plumber was. While attending the Organized Crime Institute in Ft. Lauderdale, Florida, the instructor went over the heads of the Italian Organized Crime Families and there he was, Sam DeCavalcante, Capo of the Northern New Jersey family; the Sopranos TV series was based on his life. Nevertheless, I owed him my life. It turns out, killing a cop was bad for business and besides, Jose Miguel Battle worked for the NY Family, not his.

Jose Miguel Battle, better known in the Cuban community as "El Padrino" was convicted in Federal Court in Philadelphia, mostly on my testimony in 1977. I was already a Homicide Detective in Miami when I was called to testify. A year later, he was again indicted for Conspiracy to Commit Murder, and I arrested him again and extradited him to Miami from New York. In the plane en route to Miami, he said to me, "it is my bad luck to be arrested by the only honest cop I ever met." I took that as a compliment!

Going back to Union City in 1974, a few months after the Battle incident, at about 1:00 p.m., I stopped for Cuban coffee in Bergenline Avenue, the city's main street, and met with my good friend, Detective Nicky Guirado. We spoke briefly and he said, "Diego, I'm working on something; I will meet you tonight to tell you." I said "alright" and left to the station to close out my shift. Little did I know the tragic event that would follow.

As I was turning in my paperwork from my 6am to 2pm shift, and was ready to turn the car keys in, a call came over the radio of a shooting in front of Rapido Taxi and that cops were "down." I had a very bad feeling! This location is only about 6 blocks from the Station. I rushed outside and got in my police car. I was travelling very fast on a one-way street and arrived in about two minutes. As I pulled in front of the taxi office, I saw Nicky's partner on the ground, clutching his bleeding leg, and Nicky on the ground, bleeding from his neck. Nicky's partner yelled at me, "shooter went around the corner." I ran to the corner and, as I negotiated the turn, I saw a man face down on the sidewalk; I checked and he had no pulse and was not breathing.

I come back to Nicky and he is still alive, but bleeding profusely. I called the dispatcher and asked to alert the emergency room at Hudson Hospital that we had a bleeder. This hospital was only a few blocks away. By this time, a motor officer arrived and between us, we got Nicky in the back of the car, and while I put pressure on his wound, the motor officer drove to the emergency room, but to no avail. The doctors were not able to stem the blood flow and he passed away. I lost a great friend, a superb police officer, and he left behind a wife and two sweet daughters. It seems that the man that killed him died from shots that Nicky's partner fired while wounded on the ground. This criminal had shot a Miami Police Officer and was wanted by the Miami Police Department when he was stopped by the two detectives. After this tragedy, I started to think that it was time to leave Union City behind.

Late in 1974, I was sent to Miami, Florida, to follow-up on a homicide investigation. After a check-in with the then Public Safety Department in Miami, two Cuban-American Homicide detectives were so glad to meet a Cuban American cop from New Jersey that they offered their help in following my leads. Once the investigation was done, they asked if I was interested in coming down. You can guess my answer; I applied to the Public Safety Department (later named Miami-Dade Police Department) and was accepted for employment. I packed my mother and sister in a truck with a few pieces of furniture and drove down to the Sunshine State, with the blessings of the Union City Police Chief. In April 1975, I attended the Southeast Florida Institute of Criminal Justice and started a new chapter in my life.

A Miami Cop

I was again blessed that I had the opportunity to start in a large police department that was in the initial steps of professionalism. I said "initial steps" because the department was not without problems. It was starting to grow and had excellent leadership at the top, but lacked diversity and understanding of some of their communities. The road to progress was hard, divisive at times, and dangerous. I had to deal with corrupt cops, non-acceptance, and lack of support at the beginning. I had to look back at my experience in the North, and found a Hispanic Police Lieutenant, one of two among 1,200 officers, and started a friendship that only ended when he passed away in 2014. He was Eduardo "Eddie" Gonzalez; he rose to Deputy Director of the Miami-Dade Police Department, Chief of the City of Tampa, the longest serving Director of the U.S. Marshalls Service, and the most trusted human being I ever met.

Together, Eddie and I and a few others started the Hispanic Police Officers Association to recruit and advance the careers of Hispanics in the Department. He appointed me, when I was promoted to Sergeant, the Departmental Recruiter, and in 1984/1985 brought in over 5,000 candidates to include blacks, Hispanics, and women to the force. In 1986, Eddie and I joined the newly created Hispanic American Police Command Officers Association (HAPCOA), a national organization, consisting of Hispanic executives from across the United States that had representation in Washington, D.C.

I held a number of positions in this organization and rose to be First Vice-President. I was very proud to represent the organization and work as part of President Bill Clinton's crime bill in Washington, D.C., and was present at the signing of the bill at the White House. I also worked with the Community Relations Service (CRS) of the Department of Justice and produced a video and program entitled Law Enforcement Safety Tips that was intended to reduce the level of violence between Latinos and law enforcement. This program won an award by the National Association of Counties for its impact in Latino communities.

As President and co-founder of the Survivors of Guantánamo Bay, I also worked with CRS on the Cuban/Haitian Task Force to assist refugees at Guantánamo Bay in 1994. I helped organize the camps and mediate problems. During this time, I also provided training for two Military Police Battalions on the historical overview of Cuba, political views, immigration policies, beliefs, and customs.

During my 30-year career at the Miami-Dade Police Department, I worked in a number of positions such as road patrol as a police officer and corporal. I was a Homicide Investigator, handling special cases involving narcotics related killings, Cuban related anti-terrorism, and organized crime cases. As I rose through the ranks to Corporal, Sergeant, Lieutenant, First Lieutenant, Police Commander, and Captain, I was involved in a variety of assignments, which gave me an all-around experience that will benefit me greatly in years to come.

Knowing well that education is also a major requirement in supervision

Basic Law Enforcement (BLE) 22. Miami, Florida, September 1975 (Diego Mella).

and management, I worked very hard for a period of ten years, attending first Miami-Dade College, received my four-year degree from Barry Catholic University in Professional Studies, and my Master's Degree in Public Administration from the University of Miami. These steps opened many doors for me after retirement.

I retired honorably in 2005, but not before I was called to assist the U.S. Department of Defense in the preparation of the security for the Greek Olympics in 2004. Working closely with the National Strategic Gaming Center at the National Defense University, I traveled to Germany as part of a team to train the Greek leadership, and later to Athens, Greece, for the training conference of the 8-nation coalition for the security of the games. For this work, I received a Commendation from the Greek government, and was designated an Honorary Wargamer and received a commendation by the National Strategic Gaming Center.

Life After Retirement

Shortly after my retirement in 2005, I was asked to accept a position under a contract with the U.S. Army Management Staff College, and join a team to train U.S. Army bases in the United States and overseas on security and safety. For four years, I traveled to 32 Army Garrisons, from Korea to Europe, and in the Continental United States.

My experience as a law enforcement officer, my dealings with federal agencies in my career, and my Army service were instrumental in assisting the U.S. Army with this assignment. The team was named the best small contract in the Department of Defense in 2009, and my sincere thanks go to Colonel Mitch Mitchell, U.S. Army (ret) for his guidance, trust, experience, and the friendship he always manifested towards me, and to the best team members a person will ever have.

In 2009, I was offered a position with the U.S. State Department, as a Professional Mentor to the Chief of Operations of the Afghan Police and later the Chief of the Border Patrol, in Afghanistan. I served in that capacity for 18 months, and received a Commendation from the Deputy Minister of Security for my work in training the Afghan Operations Staff on police tactics and strategies.

Lastly, upon returning to the States in December of 2010, I was offered and accepted a position with Warshaw and Associates, to perform training and police reforms for the Puerto Rico Police Department. A good friend, former Chief Martinez, Miami Police, and I were instrumental in developing "Zones of Excellences" for a police force of over 16,000 members. To the people of that wonderful island, it was a great pleasure and honor to work alongside so many police officers and commanders for the betterment of their police force.

Most Important Topic

While this topic is at the end, it is the most important item in my life. In the beginning, it was mostly survival, later it was security for my family, then it became career orientation, and finally, it was all about family and community. I could not have done all things here and others that could not be said without their support, patience, tolerance, and forgiveness for all the time away from home, and mistakes/omissions that I made.

My wife Lourdes, son Diego Jr., and daughter Monica are the engines that kept me going. They supported me so that I could go and work for the safety and protection of the United States of America and its citizens; the land that offered a refuge, a future, and delivered handsomely.

My children also benefited from our examples of how to live, how to behave, and what to defend. They know the price we pay for freedom is not cheap; it was and it is paved with blood and hard work. The price for success is steep and requires hard work, education, and perseverance. It is a source of pride when we look at the wall in my small office and see all the college and university diplomas we all earned.

As I look back in time, I also give thanks and praise to my father, Jose Mella Barrios, my mother Nilda de La Torre, and my grandfathers, Jose Mella Monterroso and Diego De La Torre, for their inspiration, hard work, and dedication; examples that guided me in my life.

May we all see a Free Cuba in our life time!

All we need in the United States of America is a unity of desire for freedom, hard work for a new life, a path to health and the pursuit of happiness, and the strength to defend it against all enemies, foreign and domestic. GOD Bless The USA!

Diego (left), flanked by two of his mentor partners outside Camp Dobbs in the hills of Afghanistan, 2010 (Diego Mella).

The Journey
Faith and Trust in a Time of Uncertainty

Ernest G. Vendrell *and*
David Ernesto Vendrell

Introduction (by Ernest G. Vendrell)

There are many stories about the Cuban exile experience that deserve to be told. They are stories rich in historical significance, affecting a wide-range of individuals and families. Each undoubtedly comprises a multitude of challenges, sacrifices, and significant risks undertaken to escape communism and establish a new life in a free society. For example, what would drive a man to burn down his own property and risk his family and everything that he had worked for his entire life? This is one of those stories.

My name is Ernest G. Vendrell. I was born in Havana, Cuba, the 2nd oldest of what eventually turned out to be 2 boys and 2 girls. My family lived in the town of Morón, in the province of Camagüey. From past recollection, films, photographs, and family descriptions, it can be said that we lived a very comfortable and happy life on an extraordinarily beautiful and diverse island nation—one that was often referred to as the Pearl of the Antilles.

As is often the case, many Cuban American families will recount stories from the Cuba of yesterday, sharing these experiences with their extended families. It is an important way for families, particularly the younger generations, to learn about their heritage, appreciate Cuban culture and traditions, and understand why life changed so drastically for many Cubans after Fidel Castro rose to power and began consolidating his dictatorial grip on the country.

In our family, the principal story-teller continues to be my father, Ernesto Antonio Vendrell-Pelegrin. At 90 years of age, this incredibly passionate and intelligent man loves to talk about the political, economic, and social conditions that enabled a man like Fidel Castro to assume control of Cuba and maintain power for more than 50 years through a repressive and brutal communist regime. Although his compelling stories have captivated our family throughout

Story time. Ernesto Antonio Vendrell-Pelegrin with Ann and Ernest (Ernest G. Vendrell).

the years, perhaps no one has listened more intently and had more one-on-one discussions with my Dad regarding the decisions that brought our family to the United States, and the Cuban Exodus in general, than my older son, David Ernesto Vendrell. Therefore, David's direct recollections and insights are interwoven throughout the following account. In particular, having recently traveled to Cuba, David will also provide important perspectives based on his observations and conversations with every-day Cubans toward the end of this essay.

However, to fully understand the conditions and decisions that were made to enable our family to escape Cuba, it is important to go back in time and become familiar with the principal story-teller in our family, my father. In essence, he is at the center of our family's account of the struggles and risks that we experienced in leaving Cuba, and the challenges that we needed to overcome in acclimating to our new home in the United States. So, when David and I first approached him about writing our family's story as part of a larger volume of similar experiences, he was quite enthusiastic about the opportunity, particularly what it represented for the Cuban Exile Community. As an avid supporter of freedom for Cuba and its people over the years, he felt that these were stories that needed to be told. Besides chronicling the challenges, hopes, and dreams of Cubans forced to flee a brutal regime, it would help to leave a lasting legacy for Cuban immigrants everywhere. Therefore, the majority of this story is written through my father's (Ernesto's) eyes.

Why Family Matters: The Early Years
(by Ernest G. Vendrell and David Ernesto Vendrell)

Once again, he cried himself to sleep. At 8 years of age, Ernesto felt overwhelmed by his surroundings. The endless cycle of a rigid school regimen, the unrelenting noises of so many students during the day, followed by the deafening silence and sense of being alone at night, proved just too exhausting time and again. The Escolapios de Guanabacoa boarding school, although relatively close to Havana, was difficult to get to back then, requiring that travelers trek by boat to a remote location far removed from the conveniences of the day. Perhaps it was this sense of isolation that prompted officials to locate the school there; it required students to focus on the rigorous curriculum, absent the typical distractions associated with a school in a more urban environment. Regardless, he would later recount that "even though I had extended family living in Havana, I was far from my home in the small town of Pina, in the Province of Camagüey, and could not bear to be separated from my parents and sisters. It is difficult to understand how much I cried and suffered at that school."

But, how did he end up there? Month's before, his parents decided that he should attend a more "sophisticated" school in the City of Morón, which was approximately 13 miles from his hometown of Pina. La Trinidad primary school did offer more educational opportunities, but since it was too far from home to commute on a daily basis, he had to enroll as a boarding student. Missing his family terribly, he would escape from the school whenever possible, board a train, and, much to his parent's dismay, appear back home late at night. Ultimately, they matriculated him in a far-away school in Guanabacoa, close to 250 miles from Pina, knowing full well that the distance and remote location would solve the problem of him leaving at any time. Unfortunately, during his time in Guanaba-

A young Ernesto Antonio Vendrell-Pelegrin, eight years of age (Ernest G. Vendrell).

coa, he would return home only during the Christmas break, as well as the summer months.

Eventually, when he was 10 years old, his parents matriculated him in the Colegio de Belén, a prestigious Jesuit school situated in Havana. It was here that he first met Fidel Castro, who was a few grades ahead of him. Being new to the school, he made a habit of observing others and gauging their intentions; something that he had learned to do during his time at Guanabacoa. Before long, he came to the conclusion that Castro was a bully who would take advantage of others at every opportunity. It was no surprise to him that most of the younger students, and some of the older ones as well, avoided him whenever possible. He was no exception.

Fortunately, by this time, his two sisters (Antonia and Carmen), as well as two cousins, were attending a nearby school—the Dominicanas Francesas Catholic School for girls. Just like him, they were sent to Havana to attend boarding school. Finally, he felt more relieved knowing that at least his sisters were less than a mile away, although he could not see them unless it was a holiday. However, after several years, he was old enough to sign himself out of school one weekend day a month, and he would enthusiastically use that time to visit his sisters. The routine was always the same. He had 1 peso to work with; he would use 5 cents to take the trolley car to his sisters' school, then 50 cents for lunch at their school, followed by 30 cents for a movie at a theatre nearby, and then another 5 cents for the return trolley car fare back to El Colegio de Belén. The Cuban Peso was tied to the U.S. Dollar—the only country in Latin America to do so at the time. So, for less than $1.00, he was able to spend a great day with part of his family, and this served to restore his sense of sanity.

Nonetheless, Ernesto swore at an early age that he would never send a son or daughter to boarding school. Instead, he vowed that he would keep his family close, and that they would be at the forefront of any decision he made, regardless of the sacrifices or consequences. In addition, he learned a very valuable lesson early on in his life: Fidel Castro was an opportunist and a bully—one that could never be trusted.

Coming of Age: The Entrepreneur

As the years passed, Ernesto continued with his high school studies at Instituto #1 De la Segunda Enseñanza in Havana. He quickly came to realize that he liked the business environment, and decided to make a career as a businessman and entrepreneur. His first job was during the summer months, when he worked at the family pharmacy in Pina. He would order supplies, assist in the preparation of prescriptions, coordinate the dispatching of medicines, and would work the front counter as well. In particular, he enjoyed the business side of the operation, and figured out early on that he was well suited to management and finance.

After high school, Ernesto remained in Havana, hoping to find a business-related job. His intentions were to work, and to attend college part-time. At 18 years of age, he was eager to set off on his own, making his own decisions and plans for the future. It was during this time that he landed a job in Havana with Previsora Latino Americana in the Accounting Department. Previsora was really a groundbreaking venture in Cuba. It enabled ordinary citizens to make regular deposits into a private account, so that they could eventually arrange for the building of a home on their own land. Since home mortgages did not exist in Cuba back then, it provided an important avenue for home ownership in Cuba during this period. Working in the Accounting Department also allowed him to experience the finance side of the operation, and he found that he liked this facet of business very much.

In fact, nothing gave Ernesto more satisfaction than handing over a check to an account holder, since it represented a dream come true. Nonetheless, after several years, he was promoted to work in the *Inversiones* (Investments) Department of Previsora Latino Americana, where he was directly involved in the development of new business ventures and site locations throughout the country. Later, at the age of 26, he was tasked with opening, and managing, Previsora's new office in the City of Camagüey. The company was expanding throughout Cuba, a country that was experiencing considerable growth and prosperity in Latin America in the post–World War II environment. At the time, Cuba was ahead of every Central and South American country economically, and the prospects looked good for the future. Along these lines, working in the Investments Department re-kindled his entrepreneurial spirit, and helped him to see the possibilities for additional business opportunities in Cuba. It was at this point, that he considered going into business for himself.

Previsora Latino Americana. "Your Own House for Less than the Cost of Rent" (Ernest G. Vendrell).

Ernesto Antonio Vendrell-Pelegrin, handing check to Previsora Latino Americana account holder (Ernest G. Vendrell).

Starting His Own Family and Business

Later, Ernesto returned home to Pina to take some preparatory courses at a private school, Academia Torrado, in nearby Morón. As luck would have it, while there, he met Oneida Rodriguez-Ramos. She was in her final year of high school at the Instituto de la Segunda Enseñanza in Morón, which was situated directly across the street from Academia Torrado. Within a short period of time, the young man fell in love, and he began to pursue Oneida, often writing her letters. As Oneida would later say, "…he made his intentions clear from the start. I wish I still had all of the letters that he wrote to me. I am sure that he would be very embarrassed."

Reminiscing of Cuba prior to Castro taking control of the island, Oneida would recall how happy her family was during this period. Her extended family had worked very hard over the years, building a good life for the future. In particular, part of her family consisted of ranchers and farmers, and she remembered the times that she would go to her grandfather's farm, El Quemado. To her, it was additional tangible evidence of the hardships that her family had overcome to establish themselves in Cuba.

Oneida would also recount that although there was considerable political turmoil, Cuba was considered a democratic country with an abundance of natural resources. Coupled with a rising middle class possessing a strong

96 Escape from Cuba

Oneida Vendrell at the family farm, El Quemado (Ernest G. Vendrell).

work ethic, this bode well for Cuba's future. Additionally, the country was beginning to reap the benefits of many modern conveniences. Moreover, there was a sense of optimism, particularly among the middle class, to include professionals and entrepreneurs.

Oneida eventually moved to Havana (accompanied by her mother at her father's request), entering the University of Havana to major in public accounting. Since Ernesto was also working in Havana at the time, it wasn't long before they began dating. As Ernesto would later recount, "...there was no such thing as dating by yourself at that time. We would always be

Modern Conveniences. Oneida Vendrell at the Morón house (Ernest G. Vendrell).

Cousins enjoying Varadero Beach. Lourdes, Ann, Francisco (Pancho), Ernest, Joaquin, and Hugo (Ernest G. Vendrell).

accompanied by her mother, or one of her mother's cousins. It taught me a lot of patience...." However, in December of 1950, Ernesto and Oneida were married in Morón, Cuba. They settled in Havana. Before long, Ann was born, followed by Ernest, Lourdes, and Joaquin. Recollecting on his memories from this period, Ernesto would state that "...Cuba was prospering, and so were we...."

As he continued to set his sights on future business opportunities, Ernesto certainly had a good role model from the business world in his father-in-law. Bonifacio Rodriguez-San Gil was a well-respected and successful entrepreneur who built a thriving business in Morón, Cuba. An immigrant from the Canary Islands, Bonifacio arrived in Cuba at the age of 17, joining an older brother who had established a small business in Palenque—a small town amidst a rural setting. He worked hard, and overcame many obstacles in the hopes of building a better life for himself and his future family. Eventually, he would move to the larger town of Morón, where there were more business opportunities. There, he would establish a business, and later meet and marry the love of his life, a local girl by the name of Maria Ramos-Ramos. Together, they would have two daughters, Oneida and Antonia, who became the focus of their lives.

In particular, Ernesto marveled at how, over the years, Bonifacio built a sprawling business complex close to downtown Morón. There was a hardware store, a food store, and warehouses to store a variety of foods, beers, liquors, hardware items, paints, and fertilizers. In addition, Bonifacio was a

Bonifacio Rodriguez San Gil Store in Morón, Cuba. Oneida Vendrell in Center as a young girl (Ernest G. Vendrell).

major representative for various products, to include important brands such as Bacardi, Canada Dry, and Glidden Paints. He had also established the logistical network and trucking capabilities to transport and sell these items throughout Cuba. Viewed from this perspective, it was a flourishing business with tremendous potential for the future.

However, Ernesto fully realized that Bonifacio's success did not come by accident. Bonifacio had worked very hard to establish his business, and overcame many obstacles in the hopes of building a better life for himself and his family. Certainly, the climate for doing business in Cuba was good at the time, but success often required expending plenty of sweat, not to mention some tears. It also required that entrepreneurs dream big, and put in place a long-term strategy for the future. In essence, as long as businessmen were willing to work hard and invest in the future, the returns under a free capitalist society were good. These lessons were not lost on the young man, as he considered future opportunities.

Consequently, in 1956, after careful consideration, Ernesto opened up his own modern supermarket in Morón, Cuba. It was certainly quite different from what most Cubans in the Province of Camagüey were familiar with at

Vendor Representatives Conference in Cienfuegos, Cuba. Bonifacio Rodriguez-San Gil, left center of picture in beige suit and glasses (Ernest G. Vendrell).

the time. In particular, the Vendromax was the first in the province to institute the concept of self-serve isle displays, push carts, and state-of-the-art checkout registers. The business proved immensely popular and profitable, and, although the store no longer exists, even today, the locals refer to the building where the business was housed as the Vendromax.

The Impact of Castro's Rise to Power

Although at the time, Cuba, including many businesses and entrepreneurs on the island, had been prospering and had good expectations for the future, the political climate had been rapidly changing on the island. In particular, by late 1958, Fidel Castro, who had been waging a successful guerrilla campaign against the Batista government for several years, based on communist guerrilla tactics, coupled with carefully orchestrated propaganda geared to amassing peasant support, defeated the government forces. Batista fled the country on December 31, 1958, paving the way for Castro to assume power in early 1959. Castro, an intelligent and ambitious attorney by trade, and a Marxist-Leninist revolutionary, quickly took over as head of state and began efforts to consolidate his power.

Oneida Vendrell, shopping at the Vendromax on opening day (Ernest G. Vendrell).

As Ernesto would recall, this is when things began to change dramatically for our family. As previously mentioned, at one point, he had attended the same elementary school with Fidel Castro, and felt that Castro was both a bully and an opportunist that could not be trusted. Additionally, he had become increasingly concerned as Castro began to wage his guerrilla campaign in the mountains of Oriente Province, achieving greater popularity and military success as time passed. Once Castro assumed power, and his intentions became clearer to the West, he was convinced at first that the United States would never permit a communist regime to remain in power so close to its shores. However, those hopes were soon dashed after Castro started confiscating and redistributing land holdings, jailing dissidents, taking control of private businesses, nationalizing the operations of U.S. owned companies, as well as appointing communists to key government and military positions. Furthermore, the Castro government created and armed a militia made up of citizens that supported the revolution, and also established a nation-wide neighborhood spying organization designed to identify and quickly suppress counter-revolutionary activities. But the final straw for him was when Castro declared that, moving forward, the central government would be in charge of children. It was at this point that he knew that he and his family needed to leave the island at the earliest opportunity. According to Ernesto, "...important goals of communism are the taking away of private property, diminishing the role of families, abolishing religion, etc. I saw firsthand what was coming...."

Ernesto was not alone in this thinking. Many Cubans left the island immediately after Batista resigned from office. For example, Ernesto's brother-in-law, Juan Caballero, who was a former Congressman, and later the Administrative Director of the Interior Ministry under the Batista government, took the last plane out of Havana shortly after Batista handed over the government to one of his generals, who in turn handed over the government to Castro. Had he not left immediately, he would have undoubtedly been imprisoned, and possibly executed. His wife (Ernesto's sister) and two sons were able to leave a year later, after all of their property had been confiscated. Likewise, many other middle class Cubans began planning their migration to the United States. The resulting exodus of highly skilled professionals ultimately had a negative impact on Cuba and its economy.

Then, in late 1959, a tragic event occurred. While Bonifacio Rodriguez-San Gil was working inside his business complex, a local attorney, who was a Castro supporter, entered the store and approached him, yelling "...you see everything that you have here—everything that you worked for—we are going to take it all. We will leave you with nothing, you vermin.... This belongs to the revolution...." Minutes later, having been traumatized by the event, Bonifacio collapsed, suffering a severe stoke that left him in a comma for 3 months. Ernesto, Oneida, and the kids, immediately packed up and went to Morón, moving into the Rodriguez-San Gil residence to help the family during this difficult period. In particular, Ernesto took over the management of Bonifacio's business, knowing full well that it was only a matter of time before the government confiscated the company and its assets. Nonetheless, out of respect and admiration for Bonifacio and everything that he had built over the years, he vowed to find a way to ensure that this would never happen.

As 1960 rolled around, Castro continued efforts to consolidate his power. Later, as summer approached, friends with ties to the Castro government confided in Ernesto that the Bonifacio Rodriguez-San Gil business complex would be taken in the next round of confiscations. Having previously heard that the Cuban government would be assuming responsibility for children, Ernesto had already been making plans to leave with the family for the United States. Once safely in the U.S., he would work on bringing Bonifacio and Maria, as well as the rest of his extended family, over as quickly as possible. However, he did not have much time left to put a plan in motion to prevent the government from taking the business.

In Cuba, as in many Latin American countries, it is customary for businesses to open at around 8:00 a.m. in the morning, close for lunch/siesta at noon, reopen at 2:00 p.m., and then close for the day at 6:00 p.m. Essentially, everyone would leave the business during the scheduled lunch/siesta. This two-hour period afforded employees sufficient time to go home, have lunch, and spend time with their families. In particular, the Bonifacio Rodriguez-San Gil business complex was in the middle of the town of Morón. A short distance away was Bonifacio's home; prior to his stroke, he often walked home for lunch during the siesta. Since taking over management of the business, Ernesto had fallen into a similar routine. As Ernesto considered what to do next, he factored this time and distance into his planning, devising a strategy that would make sure that the company would not fall into the government's hands, while ensuring that no one was hurt in the process.

Finally, on a Sunday in September of 1960, Ernesto made preparations to burn the store down by arranging a candle, surrounded by paper and straw, on top of cans of turpentine and paints in an isolated area inside the paints and related supplies warehouse room. Then, at noontime the following day, when the business closed for the customary siesta and all of the employees left to have lunch and to be with their families, Ernesto lit the candle, locked up and left with several waiting employees, which he dropped off at their nearby homes. As Ernesto then proceeded to Bonifacio's house, he began hearing news accounts on *Radio Morón* that the business was on fire and shortly after arriving home, several employees appeared at the house with the news. Acting surprised, he immediately left for the business, which was completely engulfed in flames by this time. Upon arriving and running towards the chaotic scene, Ernesto was almost shot by a member of Castro's secret police who thought that he had come from the rear of the business where he had been hiding after apparently setting the blaze. What saved him was a passerby getting in the officer's line of fire. He was immediately placed under arrest by the town's army detachment,

Oneida Vendrell and Ann in front of the Morón home, a short distance away from the Bonifacio Rodriguez-San Gil business complex (Ernest G. Vendrell).

and placed in a jail cell pending an investigation. Later, he was transferred to house arrest after he and some of his employees convinced the army commander that he was a responsible citizen and family man who owned other properties in town, and had no plans to leave the country until the investigation was concluded.

In the days that followed, Ernesto continued to speak with his employees, the majority of which were avowed communists by this time. He convinced them that they had to speak up on his behalf, since he was not the type of man to destroy his livelihood. In particular, he emphasized that if he did not collect on the insurance, the business would not be rebuilt, and they would all be out of jobs. It worked. The employees collectively exerted great pressure on the local authorities. In the final analysis, the official cause of the fire was determined to be an electrical short circuit, and he was released. Eventually, Ernesto collected on the insurance in Havana. The event made news nationwide, and it turned out to be the last private insurance claim payment that was made in Cuba.

Upon his return to Morón, to buy time, Ernesto made it clear that he planned to rebuild the store with the insurance money. However, he continued to be jailed periodically due to employee dissatisfaction with pre-revolutionary management practices. In time, he solicited the assistance of one of the top local government officials, a friend who used to work at Bonifacio's business as an accountant. Ernesto explained to him that he could never live under the present system of government and that it would be best if he would help clear the way for his family to leave the country quickly, since once he was gone, the local officials would be able to take control of all of his properties and run them as they wished. In Ernesto's view, the Castro government could certainly re-build the business based on their own sweat equity and business acumen, but he would not allow them to reap the benefits of Bonifacio's past efforts, particularly after what they did to him.

The strategy proved successful. On December 3rd, 1960 Oneida, with her 4 kids in tow (Ann, Ernest, Lourdes, and Joaquin), boarded an airplane in Havana with round-trip tickets bound for Canada with a stop in New York City. Upon arriving in New York City, Oneida and the kids disembarked. They had two suitcases and the equivalent of $5.00 in their pockets. Oneida immediately requested political asylum, which was granted. Waiting for them was Ernesto's sister, Carmen Caballero, and her husband, Juan Caballero, who were living in Fairfax, Virginia, at the time. They took the family in.

All along, Ernesto was convinced that the Castro government would not allow him to leave the island; instead, he feared that he would be jailed once again. Since he did not want to jeopardize the rest of the family leaving, he sent Oneida and the kids first. Nonetheless, Ernesto boarded a similar flight bound for Canada two weeks later, requesting political asylum when the plane made a re-fueling stop in New York City. At last, after considerable worry and lack of sleep, he was able to join the family.

Starting Over: The Challenges of Building a New Life in the Land of Opportunity

Shortly after arriving in the U.S., Ernesto and Oneida were able to obtain a job managing a small hotel in Somerville, New Jersey, through the kind assistance of a family friend, Rafael Díaz-Balart. As Ernesto would recall, "... At the time, we could not speak English, and did not live close to anyone that spoke Spanish. Also, we knew little about the hospitality industry in our new country, but it did not matter. We needed to provide for ourselves and our 4 children, so we learned as we went, and took advantage of every opportunity...." Recalling this uncertain time, Ernesto and Oneida would state "... we were so blessed to have met John and Rita Pecuch, and their two daughters, Mary Beth and Barbara, upon settling in Somerville. John and Rita sort of adopted us. They were like our guardian angels—they helped us to navigate and understand our new home, and assisted us in so many ways. They were the kindest and most genuine people that we have ever met. They were of Czechoslovakian descent, and Rita made some of the most delicious meals and desserts. They treated us like family, and we are indebted to them...." Ernesto and Oneida would remain friends with John and Rita for many years—until both friends passed away.

In time, Ernesto would focus on managing the motel at night, handling evening and early morning check-ins, and completing any necessary repairs. Oneida would clean rooms during the day, and manage the front desk while the kids were in school. During the day time hours, Ernesto obtained a full-time job at a fertilizer plant. His job was to fill fertilizer bags, and load them onto trucks. In the

Winter time in New Jersey. Ernest, Ann, Joaquin, Oneida, and Lourdes (Ernest G. Vendrell).

evenings, Ernesto would also attend classes at Rutgers University, where he studied English and Accounting. In addition, on the weekends, he obtained a part-time job as Head of Cashiers at a local retailer. They did this for three and a half years, until they had saved enough money to buy their own house in Raritan, New Jersey, and open a bakery nearby. Unfortunately, the bakery business venture failed. But, as Ernesto and Oneida would recall, it provided them with a great learning experience, and they viewed the setback as a stepping-stone for future success.

Working at the motel: Ernesto and Oneida Vendrel, with Ernest, Lourdes, and Joaquin (Ernest G. Vendrell).

Unfortunately, during this time frame, Ernesto and Oneida received the news that Oneida's mother had passed away in Cuba from cancer. However, through the intervention of the American Red Cross, they were able to bring Bonifacio to the United States, and he was able to live as a free man once again. Sadly, he passed away from another stroke a few years later.

After the bakery experience, Ernesto and Oneida resolved to obtain positions in the accounting field, a focus that they maintained for most of their professional careers from this point forward. They moved the family to Collingswood, New Jersey, where we lived for three and a half years. Ernesto obtained his first accounting job at a hotel in nearby Cherry Hill, while Oneida obtained a bookkeeper position at a business in Philadelphia, Pennsylvania. Having achieved more

Maria Ramos de Rodriguez and Bonifacio Rodriguez-San Gil (Ernest G. Vendrell).

stability in their professional lives, they began taking the family on summer trips to the Jersey Shore (Ocean City and Wildwood), as well as trips to our nation's capital and New York City.

However, although they were grateful for their work in New Jersey, Ernesto and Oneida's goal was to eventually move to South Florida, where the weather was far warmer, and the Cuban exile community was growing rapidly. This goal was realized in 1968 when Ernesto obtained a job as the comptroller for a large hotel in Daytona Beach, Florida. Likewise, Oneida obtained a job as a bookkeeper at a local hotel. One year later, they moved to Miami, where Oneida obtained a job as an accountant, a job that she would have for the next 26 years. Ernesto would work as a comptroller for large hotels in the Bahamas, the Dominican Republic, Vero Beach, and Miami for close to 25 years.

Ernesto and Oneida Vendrell with Ann and Ernest visiting the Empire State Building in New York City (Ernest G. Vendrell).

After retiring from accounting, Ernesto became very active in ministry and evangelism. In particular, he became involved in radio ministry, and was selected as the head of religious programming for *Radio Mambi* and *Cadena Azul* in Miami, positions that he held for approximately seven years. It was during this time that he was also led to investigate the possibility of broadcasting the Gospel to Cuba, and he traveled to the Turks and Caicos Islands where there was the potential to establish a television broadcasting facility that could easily reach the island nation. This did not materialize. However, undaunted, Ernesto applied for a television license that became available in Key West, Florida, that would likewise be capable of reaching Cuba. This required that Ernesto give testimony in Atlanta, Georgia during the application process. However, the license was eventually granted to another, more experienced applicant. Nonetheless, Ernesto continued traveling throughout the Caribbean and Central America on various mission trips. His service to ministry and evangelism led to the Hispanic American Family of the Year Foundation nominating the Vendrell Family for this award in 1989.

Later, after considerable study, Ernesto was ordained a minister. He immediately began preaching in the Miami area, and eventually became the pastor of a local church. His pastoral duties also led him to preach the Gospel at various jails and prisons, as well as visit and comfort the sick at local hospitals, assisted living facilities, and nursing homes. Although he no longer is the pastor of a church, at the age of 90, he still studies the Bible every day, prepares sermons on a regular basis, and preaches several times a month. As he often mentions to family and friends, he prays that a religious revival will occur in Cuba. In his view, such a revival would have a very positive impact on Cuba and its people.

Top: The 1989 Hispanic Family of the Year Foundation Award. *Bottom*: Ernesto and Oneida Vendrell being honored for more than 40 years of service in ministry and evangelism at an October 2017 function (Ernest G. Vendrell).

Postscript: Reflections on My Family and Cuba (by David Ernesto Vendrell)

Growing up, I had been told endless stories about Cuba—the little island homeland that sparked both passionate nostalgia and continual heartbreak for its exiles—*my* family. There was a sense that my cousins and I had missed out on a familial experience that molded us into the unique generation that we represented.

There was *Abuelo* Cabrera, staunchly wearing his guayabera and losing himself in the details of American politics, acting as a watchdog from idealistic Communist invasion. He would share stories of chaos and imprisonment, but also of growing up across the street from his future wife, *Abuela* Josefina. There was *Abuelo* Ernesto, recalling the disastrous consequences of Castro's rise to power, and how he was almost shot by several of Castro's militiamen for simply speeding on the highway. *Abuela* Oneida would reminisce on the beauty and peace of the island nation, while also extolling the patient suffering of motherhood. These myths felt larger than life, as though they happened to some other people on some other planet. The relative ease of my American life couldn't contemplate such ingrained hardship.

But, that was the duality my Cuban-American family represented. Dreams. Struggles. Perseverance. There was a resilience to the days' endless battles in order to make it easier for my brother, my cousins and me—we would never know such a life if they had anything to do about it. I found myself particularly inspired and grateful for these stories and sacrifices, yet feeling like I was missing out on something special—something foreign and exotic that gave my roots a significant uniqueness that crossed borders and history. Something that made me feel like a small part of a bigger story.

The Journey from America to Havana

Over this past summer, I had the opportunity to visit Cuba—the first in my family to do so in over fifty years. I was going to stop for a whole day in Havana with my girlfriend, Jessica Diaz, her parents, Delvin and Ofelia, her brother Daniel and his girlfriend, Sosse. I was ecstatic to finally get the opportunity to close the gap between imagination and reality—to finally see Cuba, walk its streets and feel its energy. However, I knew that this trip would not be completely celebratory to all of those in my family. The generations before me fought tooth and nail to get *out* of Cuba, so why would I want to go *in*? I empathized with this, but I still needed to be there for myself. Luckily, I was surprised to find the majority of my family was supportive, with a mixture of hesitancy and curiosity. They wanted me to report back; how are things now? With that understanding, the voyage was set. I was going to Cuba.

On Wednesday, May 31st, our cruise ship slid into the tiny crevice of a dock in Havana. Standing at the stern, I saw over the horizon line of the city—a beautiful, crumbling façade like some long lost Spanish village. We disembarked, heading down into the bowels of the processing center that reluctantly welcomed visitors to the island. This was new to them, to us, to Royal Caribbean. Questions and anticipation swirled overheard. But, as we all made our way through the grey port, we spilled out into the magnificent Havana heat. I was immediately hit with a unique electricity—the sights, the smells, the sounds—it was almost exactly how I pictured *Habana Vieja*. Sun-burned smiles, Latin music, 50s cars. Havana was a post-card frozen in time. It is as though the world spun around the sun and forgot to take this small island with it.

Our group gathered in the monolithic Plaza de San Francisco, met our 20-something tour guide and were immediately accosted by street merchants and brightly dressed dancers. Like most Caribbean islands, everyone had a special skill to make a dollar. It seemed as if no one worked—why bother

Havana balconies (David Ernesto Vendrell).

with a job when tourists were bringing more in tips than what you could make in a day?

We took photos and then walked to a bus that would take us to our next destination. Piled in, we drove west along the *Malecón*—the long seaside wall running along the border of Havana. This is when I first noticed the disparity of the city. As Old Town faded into the rearview, the main arteries of the city passed to our left. Like veins in a sickly man, the alleyways acted as windows of crumbling paradise. I could tell the city was once beautiful and majestic, but the paint had begun to wear, the stucco was crumbling and a layer of dirt carpeted the street. It was as though we crossed a border from the first world into the third world. I turned to the right, met by the sparkling blue ocean of promise just off the shoreline.

We spent the day visiting Havana landmarks—Plaza de Armas and Old Town Square—and indulged in Cuban delicacies such as rum, coffee and cigars. We visited *El Floridita,* the famous bar that Ernest Hemingway haunted, and sipped daiquiris. We walked through the veins of Old Town, which buzzed with people, melodic voices and tiers of balconies where life seemed to be spilling out of the edifices. It was beautiful chaos—just like one

Old Town Havana (David Ernesto Vendrell).

of my family holiday dinners back in South Florida. It was the stereotypical Cuban destination dream.

Yet, I could not help but feel attuned to the secret pain all around. In a stroke that seemed antithetical to touring a Communist country, our tour guide showed us a ration dispensary. As he talked inside, I assumed it had been shut down for years, as if it were some historical landmark to show the "progress" of history. Full of scantily stocked, rusted shelves and a pitiful atmosphere, the place just felt tragic. Shockingly, he revealed to us that it was a working dispensary. It could not be true. But, he showed us his ration booklet. This was emblematic of all of the horror stories I heard growing up. These people must be starving.

Also, when we went to the Capitol building, we found ourselves being followed by an undercover police officer—another sobering reminder that this wasn't just a new tourist destination for people. It was still a Communist country with very limited freedoms.

I asked a handful of people, "how is it living here?" Most would lend a small smile and say something along the lines of "we get by" or "we're survivors." Cubans find happiness in the simple things—a good drink, a day on the beach or dinner with family. On an island that does not even have toilet paper in public restrooms, let alone most supplies we take for granted in Amer-

Ration dispensary in Havana (David Ernesto Vendrell).

ica, its inhabitants adopted a superhuman resilience and positive attitude. Tragically, to them, things seemed impossible to change, but they could at least survive it.

As we finished up our last hour in Havana, we bought some *cafecitos,* a couple of souvenirs and a postcard. Sitting at the café, I reflected on the eight-hour experience that felt like a lifetime in the making. Havana is a city of dichotomies: vibrant, yet wanting; beautiful, yet decaying; alive, yet oppressed. Though the institutions may have changed, the people are just like my family: hopeful, happy and refusing to take a day for granted.

There was a sense of clo-

Walking through the streets of Havana (David Ernesto Vendrell).

Family celebrating Christmas (Ernest G. Vendrell).

sure and completion that washed over me. All I needed was a day. I felt it, breathed it in and knew that America was home, but was so joyous to know that my roots extended beyond the borders of the States, flowed through the Gulf of Mexico and could be found buried under the streets of Havana. I felt a wholeness that had not been there before. I may be an American, but I am also a Cuban. There is enough room in my soul for both.

I finished up the postcard and dropped it in the mail, excited for this little piece of Cuba to find my family someday soon; for my words to make that perilous journey from Havana to America—just like my family all those years ago.

My Pedro Pan Story

OSCAR VIGOA

On April 27, 1962, at the age of seven, I left Cuba alone with my cousin Jesusito, who was 16 years old at the time. We boarded a KLM aircraft for the short trip to Miami. I had no idea what to think and was led to believe by my family that it would be a short trip to the eastern part of the island, and that they would see me soon. I trusted my mother and father, so I boarded the plane without hesitation. Members of my family would later comment how *hombresito* I was to walk alone to the plane, displaying no hesitation or reluctance while leaving my family behind. And so I started my journey to freedom.

A Life in Havana Cuba

I was born in Havana, Cuba, on March 14, 1955. I was named Oscar Florentino Vigoa, Jr., because my father thought I resembled a famous Cuban boxer named Florentino. My father, Oscar Vigoa, and mother, Carmen Gonzalez Vigoa, lived in Havana (511 Perez y Melones, in Luyanó, Cuba). My father's mother and father lived in Pinar del Río (on a particular mountain where all the Vigoas lived). But, after my grandparents divorced, my father (approximately 10 years old at the time), his brother Jesus (who was then 15 years old), and their mother, Celia, moved to La Havana. I grew up living in a family-oriented environment, with my *"abuelos"* on my mother's side, in a big house. Emiliano, my grandfather, was a true Spaniard; he looked the part, and spoke the part. He lived a very proud life and spoke with a heavy Spanish accent. I hardly knew my grandmother from my father's side, Celia, and never saw my grandfather from my father's side. From what I could recall, the neighborhood was a close-knit community that fostered friendship and collaboration between the families. That close relationship would end when *fidel castro* (I cannot capitalize this person's name; he is a despicable man who destroyed the Cuban culture) became the communist dictator. We were a very close family that lived in close proximity to each other; we were involved in regular family outings in different homes, a typical Cuban culture as we participated with neighbors in a close-knit community. My dad had two close friends, Ovidio and Ernesto (also true Spaniards) who would visit our home on a regular basis. They told me that I was a very active and mischievous kid. When I rode the *velocipedo*, a small tricycle that I cherished, I would run over their feet as they sat talking to my mom and dad. Years later, they told me they got a "kick" out of that. My uncle, Jesus Vigoa, would also visit our home on a regular basis. It was a close-knit family that enjoyed good food and family interactions.

I used to traverse the neighborhood with childhood friends in search of fun. I rode my bike and played in the streets. It was a safe community, and we had everything we needed to live a good life. My uncle, Rodolfo Homerlein, who was married to my mom's sister Fina, told me a charming but daring story. His son, Rudy (Rodolfito), was having a hard time learning how to ride his new bike. One day, he showed up at the house hoping that I would demonstrate to Rudy how to maneuver the bike in a slow step-by-step manner. Of course, I had other plans. We lived on the upper part of a hill. I helped Rudy on the bike, and in front of his dad, I shoved him down the hill as he drove in panic. I told him that now he will learn how to maneuver the bike. Needless to say, Rodolfo and my mom were flabbergasted. They thought Rudy would crash and get hurt. However, he did not crash, and he learned how to ride the bike. From that wild experience, he attained confidence, which enabled him to successfully learn a difficult

Emilia and Emiliano Vigoa, on their wedding day (Oscar Vigoa).

task. Those were good times. Years later, I learned that the most effective way to learn a difficult task is to do it. In other words, face the fear and do it anyway.

Famous Family in Cuba and on the Bus

Rodolfo Homerlein, my uncle of German descent, was a renowned history professor and scholar who was given the dubious honor to teach and tutor the sons of the late Cuban President, Fulgencio Batista. Although he constantly demonstrated a humble lifestyle, Rodolfo was always invited to the most sophisticated of gatherings, and in hush-hush, he told me he liked it. In all the sense of the word, Rodolfo was a gentleman and a very intelligent scholar in high demand as a teacher and tutor of famous people on the island.

Little Oscar Jr. prior to exile, Havana, Cuba (Oscar Vigoa).

My dad worked as a bus driver and mechanic for the Catholic school, LaSalle. I remember him taking me on school field trips, which he was responsible for. He would drive the bus up steep hills, deep into La Sierra Maestra, a place that contained majestic green mountains. In this capacity, my dad had the opportunity to meet famous people, the parents of the children he was responsible for, on a daily basis. Later he told me, "Life is not about famous people, it's about simple people doing famous things." As he drove the bus filled with children and chaperones, I sat next to my dad on the engine cover compartment in the middle front of the bus (not the safest thing to do), free to admire the beautiful landscape and green forests. Moments that I will always remember are how patient and focused my dad was as he drove the school bus full of kids and teachers up the mountains. You could sense how the bus was having a hard time by the growl the engine made as it crept up those towering mountains. Those were fun times.

The Noche-Buena Gathering and Subsequent Nightmare

Years later, my family and I in exile were at a *noche buena* gathering at my uncle Jesus' house in the northwest part of Miami. A distant family

My Pedro Pan Story (Vigoa)   117

The Bus. My father Oscar Vigoa at right, with fellow bus drivers at La Salle School (Oscar Vigoa).

friend saw that I would not eat from the *cochino* (pig) that was cooking on the Cuban-made barbeque. Out of curiosity, he asked my dad and me why this was so. I told him it was a simple story that occurred when I was about 5 or 6 years old. My mother's brother, named Fidel (don't like that name…), was holding a *noche buena* at his house and we were invited. As I walked into his home, it was customary that I would always gravitate to the back yard. When I approached the back door this time, at the threshold, I saw Fidel stabbing a pig in the neck with a long butcher knife and the pig making horrendous loud screeches that I will never forget. I was traumatized for a very long time and always held contempt for Fidel. I knew he was no good; he later became a *Fidelista*, a dedicated and despicable communist.

My Extended Family

My mom's brother was cool. I remember him as a tough guy; they called him *Macho*, and he had little tolerance for evil and stupidity. On some polit-

118   Escape from Cuba

From right back row: Rodolfo Homerlein, Fina Homelein, Jesusito "Jay" Vigoa and my mother Carmen Vigoa. I'm standing in front of my mother and Betty and Rudy Homelein are on the right. The three people on the left are unidentified family friends (Oscar Vigoa).

ical issues, he was in conflict with the Batista government, but he never believed the lies of that barbaric and cruel man, *fidel castro* (I will not capitalize this name). In particular, Macho never supported or sympathized with the *castro* regime, despite his concerns about the Batista government. Although he wanted to migrate to the United States, in an act of compassion and courage, Macho stayed behind to care for the remaining family. Some of our extended family and friends stayed behind. Some decided to stay to see if *castro* would be a good change for the country. Others could not leave for a variety of reasons, including the communist government terminating the exit visa format. It was important that a young tough-guy stay behind to care for the elderly of the family, and he is a hero in my book. He had to watch his every step to ensure that he would not lose his cool, be available for his family, and avoid jail under the communist regime of *fidel castro*. He hated the *Comité*, that invasive communist surveillance system (spies in action), that was installed at every block in the neighborhood to divide and conquer.

My dad's brother, Jesus, and our family were very close. He was a caring and very hard-working man. He was in the construction business and was in high demand because he was competent and ethical. I recall one conversation that Jesus, my dad, and I had when we lived in Miami. The conversation was about Batista and his alleged policing tactics and policing philosophy. I never forgot what Jesus said. He stated, "If you obeyed the law and lived within familiar basic rules and good values, you never had a problem with the Batista government." Moreover, he said, "I never had an issue with a police officer; I obeyed the laws and never found a way to get into trouble."

The Difficult Decision Parents Sometimes Need to Make

Macho in pre-Castro Cuba, standing next to Oscar Vigoa's residence in Luyanó, Havana (Oscar Vigoa).

I vaguely recall when Jesus and my dad discussed sending his son Jesusito (Jay) and me to the United States. I recall my father saying, "Before the communists get him, the Americans will." I could denote that this decision was a painful undertaking and a strain that weighed profoundly on my mom and dad, since I was their only son. The strong rumors around the island at the time were that *fidel* was going to send all kids to Russia for further indoctrination. These conversations were very confidential; I was told very little and only close family and friends were in on the plan to send me out of Cuba. As an employee of the LaSalle School, my dad was working with the priests and administrators of the school on the *Pedro Pan* connection to Miami. He skillfully negotiated with the priests and administrators at the school to fly me and Jesusito out to Miami. I cannot stress enough the confidentiality of this operation. If the communists got wind of this exodus, the entire plan would be dismantled. These negotiations did not become interesting and very personal until Jesusito and I reached the USA. Miami was a very small town at the time, and the influx of refugees from Cuba was daunting. So, the Catholic Church and Miami officials were placing us kids all around the United States. I had friends that ended up in Nebraska, I later learned. My dad was informed that I was earmarked for San Antonio, Texas.

When he heard that, he assiduously worked with the priests and high-level administrators to keep me in Miami. Thank God for that.

The Rockets Over the Bodega

While still in Cuba, up the street, and up a small hill there was a *bodega* that I would frequent with my dad and *abuelo* Emiliano. On one particular afternoon, as my dad and I were walking to the *bodega*, I saw and heard three rockets, with a glaring red flare illuminating the night sky, fly over the *bodega*. It was a frightening experience; I have never forgotten the lasting image of three flaring red-hot tubes as they appeared to be on fire screaming over the horizon of the neighborhood. My father quickly took me back home and told me to hide under the bed until he told me otherwise. Needless to say, I was scared. Unknown to me at the time, there was a civil war going on in Cuba between the Batista government and the revolutionary forces of *fidel castro*. On January 1959, *fidel* won the bloody civil-war, and took over the island with a bunch of cronies, to include the disgraceful murderer, Ernesto "Che" Guevara.

I'm proud to say that my father never fully fell for the rhetoric spewing from *fidel* or his revolutionaries for a better Cuba. He was very suspicious of their approach to the issues; they looked passionate, dirty, but not sincere. The demands put on the people were not reachable, and suspicions and imperfections permeated the new regime. My dad was troubled by their appearance and their brutality of the opposition; Cubans killing Cubans! In particular, "Che" (I can't mention his last name, it would give credit to this butcher) was a criminal revolutionary who was responsible for most executions without trial or due process. No mercy, "the end justifies the means," was the motto he lived by! This bone-headed military approach (used by Hitler and other historical monsters) began to turn-off most Cubans on the island; they began to see and feel the brutality of the firing squads and executions.

The Citizens' Committee (el Comité) *Spies for Fidel*

Fidel, being a cunning, evil, and shrewd dictator, knew the consequences of liberty and its action-oriented message. Therefore, he began to impose a *Comité* (the English translation: a form of a citizens' committee or watchdog agency) that *castro* would use as spies to surveil decent Cubans without due process. This is a system whereby every citizen is responsible to "rat" on other citizens, particularly if they violate state laws such as free speech, free assembly, freedom of religion, and so forth. If you did not "rat" on your friends and family, you would be considered a "worm" (in Spanish: *un gusano*), a term these new communists would call the decent Cubans remaining on the island or those that left the island. Those who did not inform for the government would be put in prison. Now the ridiculous began to flourish, and the communist model took control of the daily lives of Cubans. It worked. No one dared to challenge the new despots, whereby the brutal regime took hold of each neighborhood, one by one.

After the Bay of Pigs invasion, I remember I was told to attend a viewing of a film at the corner of my house in the open. The *Comité* rats were watching to see who attended and who did not. Of course, those that did not attend were suspected to be *gusanos*. The *gusanos* would not be allowed to enjoy the benefits of the revolution. Thus, all activity or food was rationed more severely against the good people of Cuba. The communists projected a movie on a paint chipped wall that showed images of a failed mission at the Bay of Pigs, as many in the crowd began to chant and cheer. I remember being troubled by the images; I saw soldiers, some wounded, being pushed along the beach. As a 5-year-old, I had no idea how to comprehend the situation, and that was the predicament that I was in. At first, I was enjoying the moment as my friends and I were out late watching a movie outdoors. I must confess, initially, I liked the new communist dictator; he was a rock-star. I remember my family telling me that they had reserved a dog's plate for the dictator's food, and I would fight them to repeal their insults. But, as time went on, however, I began to dislike the new regime. It appears the influence of my father and my good listening skills at family gatherings fueled the hatred of the violence that *fidel* brought to my homeland. All along, I did not realize that my father and mother were preparing me for a family separation and a trip to the United States.

The Secret

My parents told me over and over again that it was a secret and not to tell anyone, but I would be going on a short trip to another city in Cuba. I did not know what to feel; it seemed beyond my interpretation and conceptualization. As time went on, I grew more hostile to the *castro* communist government, but my dad told me not to be vocal and I understood. As a 6-year-old, I began to grasp the enormity of the consequences of a communist government on family unity and life. It was now about *la revolución* and all about *castro* and his cronies; the family life was dead in favor of a communist lifestyle. Now, the dreaded travel-day began to approach like the sun approaches a new day, and the secret is guarded as the sun rises from the east. We headed to the airport, but I don't remember the drive. While at the airport, I saw a lot of *milicianos, fidel's* guerrilla army soldiers acting as police officers. I don't remember the processing at the airport, but I do remember what I did while waiting to board the flight.

The Accordion Player at the Airport

I was a gifted accordion player. I played the accordion everywhere, and I could even play a request. I was self-taught to the amazement of my family and friends, and I developed a keen ear and manual skills to make that instrument sing. In the airport, I was playing the accordion to the most decent and civilized Cubans who were departing with me. Then came *miliciano* and he commended me on playing the difficult instrument. Then he asked me to play the new Cuban communist song, *La Internacional*. I pointedly and sternly told him, "Bete para el coño de tu madre." It simply translates to: "Go to hell, you son of a bitch." I guess I inherited this spirited soul from my uncle Macho. Needless to say, my mother and father almost had an instant heart attack. They almost succumbed to the reality that I would not be allowed to leave. But miraculously (praise God), the *miliciano* just grinned and walked away. My dad obviously reprimanded me and told me not to do that again, since it would compromise my trip. I complied, and the experience assured me that I could not be a normal kid in a normal country. I loved that accordion, but as in typical fashion, the communist government did not allow me to take it on my trip. The only companion that I had, an instrument that would act as a psychologically soothing object, was detached from my hands and returned to my family. It was a psychological brutality imposed on a young kid embarking on a trip of a lifetime to an unknown destination.

Leaving My Family

In 1962, on the 27th day of April, my 16-year old cousin Jesusito, and I boarded an airplane for a short trip to Miami. I did not fully understand what was happening, since I was led to believe by my family that it would be a short trip to the eastern part of the island and that they would see me soon. I trusted my mother and father. I had no idea that I was leaving my family behind. Now, at age 62, I can understand this moment better. More suited to comprehend the magnitude of the separation, I can now conclude that it was God's grace that supported my efforts to walk alone to the aircraft and not look back. Imagine a seven-year-old boy walking alone with a 16-year-old cousin toward an aircraft for the first time without the comforts and protection of a mother or father; a flight to an unknown land with an unknown language and no family and friends. It creates deep scars, but it builds profound character beyond belief.

The plane took off and I left behind everything in the world that mattered to me; my mother, my father, my relatives, my friends, my homeland, and the Cuban way of life. I don't remember how I felt. The plane ride was non-eventful, and I just sat there and looked forward with a blank stare. A couple of hours later, it seemed, we arrived at Miami International Airport, and my cousin went one way and I went the other. That was alarming; I was alone in a foreign land and did not know how to communicate in English. An unknown man (I later learned his name was George) was sent by the Catholic Church and Monsignor B. Walsh, the leader of the *Pedro Pan* exodus whom I consider to be a hero. George took my hand and gestured for me to come with him. I did, and ended up in Florida City, a community in South Dade County, where the U.S. government and the Catholic Church had established a camp for young boys. My cousin Jesusito was taken to Matacumbe (located by Tamiami Airport), a camp for older boys. I did not see him again until much later.

My Angel in a New Land

I stayed at the Florida City camp for a considerable period of time. The Catholic Church was placing boys in foster care throughout Dade and Broward counties. When it finally became my turn, I boarded a van along with other boys, and maybe an infant or two. We traveled for some time, and I watched as each boy was placed in foster care. However, when we got to my stop, the designated family was not able to take me because they already had their allotment of kids. I was very disappointed and had a defeated presence as we approached the house of Mr. and Mrs. Del Vecchio. The Del Vecchios were a middle class Italian family that were kind enough to take, and mostly adopt, babies; a harder task in foster care. I was the only boy left in the truck after the delivery of the infant to Mrs. Josephine Del Vecchio. I sat motionless and waited to be transported back to Florida City and start the process all over again some other day. You may imagine what I was thinking at the time—nobody wanted me, and I could not understand why. This was a hard proposition for a seven-year-old kid to digest in a strange land, unable to communicate. God only knew that my fate was sealed at this point. But, when Mrs. Del Vecchio received the baby, she looked in the truck and saw the defeated and hopeless expression on my face. She asked the van driver what would happen to me and why I looked so sad. The driver told her that I was not placed in a home today because the foster homes were full.

Mrs. Del Vecchio motioned the van driver to confer with her privately. She asked him to leave me with her. The driver was confused and pointed out to my Mrs. Del Vecchio that she never took in older boys; why was this an exception? She politely acknowledged, but said, "He looks so sad, I can't let him leave."

It wasn't until many years later that I learned of what Mrs. Del Vecchio had said to the van driver that day. I recalled the emotions of that day many years later when my family and I went to visit her in Ft. Lauderdale. She was so glad to see me that day, and I was so thankful. Words cannot describe the feeling. This encounter was very important to me. It changed my life. Mrs. Del Vecchio was my angel in a new country.

As I learned later in my short life, I was scheduled to be shipped to San Antonio, Texas. Nothing against the state of Texas, but I wanted to be close to Cuba. As my parents would later say, the climate was similar, and that would make my life a little easier. I was very fortunate too that my Dad worked at La Salle Catholic School in Cuba, as he was able to convince the Catholic Church to make every attempt to keep me in South Florida. In my case, the Church complied, but many boys and girls were shipped all over the United States. There were too many Pedro Pan kids, and the infrastructure in South Florida at the time could not handle it. So, the exodus continued to other parts of the nation.

My Home Away from Home

I began my life in exile, in a foreign land with different customs and norms. Imagine a seven-year-old boy from another country in foster care, not knowing the language, with no parents, no family, no friends, all alone and waiting. I had the grace of God and the Holy Spirit watching over me and protecting me. My foster parents were outstanding. My foster father was Joseph Del Vecchio, a successful truck driver. Mr. Del Vecchio (out of respect I never called him by his first name; years later, I found out it was Joseph from his daughter Loretta) and stay-at-home home foster mom, Josephine were devout Catholics, and demanded the best from you with motherly discipline and fatherly support and encouragement. They were awesome. They taught me self-reliance, good values, and respect for the Catholic religion and other people. As a traditional Italian family with very strict moral values and norms, they fostered respect and loyalty. We would have to all be seated at a certain time for dinner, with no exceptions. On Fridays, we had fish out of respect for the Catholic faith. On Sunday, very early in the morning, we went to church, and all the kids behaved exceptionally well. My foster parents had two biological children, Marianne and Matthew. They were both a bit older, but we got along very well. I became good friends with Matthew. We would play around the vicinity of the house every day, and he introduced me to all the kids in the neighborhood. I remember displaying a lot of physical strength as a kid, and that was admired by all the children. In particular, I remember lifting the angle rides in the playground to the surprise of the other children. With the help of Matt, I was treated with respect.

The Fall in the Lake—A "Real" Learning Experience

I will never forget what happened to me one particular summer day. Since I did not know how to swim, Mr. Del Vecchio told me over and over again that I was not allowed to play near the canal; he made me clearly understand this rule. Well, I violated that rule on a clear day. Matt was going to the canal to play and I had to go. I felt compelled to test my foster father and my limitations, and wanted to impress upon my friends that I was not scared. Matt told me not to get close to the embankment, but of course, I ignored him. I started scaling the side of the walls when I fell in the water. Matt was in shock; he knew what was in store for him. He and the other boys quickly pulled me out. I was stupid and hardheaded. I could have drowned, but yet again, God and his angels watched over me. Immediately, I ran home to change, and Mrs. Del Vecchio confronted me at the door. She asked me why I was wet. I lied, telling her that I was playing by a kiddy pool at the home of one of our neighbors and fell in. She said, "We'll see about that."

Later, when Mr. Del Vecchio got home, he asked me why I got wet in the afternoon. I told him the same story, and it looked like he did not believe me. So, he asked me again, "Why were you wet? Tell me the truth." Again, I told him the same story. Then he asked, "Were you playing by the canal?" I said, "Absolutely not."

What happened next changed my life forever; I learned an invaluable lesson. Mr. Del Vecchio said, "OK, I guess I was lied to, I was told you were playing by the canal, but it appears I was wrong. Thus, I will take it out on Matt. He will be disciplined for not following instructions." Then he yelled, "Matt get over here," as he began sliding his belt from his pant loops to strike and punish Matt, I stopped him, and confessed that I had lied. In essence, I told Mr. Del Vecchio that I was playing by the canal and fell; that Matt was not to blame—it was my fault. By this time, I was speaking fluent English, but words could not decipher the anguish I felt for Matt. I learned a very important lesson that day; do not lie and most importantly, be a "man" and take responsibility for your actions. Mr. Del Vecchio stressed that moral lesson and punished me for the week; no playing outside and no other activities around the house.

The Del Vecchios were a very loving and supporting family. They encouraged intellectual exchanges, but most of all, discipline, faith, and family. I even learned how to play the organ. I can recall Mr. Del Vecchio saying, "You play the accordion so well that you should have no problem playing the organ." It was a difficult instrument, but I learned to play it in a very short time. He prepared me for a concert that I would give for my father and mother when they arrived from Cuba. They made it a point to help my overall growth and emphasized the need to be a good Christian and an overall good and intelligent human being.

My Father Is Allowed to Leave Cuba and Finds That He Has a Changed Son

After approximately 6 months, my father was allowed to emigrate to the U.S., but he could not take custody of me because he had no means of support. My mother stayed in Cuba for a while longer; the communist government would not allow her to leave with my dad. As soon as he settled down in Miami, he wanted to see me, so he told a good friend and family member, *El Chispa*, to take him to see his son. This future exchange between father and son is vintage Vigoa. My father tells it like this: as he is driving in the neighborhood he sees me walking down the street, so he tells *El Chispa*, "Hey, there goes my son. Stop the car." *El Chispa* (the spark in Spanish) complies, and my dad opens the car door and leans out. I just stopped and stared at him. My dad then asks, "Don't you recognize me?" I said, "Yes," with a cold stare and chilly direct response, consistent with a disrespectable happenstance. My dad later told me he was crushed by the encounter; he could not believe the coldness of my behavior, which was downright rude and lifeless. But, you have to understand what I was going through at the time. It is very hard for a 7-year-old kid to adapt and survive in a strange environment, not understand the language, and also hold onto the past. In my mind, I dismissed the past and began a new life; a very scary thought, but a sense of reality. But, I was not able to do that without the grace and power of the Holy Spirit; God gave me the strength and solitude to withstand the pain of separation. As part of my grieving process, I remember going into the bathroom and looking at my mother's very small black and white picture (the only memento that I was able to smuggle out of Cuba) and crying. I did this once, since it was too painful to revisit these moments!

Unfortunately, I grew up way too fast in the U.S., since I had no idea whether I would see my father and mother again. I left all my friends and family, so I learned to endure and I became very independent, suppressing my feelings in order to survive. That's only one small example of my inner feelings, the rest is too hard to relive, so I mostly suppressed it. I developed a willingness to endure to persevere at all costs. I have used this painful life experience to accomplish most of my dreams. This inner struggle provided a sense of direction, focus, and determination to be the best and never look back to what I cannot control. You become hard as steel, learning not to express your emotions or to be afraid as you live a very mature and undeviating life. My family suffered with me as I had changed completely in 6 months; they now saw a young man who made his own bed and looked at life much differently, growing up real fast with the skills and traits of an adult. In essence, I was not a kid anymore. A young life lost; *fidel* takes the credit for this one. Even my daughter, Michelle, gets impacted by my experiences; she can always sense a type "A" personality in me with a passion to succeed and not show fear. This type of personality brings with it positive and negative behaviors. She also experienced a sense of conservative comportment from a changed person; something that could also serve as a detriment to a life in a democratic society. As I look back and contemplate on my experiences, I realize that *fidel castro* and his deceitful regime have negatively, grossly, and irreversibly impacted many generations of Cubans.

My Mother Finally Leaves Cuba

As my mother tried to leave Cuba, she had what was thought to be a standard visa and was ready to depart. When she approached the travel agent of sorts in Cuba, they told her she did not have the proper paperwork, she needed more documentation. She panicked and requested that my dad get further approvals. Finally, days later, she was able to get the proper paperwork and was en route to the airport. Time was of the essence because as time passed, the communist government was curtailing travel to the United States. Some families were never allowed to leave the island, thus were never reunited. Despite my trials and tribulations, I was fortunate and blessed that I was allowed to see my mother and father again. While there, she told me a story that at first, I could not believe. In her quiet, but determined, tone and demeanor, she said, "Oh yes the Cuban government officials told us women to disrobe." Some women in her company refused, but my mother wanted to leave so bad that she complied. Imagine this heart-wrenching, despicable request by men and women of uniform, to wit, a communist uniform. I later learned through family and friends that airport officials demanded that passengers disrobe, women, men, and children; it was a policy of the communist Cuban government. I guess they were looking for smuggled property that these communists thought belonged to the Cuban government, but instead belonged to good, hard-working, professional Cubans.

Exile in Miami

While in exile in Miami, Florida, I grew up in the northwest part of town. My mom and dad had to work long hours in jobs most people did not want in order to earn enough money for daily expenses. We lived in a duplex on 17th Avenue and approximately 42 Street, a few miles north of downtown Miami. At first, my father had to work in an aluminum plating company, and all day he was ingesting toxic fumes. When he came home, he would have to vomit at least once, as blood dripped down his nose (I guess the body was telling him to expel these toxins). Nonetheless, he was determined to continue this job, despite causing him dreadful ill health. As a recent immigrant, he did this job because he could not find any other type of work. By trade, he was a car mechanic, and he was a good worker, demonstrating the art of patience with machinery and its intricacies. I was very thankful, as his example served me well later in life.

My dad was always fascinated by the engineering that made the old cars function effectively; the excellent simplicity and sturdy structure of automobiles. My mother, Carmen, was a stay-at-home mom at first, but later she had to work, and found a job in factories. We shared a duplex with my cousin Rudy's family. Across from the duplex, I met a friend named Franklin (I don't remember if it is a last name or a first name). He was an older chap (much older than us; kind of like a big brother) who cared about young immigrant kids. He taught us how to play sports. In particular, we played football at the open corner lot, similar to the movie *The Sandlot*. Now I recall why I like that movie so much! Franklin's father was a merchant marine, and his mother was a stay-at-home mom. They lived in the U.S. a few years. They were a stable family, with a stable income.

Another lesson learned in exile was one day when my cousin and his friends spray painted graffiti on Franklin's duplex for fun. Franklin was very upset and he refused to play with us again. He taught us the importance of loyalty and fostered a right

Left to right: Little Oscar, Rudy, and Betty at the Duplex on 17th Avenue and 42 Street in 1963 (Oscar Vigoa).

and wrong attitude that permeated my life. I now understood the ramifications of doing wrong and the consequences that come after. After we learned that lesson, Franklin played with us again; I was fortunate that he knew the value of others making a mistake and correcting the wrong behavior.

A couple of years later, we moved to an apartment on Northwest 32 Avenue and 35th Street. The manager, "Madam" was in charge of daily operations and everybody knew her. These apartments were very spacious and comfortable, and I liked living there. It had a wall unit air conditioner, and I had my own room. I enjoyed the weekends when the room air conditioner was turned on and I could relax in a nice cool environment. However, no matter the environment, I was still concerned that I would be plucked again and sent away to a foreign land. It is hard to explain, but this trauma stays in your sub-conscience for a very long time.

Moving Up in the World—Now We Have a House

When my brother, William Vigoa, was born in 1963, my dad was looking for a house. He had found a job as a mechanic and was doing pretty well. We went to live by Miami Jai Alai, on Northwest 37 Avenue and 36 Street, in a house that was spacious and had large front and back yards. Wow, we were moving up in the world. Now we lived in a wooden house. I liked it there. It was in a dense wooded area at the time, and my dad liked it too; he could walk to the Jai Alai fronton and hang out with friends. As I contemplate my values, it is important to make the following assertion: I never saw my dad drunk. He made it a point to never drink to the point of losing control, and he never spent his hard-earned money gambling. He was very mature and always understood his priority in life—

Left to right: William Vigoa, Jay Vigoa and Oscar Vigoa, Jr., at William Vigoa's police officer graduation on January 5, 1985 (Oscar Vigoa).

family. My mom and dad were blue-collar folks that did everything they could to provide for my brother and me—the best opportunities life could give. They worked very hard all week and sometimes into the weekend to make sure all the bills were paid, and then some. My mother was even sending money to Cuba to help relatives, lots of money I later learned.

The Accordion

Years later, my mom told me that she had a surprise for me; I was hoping for a gift, but had no clue what I was about to receive. It appeared that a family from Cuba had just arrived, and they were able to smuggle into the States my long-lost accordion. I had cherished it so much, but the *castro* regime had taken it from me when I left Cuba at seven years of age. I still have this accordion, and I treasure it with my life. These simple moments that capture your expectations and dreams of a more stable home life and secure family are paramount for a profound sense of happiness and ultimate psychological recovery.

Photograph of the accordion (Oscar Vigoa).

Learning More Lessons in Exile—It Is All About Good Values and Norms

As an immigrant child growing up in a strange place, I wanted to impress my peers in the way of leadership and, unfortunately, this turned into mischief—negative impulsive-leadership I later learned. My cousin Rudy and I got into trouble and both our parents were requested to come to the school. But before I talk about this situation, I have to provide some foundation about discipline at the Vigoa house. Our parents spent much time devising strict disciplinary strategies for us not to get into trouble. But, on a summer day that I will never forget, my dad executed this strategy to the fullest after I was disrespectful to a neighbor as I walked home with friends. The following day, my father met me at our neighbor's home and I received a "Cuban-style, Stage 3" whooping that lasted a lifetime; he was adamant that I become a model citizen who showed respect for other people. Trust me, I got it, especially after that memorable physical encounter in the Miami streets in front of family and friends.

Unfortunately, I kept getting into trouble, since my hot-tempered Cuban psyche kept getting in the way. This time, my cousin Rudy and I became disruptive students at school, and the faculty instructed us to contact our parents for a meeting the following day. Needless to say, I was distraught; the mere fact that I had to tell my father that I had messed-up again was beyond comprehension. I decided to read religious books and pray all night and repeatedly asked God to "take this cup away from me." I was in total spiritual distress, and I asked God to please temper my father's wrath as he learned of the bad news. In fact, the day of the meeting, my father was scheduled to open a new business, a Texaco gas station on S.W. 8 Street and 42 Avenue in Miami. He was excited, but stressed-out. Therefore, I did not tell my father about the meeting that night, as I did not have the courage to burst his bubble of a new business venture and feared his wrath again. Early the next day, my uncle, Rudy's father Rodolfo, came to the house and told my father about the meeting. Miraculously, my father just looked at me and turned away mumbling that "a new disciplinary strategy would be put in place to set this kid on the right track again." The new strategy revealed that I was now going to work with my dad every day after school, and in the summer, spend the entire time with him and my uncle Jesus at the gas station to learn adult norms and values, and to work and learn a trade. I loved sports and played it every day, but this new strategy erased my dreams of playing sports in school. As a result, I learned that there are consequences to making bad mistakes, and this served me well when I was growing-up. After school, I had to take two buses to get to my father's garage, the number 30 from Miami Springs to Lejeune Road, then a second bus to S.W. 8 Street. My father told me, "You better not miss the bus. This is your last chance of showing us you are a true Vigoa—a model citizen with ethical values and norms."

Determination: No Sports, Just Work and Earn Respect Again

I loved sports and I would stay after school trying out for different types of teams. After practice, I had to run from the school to catch the bus on Northwest 36 Street, a few blocks away from the field. One day, I stayed late trying out for the volleyball team. I made the team, but I missed the second bus. I said, "Oh my God," and began running and walking from N.W. 36

Street to S.W. 8 Street on Lejeune road. That's a distance of at least five miles. My Dad was waiting for me when the second bus arrived at the gas station. I did not exit the bus, and he became very worried. Then, about two hours later, he saw me arrive, sweaty and disheveled. He realized that I was on the path to recovery, but he stressed to me, "If that happens again, do not walk and run your way to the gas station, call me." I had gained the respect of both my father and uncle; they saw my hard work and dedication in becoming a good and dependable kid.

My family and I settled in Miami for a very long time. Thank God, I went to school in Miami, Melrose, and Miami Springs. I did well at the schools and played sports, such as football and baseball. I also enjoyed Jai Alai; I guess I inherited this from my Basque/Spanish background. In addition, I married my high school sweetheart, Maria. Afterwards, I was attracted to police work, and a passion to serve others.

Photo of Oscar and Maria Vigoa, Jr., on their wedding day, 1974 (Oscar Vigoa).

Important People Behind the Scene That Helped Us

As I sit here and write this important biography, I'm not surprised to learn of more Cuban Americans that impacted our lives during the Pedro Pan Exodos. I just learned of a very courageous lady named Albertina O'Farrill, who along with Polita Grau, helped the Catholic Church with Operation Pedro Pan. Like many Cubans on the island, they saw the devastating regime of *fidel castro*. At the expense of their freedom, they assisted members of the Catholic Church in getting kids out of Cuba. For their participation and courage, they both received prison sentences. Albertina was arrested in 1965, tried in a "kangaroo" type court, of course with no due process, and sentenced to 14 years in prison. Albertina was a young lady, courageous and bright and with a promising future. She endured torture and hardships at the hands of her tormentors for the sake of justice. Moreover, she decided to postpone her life, suspend it for a time if you will, in order to help kids leave a communist dictatorship that would have all but eliminated our hopes and dreams of living in a free society.

The Story of the Vazquez Family

As Mrs. Del Vecchio and my parents, Oscar and Carmen, and the rest of my family stressed to me on a daily basis, God helped and supported me for the anticipated service that I would provide my fellow brethren throughout the years in the United States and the world; I believe that. As I matured, at age 19, I married Maria Esperanza Vazquez, a wonderful and very religious lady who has been my best friend and loyal partner for over 42 years. She came from a wonderful traditional family. Her parents, Santiago ("Neno," as he was known in Cuba) Vazquez and Ofelia Vazquez, did a superb job in teaching Maria and her brother Sam (Santiago Vazquez) a profound religious

The Vigoa's immediate family. Upper right to left, Emma, and Ricky, lower right to left, Michelle, Maria and Oscar Jr. (Oscar Vigoa).

way of life. Maria and I had a great kid, Michelle, who is a wonderful teacher, dedicated, intelligent, and beautiful, and by far our best "invention" (Michelle will know what that means; it's an inside family motto). Our extended family brings Emma into the fold, a wonderful and bright child that resembles my daughter Michelle in every way. In addition, we are very fortunate to also have Ricky, my son in law, who is a self-made man as the Director of ITD for the City of Hialeah. I have been blessed with a perfect family and wonderful friends.

It appears most good law-abiding Cubans have a story to tell about the horrible communist regime in Cuba. The Vasquez family also escaped the grasp of communist Cuba. Neno and his wife Ofelia (my wife's father and mother, respectively), lived in Central Hershey, Cuba, a very prosperous small town that produced Hershey chocolates from a major manufacturing plant owned and operated by an American corporation. Neno worked at the plant in the manufacturing side, and they had a good life. Unfortunately, when *fidel* took over, the families of this small quaint town were torn apart by families who sided with *fidel*, versus others like Neno, who knew better. This type of strife created divisions between families that once cared for one another. This is the communist way of life, "divide and conquer," and the family is dead!

As the Vazquez family lived under this communist regime, they had to be very careful not to upset the head of the *Comité*. Neno, like my father Oscar Vigoa, Sr., had a negative premonition about *fidel castro*. Deep down inside, both of them knew that *castro* was no-good, and that they would have to pluck their families from the island and emigrate to the United States. Unfortunately, Neno encountered lots of turbulence when he requested an exit visa to escape the com-

Neno and Ofelia Vazquez on their wedding day, in Herhsey, Cuba, 1953 (Oscar Vigoa).

munist country. The "trick" was up; *castro* learned that good, intelligent, and professional people wanted to leave his hell-like country to a better life abroad. Therefore, he put a temporary stop to most emigration. It took a few years for the communists to grant the Vazquez family an exit visa, and in 1970, the family finally emigrated to the United States, arriving in Miami. It is important to understand that before Neno got his exit visa, he had to work in the fields. His job was to milk cows, a job that was arduous and very difficult for him due to his delicate health condition. Although Neno suffered from migraine headaches, and this grueling work would cause more grave medical concerns, the communists were not concerned for his welfare or health. They demanded that he perform this service or else there would be no exit—further punishment for a family seeking a better way of life.

The transition to American life was especially difficult for my wife Maria because she was older than me when I came over. At 15 years of age, it was much more difficult to assimilate into a society that has totally different cultural veins and language. But, in true Cuban fashion, she persevered and made her stay in the United States a success. I met Maria in the old "barrio" in the northwest section of Miami. We hit it off immediately and we began dating. Maria is a very intelligent and passionate woman who has a keen eye for unscrupulous behavior. As part of her dedication to her family, Maria helped her family with daily expenses. In particular, she began working at a

Promotion to Assistant Director of the Miami-Dade Police Department, 2007. Bottom, left to right: brother William Vigoa, wife Maria, Oscar, daughter Michelle, my mother Carmen, and son-in-law Ricky Suarez (Oscar Vigoa).

food processing plant in Hialeah while attending high school. Unfortunately, most Cuban kids had to work and go to school to help with family expenses. The Vazquez family lived in Hialeah on the southeast side. Maria attended Miami Springs Senior High School and graduated in 1974.

In retrospect, as Maria and I fled Cuba, at seven years old and 15 years old, respectively, we both faced insurmountable obstacles and difficulties in a foreign land, learning a new language and culture. This was a heavy cross to carry for young kids, but God has blessed us with a rewarding life and a magnificent and healthy family; we are grateful for the blessings. In addition, Maria and I were fortunate and honored to serve the citizens of Dade County. I served as a police officer for over 33 years, and Maria as a Personnel Technician for 21 years, with the Miami-Dade Police Department. I rose through the ranks, and ultimately retired as an Assistant Director. I was commended for outstanding leadership, dedication, and commitment to the vision and mission of the Miami-Dade Police Department. Toward the end of my career, Maria supported my quest for higher education, and this helped me to complete a Ph.D. program at Lynn University. I now teach at Florida International University and consult throughout the world, continuing to help people and provide a service to my community.

My family and I are very grateful to the Catholic Church, Monsignor Walsh and his Catholic Charities, and the Del Vecchio family; foster father Joseph, foster mother Josephine, their son Matthew, their daughter Marianne, Loretta and family. A special thanks to my cousin Jay for being my travel companion, friend, brother, and mentor throughout the years. Jay was a very successful businessman who through hard work and perseverance attained the CEO position of the South

PhD graduation, May 2010, with my mother Carmen at Lynn University (Oscar Vigoa).

Region for AB Malone Company. In addition, he served as a reserve officer for the Miami-Dade Police Department and Polk County. Unfortunately, Jay passed away at a very young age; he was involved in a car crash on Florida State Road 60 in 1985. I lost a brother and mentor, and it was a colossal loss for the entire family; rest in peace my brother. He would have written his Cuban story too, and I'm sure it would have been a "hit." In addition, I also want to thank all the men and women behind the scenes that made a difference to get us out of the hell-hole that Cuba had become for a better future, and then provided help and support while in this great country, the United States of America. We hope our story instills an inspiration for generations to come to embrace faith, family, courage, freedom, perseverance, and to never to give up the fight for freedom. We must never stop seeking a better way of life for our families, specifically the children who have no understanding about the uncertain and problematic future that lies ahead while living in a communist or radical dictatorship society.

A New City, a New Country, a New Life

Mirta Solis Nuñez

It has been 57 years since the day that I saw my country for the last time. Never did I think that our stay in the United States would be permanent. Never did I imagine that I would not go back and see the land of my birth.

My story begins in Santa Clara, Province of Las Villas, Cuba on May 24, 1946. I was born Mirta Susana Solis Mazarredo. My mother's maiden name was part of my complete name and that was a very important part of who I was, the youngest daughter of Maria Luisa and Fernando. I was a late baby; my parents were in their early 40's when I was born. I have one sister, Raquel, who is older than me.

For the first 14 years of my life, my home was Santa Teresita, a farm of 4 *caballerías* (around 132 acres) in the suburbs of Santa Clara. There were avocados, orange and tangerine groves. It was also a dairy farm, and cows were milked every morning. We lived a very blissful life, surrounded by family, grandparents, aunts, uncles, cousins, in a very special piece of land that had been blessed by the hand of God, or so we thought.

My house was the point of gathering for my family; we would celebrate every Sunday with family dinners after church. My two cousins, who were almost sisters, Lolita and Quetica, would join us and sometimes I would invite friends to come to my house and have lunch with us. Sundays were special. In the afternoon we would go to the movies in town. Birthdays and holidays were always celebrated with relatives coming from all over the place. My fondest memories of Christmas are having a house full of family gathered to celebrate *Nochebuena* (Christmas Eve) and Christmas Day. But all that came to a screeching halt when during the last few months of 1960, our parents decided that Raquel and I had to leave our country.

I was 14 years old and although my life was going to radically change and the proverbial rug would be pulled from under my feet, I saw everything in a cloud of doubt and uncertainty. I thought these arrangements were temporary. We would leave Cuba, wait for it all to return to normal in a couple of months, and then we would return and everything would go back to the way it was. I left my bedroom intact, with all my things there—my books, photographs, my childhood memories and trinkets. I brought a few items of clothing, mostly sweaters and skirts. I was not going to need shorts, or a bathing suit because by summer we would be back in Cuba. I said goodbye to some friends, but our departure had to be kept from many other people because it was not safe to spread the word that anyone was leaving the country.

Saturday, December 3, 1960, Raquel and I boarded a Pan American World Airways flight out of Havana to Miami. Just a few days after our arrival, we spent our first Christmas in Miami. It was quite different from the holidays that we had experienced up to that point. There was no family, just the two of us. Raquel and I went to church and then sat on a bus bench on Coral Way and 87th Avenue in Westchester, to wait for a bus to take us to our destination. We did not know that in 1960 Miami, buses did not run on Christmas Day. We sat on that bench quietly for a couple of hours, when all of a sudden, we looked at each other and started to cry inconsolably. We realized at that moment that the flight from Havana had taken only 35 minutes, but we may as well have been a million miles away, not only from our family, but from everyone and everything that we loved and that was familiar to us until that moment. We were not certain then, but in reality, we were embarking on a brand new, different, difficult journey in a new city, a new country.

Our World Began to Change

Our world began to change the 1st of January 1959. My home was Santa Clara, the capital of the province of Las Villas. That is where I was born and went to school until January of 1958.

In November of 1956, an old boat called the *Granma* landed in the Southern part of Cuba with a handful of revolutionary soldiers who intended to depose the government of Fulgencio Batista. They were commanded by Fidel Castro and his brother Raul. These few men, about 80 of them, scurried under everybody's noses and set up camp in the bowels of the Sierra Maestra mountains in the Oriente province. Nobody paid much attention to them. Everyone went about their business; nobody thought that this group of outlaws would have any consequences. What a big mistake. What a horrible miscalculation, one that would affect every single person born or to be born in Cuba for years without end.

As it usually happens, the students in the public high schools and universities started to protest and make noise. They supposedly had found a reason and a cause to behave in a reckless manner and to disrupt and interrupt. Their leader was Fidel and their only purpose in life was to overthrow Batista. For that, they did not attend school, and did not want anyone to go to school either. One day, early in 1958, when I was in sixth grade, we were getting on the school bus to go home. A group of students were coming down the street, marching and yelling *"Abajo Batista!"* (down with Batista!) and *"Huelga!"* (strike). They wanted the students in the private schools to strike and not go to class. They circled the bus where we were and were banging on the doors and sides of the bus. We were all terrified. As a result of this incident, and the havoc it created within my school, my parents decided that it was better to transfer me to a school in Havana. Their thinking was that in a big city, there would be less danger. The cities in the interior part of the island were starting to become affected by the political situation. In Havana there was more anonymity. So, in the middle of that school year, I was taken out of my elementary school, where I had gone since I was 4 years old and moved to a school in Havana. Of course, I would continue going home on long weekends and vacations, but that was the first disruption of many in my very sheltered and protected childhood.

I liked my new school, Lestonnac Academy in the Biltmore section of Havana. It was a beautiful school, and the nuns of the Company of Mary and the other students were really nice. I made friends fast there. I was living in my aunt and uncle's home, who I loved like a second set of parents, and my sister, Raquel, who was attending the University of Villanueva in Havana, lived there too. She already had a car and took me places and life was pretty good. However, I missed my parents, my family, my old school and my friends who were left behind. In Havana there was not as much political turmoil as in the smaller towns, although sometimes the "revolutionaries" would place a bomb in a theater or some park, just to create panic. But in general, life was normal.

At the beginning of December of 1958, things started to get very difficult in Santa Clara. There were rumors that the revolution was gaining strength and they were "coming down from la Sierra Maestra." For Christmas that year, my parents decided it was best for us not to go home; they would come and spend the holidays with us. On December 28th Che Guevara and his band of "rebels" (outlaws) descended on Santa Clara. There was a 3-day war on the streets and on the 31st of December, Batista left Cuba with his family, and the unraveling began.

I remember waking up on New Year's Day 1959. There was an eerie silence outside the house in the Vedado section in Havana. No buses, no cars, no street vendors, and people were calling on the phone to say that Batista was gone. There were looters on the street, taking what they could from houses that had been abandoned in a hurry by their owners, functionaries of the previous government. Uncertainty reigned and filled the air. News started pouring in from Santa Clara, and we found out that for three or four days there had been an all-out war in the city. The most horrific news we received was that my little 10-year old cousin had been killed by a stray bullet, while standing at the door of his house. We were all in shock trying to absorb the horrible news. He was the grandson of my father's sister. The family was devastated.

On those first, sad days, we were all in a haze. My father went to put on a shirt, that someone had given him for Christmas. The gift box was from El Encanto, a very beautiful and luxurious store. He took the brand new shirt and made a very profound affirmation, "Let me put on this shirt, it may be the last shirt from El Encanto that I will own." We did not quite understand, and he had no idea either, but his words turned out to be prophetic. El Encanto was a symbol of capitalism, luxury and well-being, and a couple of years later it was burned to the ground. Nobody knows who did it.

Fidel Castro entered Havana on January 7, 1959, in a triumphant caravan, and he gave his first speech, a very long diatribe that lasted 7 or 8 hours. Most people were deliriously elated. Castro was going to be Cuba's salvation. There would be honesty, transparency, freedom and integrity in the new government that was being established. Cubans thought the second coming had arrived. *"Fidel, esta es tu casa,"* (Fidel, this is your house) was the happy chant of many. Most Cubans were enthralled in adoration of what they believed was a messiah.

I was only 12 years old, but I knew things were changing. My parents were not enthusiastic at all about the new government and they had a premonition that the changes were radical, drastic, and would alter our way of life. From the beginning there were rifts and disagreements within families. Friendships were destroyed. It started to be "them" and "us." I was told to be careful of what I said and who I said it to because it could cause problems for me or my parents. I had never known what it was to fear people around you. People that I knew and trusted had to be checked and treated with care. You had to tread very carefully.

We were considered an upper middle-class family. My father inherited farmlands from his parents. My grandfather had purchased a fairly large piece of land when he arrived in Cuba from Spain in the late 1800s. He would not enjoy his life in Cuba very long, as he passed away when my father was 2 years old. By the time of his death, early in the 20th century, his property was heavily mortgaged. My grandmother decided that she would do everything in her power to free her family's property from debt. This was her family's only means of support and she was going to do whatever she could, so that her children would be cared for. This was unheard of at that time. A widow with small children was not supposed to work outside her home, much less ride horses, work the field, and carry a gun for protection. Yes, she did everything that needed to be done, and little by little, the debts were paid, and the land was theirs. At the time of her death, the property would be divided among the five surviving children. I go into this detail to explain that although we enjoyed a comfortable financial status in 1959, it had not been easy or free of grief and struggle. My parents were not slave drivers or *latifundistas* like the new regime started calling anyone who owned land that produced. It produced because someone worked it and got paid for doing so.

My father was a physician; an ear, nose and throat specialist. He had attended the School of Medicine at the University of Habana and graduated in 1923. His mother had sent him to school to become a doctor, and that he did. You did not argue with her. So, he became a doctor, but his passion was his land. He practiced medicine for a while, but his life was the land. And that is what he intended to do. He had a group of men working for him, but he was personally involved in the functioning of the everyday life and struggles of his farms. The people that worked for him were good and loyal, he thought. He was caring and giving to all his workers. He paid them well, took care of their medical needs, provided housing for them and allowed his workers to cultivate the land around their houses to provide crops for their own consumption.

My father was not an abusive landowner. He was a generous man to everyone—his family and the people who worked for him. In the late summer 1960, a government agent went to his properties and padlocked the gates. When my father got there and started asking what was going on, one of his former employees told him he could not get anything out of there, not even an egg. He told my dad that these farms now belonged to the workers not to him. That was a result of the Agrarian Reform. The Agrarian Reform took farms, cattle, whatever they found, away from the rightful owners, not to give to the poor, as they originally claimed. The government became the sole owner of everything that had been previously privately owned. That land was eventually abandoned and no crops were planted, nor did cattle and horses roam around anymore. Everybody lost. Only the regime got ahead. Anyway, my father was devastated by the unfairness of these actions and he went to headquarters offices in Havana to plead for the return of his property. That night, when he got home, I saw him as I had never seen him before. My father was defeated. He sat with us in the living room and said, "They have taken away everything I owned."

Our home was a nice house surrounded by a small farm, on the outskirts of Santa Clara. The name of the farm was *Santa Teresita*. It was a beautiful place, with a small river and brooks running through it. One day, a few weeks after the revolution had "triumphed," we had some visitors—a couple that we knew, come to "pay their respects" in a military Jeep. The husband, a foreigner, a member of the international communist party, was now a high-ranking officer in the army. They had an escort of heavily armed soldiers as their bodyguards. They came to look around, to see what we had. It seemed like they were assessing how we lived. They left and my whole family was uneasy. I remember thinking, "What did they really want?" The lady was well known to us, always very nicely dressed, very classy, and she was a part of this charade. People that we used to know, now they seemed to be snooping around in an army vehicle, with a group of soldiers heavily armed like they were going to war. This was our home; what were they doing there? What did they really want?

One day I was on a school field trip and all the students were singing in the bus. We were singing some religious songs. This was a Catholic nuns' school. After a while, one of the girls in the bus said, "Do not sing any more church songs, let's sing now the song of the July 26th Movement," which was the revolution's song. We all got quiet, we did not want to sing that, the girl and a few others sang by themselves. We were scared, but there was no way we were going to sing that song. The mood in that bus had changed. We were young girls that felt threatened because we were told to sing a revolutionary song that we did not feel like singing. That mood spread all around us.

People were being imprisoned, for no reason. We heard of people being put to death for their ideals, without any legal process. If you were middle class, you owned property, and your children went to private school, you were automatically *un enemigo de la revolución* (an enemy of the revolution). You could be accused by any of them at any time for anything that they did not like or agree with.

I had a friend whose 17-year old brother was sent to prison for being accused of counter-revolutionary activities. He distributed some leaflets in the high school inviting students to join the *Acción Católica* (a Catholic youth group). They planted a gun in his bag. This is the reason they gave for sentencing him to jail. He was just a young kid. His family never heard from him again.

We would wake up every morning to news on the radio about companies, banks, private business being "nationalized," in other words, stolen by the government. My parents started to entertain the idea that we would have to leave. They wanted to get us out of the disaster that was beginning to take place. They knew in their hearts that things were not going to get better.

To get out, I needed a new passport and an American visa. I got my passport, but the visa was another matter. The lines at the American Embassy were getting extremely long, and they were not issuing new tourist visas to anyone. My father was in line one day from 2:00 o'clock in the morning. When they finally took care of him, he was told that the only way for me to get into the United States was with a student visa and registered in a school in the United States. We are talking September-October 1960. My mother was beside herself. She had to get me out as soon as possible. She taught English at the Public High School in Santa Clara, and she had heard rumors of how they were going to take the young people and put them in concentration camps (It was not exactly like that, but close. I will come back to this later). My uncle saw how worried my mother was and he decided to assist in the pursuance of the student visa, which was not an easy feat. He had business with firms in the United States, and he asked them to deposit the money they owed him in a bank account. He paid for my registration, tuition and boarding at Mary Immaculate Catholic School in Key West, and he made sure that there was enough money left to give me a weekly $3 allowance; he planned all of that. I know that I was blessed with members of my family who cared so much for me and my parents. Although at the time I really did not fully appreciate how fortunate I was. However, I was able in future years to show my uncle and my aunt how much they meant to me and how grateful I would forever be for their generosity and selflessness.

However, at the time when I was told that I was leaving Cuba, I was devastated and very sad. It was a very somber time. I was being told that I would have to leave everything behind that was familiar and loved. I was going to a boarding school in Key West, where I did not know anyone. I could speak about my trip with most of my friends, but I was told to keep my mouth closed, and my head down about my trip. I had a few friends whose parents were very much a part of the new government and we did not know what they were going to do. Although eventually every single one of them left. But during the last few months of 1960, things were very different. They thought that everything in Cuba was perfect. Why would anyone want to leave? You were told to stay and work for free and help build the new "wonderful" regime, and become part of all that. Previously, I made a comment about my mother being very afraid because of rumors that were spreading at her school. One of these rumors was that everybody who wanted to leave the country had to work in "agriculture" for whatever time was assigned so that you could contribute to the well being of the revolution. That did not materialize until about a year after I left, but my cousin and many friends, young girls from very well-known families were forced to work the fields to do farm work. They were humiliated because they were called worms for wanting to leave the country, and were constantly threatened that if they did not do what they were told, they would withhold the permit letter that would allow them to leave the country. I heard horror stories about the humiliations and abuses they had to suffer at the hands of these *milicianas* which imposed the forced

A New City, a New Country, a New Life (M.S. Nuñez)

slavery. So, I am so grateful to my mother for her determination and resolve to get me out before I had to endure this infamy.

In October of 1960, I went for the last time to my home in Santa Clara. Goodbyes were said to my father's sisters and my cousins. But I really did not grasp the enormity of this. Many of these family members who had been a very important part of my childhood, I would never see again. There was a lady who had worked in my house since before I was born; her name was *Iluminada.* When I started talking, I christened her with my version *"Nana."* And so it was; for everyone she was *Nana.* She was a super loving, sweet lady, who totally loved my family, but I know she adored me. I was her little girl. She was crying when I said goodbye. I never saw her again.

My family owned a summerhouse in a small key in the Bay of Cienfuegos. This piece of Paradise was called Cayo Carenas, or el Cayo, for short. To me that was a piece of Heaven here on this earth. We spent summers there. There were about 20 families that owned houses there, and during the summer, these houses were filled with families and many kids. There was no electricity; we had a generator for lights at night. Cooking was done in a kerosene stove, but there were no phones, no television, no electronics of any kind (Imagine today's generation under those conditions). The summers were always busy at el Cayo. You walked everywhere, as there were no roads and no cars. I did have a bicycle. The entire day was spent fishing, sometimes in boats and sometimes from the wooden pier, climbing trees, swimming, and paddle boating (five or six of us in a wooden paddle boat). Everyone paddled across the bay to this deserted beach with deserted hills that we would climb and have picnics, and nobody would bother us or do us harm. We had parties, sang, and danced. We were a group of children (boys and girls) of all ages, who simply had fun. I will never forget those wonderful summers that we spent there. When I found out that I was leaving Cuba, I asked my parents to take me, one last time, to Cayo Carenas. You could only get there by boat. We got on the double-decked boat, *El Pura,* and returned that afternoon to Cienfuegos on the last 6:00 p.m. ride. There was nobody there. I remember walking around the now deserted Cayo and thinking that I would be back. The sunset that day was beautiful; I still remember it. I always heard that the sunsets in the Cienfuegos Bay were spectacular; they were. That was my perfect place. It still is to this day, 57 years later. The greatest hurt is that I could never share that place with my husband and my daughters. Only 90 miles away, and what seems like a century ago.

When I was packing my suitcase, I did not want to bring many things because I was sure I would be back in Cuba by summer. My parents had worried about getting us out, but they had never mentioned the possibility that they would eventually leave too. It was understood that these were temporary arrangements. My parents were not going to leave Cuba, leave our home, leave their lives, and come here. My father had stated and repeated that he would never leave. So, we were coming back because by June, we thought, the Castros would be gone.

Back to the trip—my sister, Raquel, had her passport and a valid tourist visa. The plan was that we would arrive in Miami that Saturday, December 3, 1960. Our cousin, who had arrived a few weeks earlier with his wife and three children, would pick us up at the Airport in Miami. They were to take us downtown to the Hotel Leamington that our uncle had reserved for us, right across the street from the Greyhound bus station. This was another detail he had taken care of to make everything as easy and smooth as possible for our arrival. The morning we left Cuba was cold; it must have been in the low 60s. I was wearing a light blue woolen suit, which had been purchased for me for the occasion. The whole process of the Rancho Boyeros Airport in Havana is like a bad dream. I was 14 years old, and I was leaving my country with my older sister. I remember we were brought into a room and a woman patted me down and checked inside my purse. By this time, we had said goodbye to our parents, aunt and uncle, and a friend of mine with her family that had gone to the airport to see us off. We were inside this room, and then we were called to board the plane. This was 1960; you walked onto the tarmac and then went up the portable stairway to board the plane. My sister told me to look, and she pointed to a link fence, and there was our whole family waving goodbye. I remember looking at them and at the blue crisp Cuban sky, and then going inside the airplane.

Sitting inside that airplane the thought came to my mind: what had just happened? Where were we going? What were we doing here? Less than an hour later we were in Miami. The airport terminal was a tiny little building with no traffic, and no people. We saw our cousin and he took us to his car, an old Ford that had to be started with a pair of pliers. We stopped at the small efficiency where he and his family lived. It seemed unreal to me that these people were crammed up in this apartment. The reality was that we had our two suitcases and $10 to our name. It seemed that I was stunned, and nobody had come to wake me up from this nightmare.

A New Beginning

The next day, a Sunday, would take us to Key West. Raquel would then return to Miami to eventually leave for Denver, Colorado, where she had a friend from school that had invited her to go there. Supposedly, she would find work and eventually we would all reunite. That trip to Key West on the Overseas Highway was so long, and so lonely. Hurricane Donna had hit the keys earlier that year and you could still see the destruction. Trees fallen, buildings down, and a radio station with the antenna on the ground broken to pieces. When we arrived in Key West, it was a sleepy southern small town, with a Navy base, and Duval Street was the center of town. My school was an old beautiful white wooden building on Truman Avenue. The dormitory for the boarding school was on the second floor of a building. There were about 30 boarders. I had a bed with a chest of drawers next to me and a curtain around it for privacy. Raquel helped me put my things away in the drawers, we said goodbye and then she left. When the nun in charge of the dormitory, Sister Theresa Cecilia, and the girls started talking to me, I realized I did not understand a word they were saying. This was not the English that I had learned in school in Cuba. That is when it all came crashing down on me. My sister had just left and she was going to end up in Denver. We were a couple of weeks from Christmas and I had nobody. I was alone, in a different world, surrounded by strangers that I could not communicate with. I cried for hours, inconsolably. I wanted to go home. What was I doing here?

Well there are many things that I remember from my first few weeks in this country. Life in boarding school was a new experience. I found out that I could write English much better than I could speak or understand. Some people spoke Spanish and they helped me out. At the time I got there, I was the only Cuban "boarder," which is what we were called. A few girls were from Venezuela, one from Puerto Rico, and one from Costa Rica. I thought I would have to spend Christmas in the boarding school; that is what I had been told. Some of the girls could not go back home for the holidays, so I would not be the only one. But I was miserable. I had one special English teacher, Sister Rosemarie and she was really sweet. One day, I was feeling really sad and I told her, "I am going to be far away from everything this Christmas." The next day, she gave me a little card with Baby Jesus and on the back she wrote: "May Baby Jesus be your 'everything' this Christmas." I still keep the card, and will always remember her kindness. A few days before Christmas, I received a phone call at the school. They got me out of class to get the call. This was very unusual, calls from Cuba were impossible at the time. Who was calling me? Well, it was Raquel to tell me that she had decided to stay in Miami and had found a job. She said that I was coming to Miami to spend Christmas. My godfather and his family had arrived from Cuba a few weeks earlier; they were renting a house in Westchester and were sending me the bus fare. I felt like I had won the lottery. I was so happy and grateful that I was going to spend Christmas with family, and not be alone in a boarding school.

My sister had found a job in an office and she got paid $30 weekly or so, but at least it was something. I mentioned in my introduction how important Christmas was in my family; we always had our house in Santa Clara filled with family that came from all over the island, and my uncle Ray and his wife who drove from New York City and then took the ferry to Cuba. The month of December had always been a month of celebration for my family in Cuba. So, I was very happy to come to Miami from Key West for those holidays in 1960. One of my friends who left Cuba before me was living in Miami with her sister and family, and we were able to see each other. So, it was not bad at all, except on Christmas day. After going to mass at St. Brendan's Church, we walked to the bus stop to take a bus and go downtown to window shop or go to a movie. We spent the whole afternoon siting there on that bus bench because no buses ran in Miami on Christmas day, and we both cried, missing our family and our home at Christmas time.

After the Christmas break, I again got on the Greyhound bus back to Key West. Of course, young as I was, I was learning English fast and adjusting to my new life. The morning of April 17, 1961, I woke up to the news that a group of young Cuban men and the United States Armed Forces were invading Cuba; the Bay of Pigs Invasion had begun. This is what we were waiting for; this was to be the end to this "exile" experience. We were going back home. Needless to say, that did not happen. The letdown after that was overwhelming. We were starting to lose hope that we would return soon to our beloved Cuba. I finished the school year in Key West and without any problem, waived goodbye to the boarding school and came back to Miami to join those that were already here. My cousins, their three children, and my sister had rented a three bedroom, one bath house with two storage rooms, which were quickly converted to bedrooms, and the family from Cuba started to come. We got to a point where we had 14 people staying there. They had room and board, and everyone started to find work, wherever they could. We had a bathroom schedule in the morning where those who had to work or go to school would have priority, and it all worked out fine with just one little bathroom. Then we heard from our parents that they had decided to leave Cuba. We were able to get them on a visa waiver program that had been granted by the United States government for Cubans wanting to leave. Of course, we knew this was another nail in Cuba's coffin. The fact that our parents, especially my dad, had made the decision to leave Cuba meant that things there were really bad. They arrived here with nothing. No money, no job, and in their early 60s. My father did not speak a word of English. They had just endured the experience of placing their entire lives in two suitcases, leaving their country and facing an uncertain future in a new country where they would have to start from nothing. But they survived, they overcame, and they succeeded.

In September of 1961, I was registered in Immaculata Academy, which later would become LaSalle, in Miami. I attended my last two years of high school and graduated in 1963. Those years were hard. But as in every situation in life, there were always glimmers of hope. My father had a life insurance policy with a company in Canada. They agreed to pay him the amount that was available at that time. It was not much, but enough for them to give a down payment on a duplex in a neighborhood around the airport in Miami. One was rented, and this helped us pay the mortgage. We moved in the other one. It was a two-bedroom apartment with one bath. My sister was the only one person in the household earning an income. She needed help supporting the family. My father decided to go to Puerto Rico, where he had received information that the Puerto Rican government was allowing Cuban doctors to take the Foreign Medical Examinations in Spanish. So, he left for San Juan, Puerto Rico with a one-way ticket and $100. One of my cousins, who worked for an American Company in San Juan, offered him room and board. He had been there for about a week, when while riding a bus, he got pick-pocketed, and all the money that he had left was gone. We did not find out about this until much later, since he did not want to worry us. After a couple of months, he was hired, but he had a time-limit to take and pass the tests. Though the tests were in Spanish, the textbooks he had to study from were in English. My mother took those textbooks and translated them to Spanish. There were several notebooks handwritten by her with the lessons he had to study to take his tests. He passed, and for the next ten years he worked at the Health Department Center in a small city near San Juan, called Las Piedras. He was the general practitioner at the health center, and saw patients with all kinds of ailments, from colds, to heart attacks, to delivering babies. He worked day and night, because whenever they needed him to take night calls at the hospital, he would be there to get the extra money in his paycheck. For a couple of years, he would drive back and forth every day from a house they had rented in Rio Piedras to Las Piedras, a one hour drive each way, on a steep, curvy and hilly country road. At the end of their second year in Puerto Rico, they were able to purchase a house in the outskirts of the little town of Las Piedras, thus avoiding the long commute.

In the meantime, when I graduated from high school in 1963, I had to move to Puerto Rico with my parents. My sister had gotten married and we all were supposed to get on with our lives. That was another change, another trauma in my life. I was used to Miami, I had made friends here, and I knew my way around there. I really did not like living in Puerto Rico in 1963. I was there for a couple of months, but really I was not happy. I needed to go to school, work, and get around. The only car in the house my father had to use to drive to work one hour away, and many nights he had night duty and would not be home for a couple of days. The bus system at that time in Puerto Rico was not adequate, and I was not allowed to take a bus by myself and move around on my own. My mother had to come with me everywhere. I did not mind being with her, but she was not always available to leave and go out with me. I felt completely tied up in knots. I wanted to return to Miami.

I had a friend who had registered at Charron Williams Commercial School in downtown Miami. This school would prepare you in one school year from September to June to work in the secretarial field. It was a very reputable and well recommended school, and they would also find a job for you after graduation. So, my parents accepted, and my sister and her husband said I could come and live with them and I would attend school in Miami.

I came back to Miami at the end of August, so happy to be back, looking forward to the new school year at Charron Williams, and at the same time, I felt very bad leaving my parents behind in Puerto Rico and being away from them. But life had to go on. As it happened, a couple of days after being there, I went to visit one of my friends from high school, the one that had referred me to the new secretarial school. Her mother, who was a very sweet lady and had taken a liking to me, wanted me to visit with them and they invited me to have dinner with them. I was 17, and the three-mile walk to her house did not faze me. I would take the bus back home after dinner because by then it would be dark. As fate would have it, that night in that house I met, Luis, the man that would be my husband. He was also a friend of the family and had decided that afternoon to visit the family and we met. We clicked. I remember seeing him and thinking he was a nice-looking guy, and my friend's mother had already filled me in, about his many qualities, merits and abilities. He drove me home that evening after dinner, and many more evenings after that.

Left to right: My mother-in-law Pilar, my father-in-law Eloy, my mother Luisa, and my father Fernando (Mirta Solis Nuñez).

A New City, a New Country, a New Life (M.S. Nuñez)

Mirta and Luis 1963 (Mirta Solis Nuñez).

We liked each other and although I was very young, he proposed a few months after we met. He gave me an engagement ring and we were married on December 26, 1964, and we will celebrate our 54th year anniversary in just a few days. We have three awesome daughters that are very close and attentive to us. They are all married to excellent guys and we have five incredible grandchildren that also love us dearly. We have been blessed by God with a terrific family; they are the reason we wake up every morning.

In June 1965 we drove to Toronto, Canada to get our residents' visa and in January 1970, we became citizens of the greatest country on God's earth. I love this country with everything I have. My daughters were born here. We were able to raise a family, go to school, work, grow, evolve and thrive and I am a very proud American. That does not mean that I will forget the country where I was born.

I have never returned to my country of birth. I would not recognize it now. I will not return because the reason why we had to leave is still there. The same government that kills so many, that tortures and harasses, that humiliated my parents, that took everything away from us, that called us names, that destroyed our way of life, that same government is still there. They have outlived our parents and most of that generation of steel titans who had to leave and start from the bottom at an age where most people are retiring. They had to pick themselves up by the bootstraps and do what needed to be done for the next 40 or 50 years, and proudly most of them made it and reached their goals. My parents goal was to finish working in Puerto Rico, which my father did for ten years. They sold the house there and came back to Miami where they bought a house in the same neighborhood where my sister and I lived with our families. So, their dream of being close to their grandkids and us became a reality. They are all buried in American soil, in Miami. They went to their deaths without ever losing the dream that Cuba, one day soon, would be free again, and they were ready to go back as soon as the Castro family was gone. But the Castros never went away. On the contrary, like toxic venom, they have spread and multiplied. As long as there is a remnant of the metastatic cancer that destroyed my beautiful homeland, I will not set foot there.

Cuba is lost. The Cuba that they have destroyed, ripped apart and devastated is not my Cuba. That one they can keep, whatever is left. But the Cuba of my dreams will never die. It will always be there, with the beautiful beaches, the breezes, the delicious fruit. I will keep and always take care of it.

Mirta and Luis 2015 (Mirta Solis Nuñez).

Return to Playa Larga
The Story of Jesus Delgado

Luis O. Rodriguez

This is a story of total dedication to the ideals of freedom and duty to the fatherland. It is a narrative of one man's moral stand against insurmountable odds at the juncture of arguably Cuba's most defining moment. It is a story told by Jesus Delgado, a Cuban exile now aged in his mid-seventies, who was once a vibrant 19-year-old Brigade 2506 combatant. This is an account by a representative of a generation caught up in a high stakes political game between the U.S. and Cuba. This story is written in the first-person narrative, as it was relayed orally to me by Jesus.

The Early Days of the Revolution

In 1958, at the age of 17, I was a young man in the midst of pursuing a technical career. I was able to enroll at the technical school of Rancho Bolleros Airport (now José Martí Airport), where I sought to become a machinist. At the time it seemed to be a good career that would lead to a good life. On January 1, 1959, just prior to my graduation, Fidel Castro overthrew the government of President Fulgencio Batista, and thus, what appeared to be a bright future for Cuba and a prominent profession for myself came to a sudden end. Just prior to my graduation, Castro's new government officials arrived at the school and claimed that I had been permitted to enroll at the technical school through a presidential decree and as such, I would not be permitted to graduate with the rest of the class. At the tender age of 18, the described incident became the first personal slight by the government against me and a realization for myself and the rest of my family that our country was headed towards a totalitarian regime.

The early months of 1959 were a true revelation of things to come. Cuba's society was engaged in a topsy-turvy upheaval and the code of moral values that generations of Cuban citizens had lived by no longer seemed to apply. It was a common occurrence in 1959 for those who had enjoyed professional careers such as judges, attorneys, and public officials to be publicly ridiculed and both physically and emotionally harassed by the lowest echelon of Cuban society. Many known criminals and citizens of lower moral values had seized the day by claiming allegiance to the new regime. The simple act of wearing an olive green shirt and sporting a beard by such opportunists was a badge of honor that entitled them to commit all sorts of crimes and injustices in the name of the new revolution without being held accountable to any law or just punishment.

Chief among the hatred of the pro-government mobs that controlled the streets in those early days were places of order such as police stations, courts, etc. Groups of delinquents and drug users routinely entered police stations and assumed control of those facilities while wide-eyed officials were helpless to stop them from committing their dastardly deeds. Police officers and former Batista government soldiers suffered the harshest reprisals by far. The favorite epithet utilized by those so called "revolutionaries" to describe law enforcement and military officials was *esbirro*, which loosely translates to government minion.

My father had been a member of the military throughout his professional life. He had committed no so-called "injustices" against citizens and had simply preserved civil order in an honorable fashion. Now, in this new world we found ourselves in, my father was permitted to continue to perform his duties; however, he was forced to wear a red and black *26 Movement* bracelet as proof of his "allegiance" to the new government.

I distinctly recall a regrettable incident that involved my father that could have easily resulted in a tragic consequence. It occurred on a public bus as my father and I moved about the city. As we sat on the bus, a bearded revolutionary who appeared to be drunk and dressed in olive green garb, while sporting a .45 caliber sidearm, boarded the bus and made his way to the area of the bus where we were sitting. The individual, caught in the euphoria of the time, began to deride my father with all kinds of obscenities, as he demanded my father to give up his seat. My father immediately rose to his feet and engaged the individual in a physical altercation. At that time, the individual drew his firearm from his holster and had to be restrained from shooting my father by those nearby. Were it not for the intervention of the other commuters, the occurrence could have had a disastrous ending.

The simple act of survival in those early days of 1959 became quite a juggling act. I remember my father relating stories about the iniquities committed by the new motley crew army that had seized Columbia military headquarters in Havana. The once immaculate facility, a symbol of pre-Castro days, became the target of many offenses. My father would relate how members of the new army would defecate and utilize their excrement to write anti-Batista propaganda on the tiled bathroom walls. All in all, insanity ruled the day, as anyone suspected of any alleged crime would be dragged off to La Cabana prison or would be shot and buried on the easement of some nondescript country roadway without being seen or heard from by families ever again.

One incident that eventually made me lose hope in the possibility of a good outcome for Cuba under the new regime was that of the public trial of former Batista government Colonel Jesus Sosa Blanco, held in February of 1959, at the auditorium of *Ciudad Deportiva* (Havana Sports Palace), and in the presence of 17,000 spectators. The shameless act was televised countrywide on Cuban television. Sosa Blanco was accused of committing 108 murders while under orders from Batista. The trumped-up charges brought against him were inaccurate and lacked any legal research standard. The witnesses brought forward against Sosa Blanco repeatedly made contradictory statements at the trial and their one-sided testimony was conveniently overlooked by the prosecution and the assigned judge. Sosa Blanco was found guilty and was subsequently executed on February 18, 1959. Prior to his death, he referred to his trial as a spectacle "worthy of ancient Rome." The trial and execution were indicative of things to come.

In 1959 and the early 1960s, Cuban citizens identified as Batista government sympathizers and even those overheard by government informants to express non-conformist views of the new government would be apprehended anytime, day or night, and hauled off to La Cabana prison where Che Guevara ruled supreme and dictated over life or death. Many of the victims executed by Guevara's henchmen, some as young as 16 years age, went to their deaths with valiant cries of *"Viva Cuba Libre!"* and *"Viva Cristo Rey!"* It was at that time I came to the realization that the country I was born in had transformed into an abomination and would never be the same again.

The Resistance

As repression continued to increase throughout 1959 and 1960, resistance against Castro's government began to increase. Emboldened by their newly acquired sense of power, Castro government authorities became even more repressive. Young men, some in their late teens, began to plot against the government and they were hounded by authorities throughout Cuban cities. On mountainous regions such as Escambray and Sierra de los Órganos, well organized anti-Castro guerrilla groups began to prepare for action against the government.

As an 18 year-old-man, with solid patriotic ideals and a notion of the direction where Fidel Castro was taking our country, I felt the necessity to rebel against the growing tyranny that had swept my country and I soon joined a group of dissenting young men who shared similar political views. Though our clandestine effort was a well-kept secret, government authorities soon picked up our scent and focused on our activities.

In May of 1960, government authorities raided my home in search of subversive materials and weaponry. I had been informed of the impending raid and I had departed from the area just prior to the arrival of the authorities. I knew then I could not return home since that would have certainly meant apprehension and a quick trip to La Cabana prison. Such arrest would have meant death at a firing squad or a long prison sentence.

I had always felt that fate would eventually deal me such a heavy blow, and I had already drafted an escape plan to address such a likely crisis. For some time, I had fished the area of Santa Fe, on the northern coast of Havana, and I had spied a 20-foot vessel that was moored on a channel near a waterfront home. On May 7, 1960, myself and six other young men who were in a similar situation as I was, headed to Santa Fe and we proceeded to appropriate the vessel. We soon set course for the U.S., and eventually made it to Florida safely. Once there, we proceeded to ask for political asylum. I remember pleading at a later time with U.S. Government authorities for the safe return of the vessel to its proper owner. After all, I did not want anyone to mistake us for common thieves. The boat incident and our photograph were published the following day on the pages of The Miami Herald. Had it not been for that vessel, I believe our group could have faced long prison sentences or even a firing squad. I was just a 19-year-old man at the time and I suddenly found myself exiled and alone in a new country with a new language and culture and with very little prospects for a normal life.

Abandoned and Left to Die

In August of 1960, just three months after my arrival in the U.S., I was referred by friends to an office that was located near the vicinity of The Miami Herald building, just north of downtown Miami. The office was a Central Intelligence Agency (CIA) front known as *Centro Frente Cubano Democratico*. The highest ranking Cuban exile and principal mission commander there was Manuel Francisco Artime. It was an open secret among Cubans in those days that the CIA was recruiting exiles to embark on a military invasion to Cuba to forcibly remove the government of Fidel Castro. I am now convinced that the Castro government was well aware of the invasion plans and that they were preparing their troops for that confrontation. Many new arrivals such as myself, were pouring into that CIA office daily to volunteer for what we believed would be a U.S. backed military operation. I was happy to enlist, as were all the others. We truly believed we would reclaim our country and once again guarantee all Cubans a democratic form of government.

Three days after volunteering, I was contacted and asked to report for the assignment. I was part of a group of 33 Cuban exiles that included Erneido Oliva, who was second in command in the mission. Our group was transported via truck to a hangar at Miami International Airport (MIA) and once there, we were asked to turn in all our personal belongings to U.S. Government officials. We were then provided with U.S. Army uniforms and military dog tags that bore fictitious names. The objective of such action was to conceal our identities in the event our aircraft crashed. That detail was a prophecy of the level of involvement the U.S. government was willing to accept in the entire endeavor. We would pay for that lack of U.S. commitment months later on the beaches of Playa Larga and Playa Girón.

Our group was flown from MIA overnight and none of us had a clue as to where we were headed. We would find out the next morning at our destination that we had arrived in Guatemala for military training to prepare for the future mission to Cuba. Our group was comprised of 30 pilots and mechanics and three others including myself, who were assigned to infantry. Years later, I would come to realize that our operation could have been easily infiltrated by Cuban government informants whose task would have been to report on our progress to Cuban government officials.

The group of pilots and mechanics who were transported with me were assigned to Retouleo Air Base, while I and two other group members were transported to JMTrax Base in the Sierra Madre on the Pacific coast of Guatemala. From that location, we were transported to Finca Betia, a farm owned by a Guatemalan Vice President. The farm was secluded and located at an altitude of 7,200 feet. At that early time, we were not yet a brigade and we were divided into two sections. One of the sections was comprised of infiltration teams and the other was a guerrilla unit. The units were assigned the code colors grey and black to help differentiate their intended purpose.

I was issued identification # 2754 by the command and was assigned to train in Team J of the Black unit (known as the 2nd Infantry Battalion). My training consisted of learning how to handle explosives such as TNT and plastic explosives. The group was headed by Hugo Sueiro Rios, who would later be promoted to Battalion Chief. The infiltration unit (Gray) was headed by Miguel Alvarez. Alvarez' group would provide support to the guerrilla teams and was trained to operate Ham radios and how to conduct clandestine activities.

The brigade numbering system began at 2500 to give the impression of a larger number of volunteers. Our group became known as Brigade 2506 in memory of Carlos Santana Estevez, AKA Carlyle, who was issued that number and became our first casualty when he was killed in a training accident in September of 1960. The brigade was comprised of six battalions, which included a paratroop, an armored and a heavy gun battalion, in addition to our air force. Altogether, a total of 1,334 men would train and a total of 1,297 plus 177 airborne paratroops would eventually land in Cuba and participate in armed combat.

On April 12–13, 1961, our invasion force left Guatemala for Puerto Cabezas, Nicaragua. We were transported in privately owned vessels from the *Garcia Line,* and I subsequently traveled to Cuba on a U.S. vessel known as the Houston. The 2nd Battalion was comprised of 144 men, 36 men per company, plus staff, medic, and high command. A total of four ships with two torpedo boats as support arrived at Playa Larga on April 17, 1961, at 1:20 a.m. The men in our battalion landed at Playa Larga, while the other three ships continued on to Playa Girón. Our objective was to seize control of the roadway that led to the area and cut off Cuban government reinforcements to permit the rest of our comrades to establish a beachhead in Playa Girón.

As we were preparing to land, the noise from our crafts being lowered into the water was overheard by Cuban government troops stationed on shore and those troops began to fire tracer rounds in our direction. Their opening salvo was met with .50 and .20 caliber machine gun rounds from one of our ships as we returned fire, proceeded to land and secured the beach. It is very difficult for me to express the elation I felt at the time. There I was, a 19-year-old man, rifle in hand, fighting and reclaiming freedom for my country. For one brief moment in time, we reconquered a very small strip of land and we were planning to defend it with our own lives.

I remember securing a position along the roadway and confronting Cuban government troops as they hastily retreated from Playa Girón and headed in our direction. Unknown to us at the time was the fact that Castro had positioned 1,200 to 1,400 well-trained troops at a nearby sugar refinery complex, and in the course of the next 30 hours, he would employ upwards of 70,000 troops to repel our invasion.

Just prior to the day of the invasion, U.S. planes bearing Cuban government markings bombed various Cuban airfields and destroyed most of the Cuban Air Force aircraft. The Cuban government managed to save several of their aircraft and would employ those planes very well to attain air superiority throughout the latter part of the conflict. The Cuban Air Force utilized Sea Fury and T-33 jet planes against our B-26 aircraft. The B-26 lacked rear artillery and were mostly sitting ducks against the superior jet fighters. I believe 17 out of 21 of our aircraft were shot down during the course of the conflict.

Our battalion stood its ground from the time of our landing on April

17th throughout the following day. As Castro realized the thrust of our attack was at Playa Girón, he directed his entire army to that focal point. With diminishing air support, Cuban tanks made their way through Playa Larga and our battalion was unable to stop their advancement. I distinctly remember the Cuban tanks running over their dead soldiers as their troops made their way to Playa Girón. Our battalion had inflicted many casualties, especially to those troops assigned under Cuban General Almejeiras.

I distinctly remember the words of Commander Jose "Pepe" Perez San Roman as he spoke with U.S. high command and requested air support from the Fox and Essex air carriers, which were moored just outside Cuban waters. San Roman was well aware that without air support, we were in a bad predicament and he pleaded with the U.S. high command for aerial support. I remember hearing the discouraging statement in response to his radio request, which made us realize our fate. The voice heard over the radio claimed, "Our hearts are with you, but our orders are not to provide air support." It was then that we heard San Roman in a calm voice tell those on the other end to, "Stick your hearts in your ass, what we need is your airplanes." If there was a time when I felt abandoned in life, that must have been it. However, as idealistic as we were, we were ready to fight to our last round of ammunition.

As Castro threw more troop support into the area, we were ordered to reinforce the entrance to Playa Girón and help assist our forces in their attempt to retreat and reach the Escambray region. By that time, we were down to four squads comprised of 27 men. My assignment was that of a sniper, and as such, I had concealed myself in a rocky area while providing cover for our squad. An anti-tank grenade exploded near me and I was struck in the face with shrapnel. My watch stopped working at that precise time, thus I remember the time to this day. I was lucky though; five of my squad members were killed at about that time.

As I laid stunned from my injury, I remember my squad members calling out to me, but I could not see them. I was placed in a vehicle and driven back to Playa Girón where I received first aid and was moved to a house that was located in the area. The house was being used as a temporary morgue at the time. There I joined another injured soldier named Primitivo Aguado, who had been shot in the back. Sometime after our arrival, a Cuban aircraft dropped a bomb on the house where we had been interned, and the structure came tumbling down. Aguado and I were lucky to survive, as we escaped the rubble.

As our landing force disintegrated, we were left without ammunition or a means to escape. We were trapped in a thin coastal area comprised of a mangrove forest. We knew then, no one was coming to rescue us. A group of us entered the mangroves and wandered about for two days as we attempted to survive as best we could. Eventually, our group was detected by members of Juan Almeida's escort. By that time, the Cuban government was in total control of the situation and we all knew our mission had ended in disaster. We were then taken as prisoners and transported to Playa Girón, where we joined a large group of detainees.

Upon arrival at Playa Girón, we became aware that Cuban government Comandante Osmani Cienfuegos was already in charge at that location, and his duties consisted of providing transport for the prisoners from the area to Havana's Sports Palace. A group of 147 of us were tightly packed by Cuban soldiers in a refrigeration trailer for a trip to Havana. The trailer had no ventilation ports and as such, breathing became extremely arduous from the inception of the trip. The group was directed into the trailer by force at bayonet point and under orders from Cienfuegos, who personally oversaw the operation and was overheard to state, "Fill up the trailer so they may die as pigs."

It became apparent to us that ventilation would be a problem and Primitivo Aguado managed to pry a small orifice on the side of the trailer with his belt buckle prong. A total of eight or nine of us utilized the orifice made by Aguado as a breathing port for the remainder of the trip. The trailer made a sudden stop approximately three hours later at the entrance to the small town of Jovellanos, and the doors were opened for a few minutes to permit ventilation throughout the trailer. Though we forcefully complained about the condition under which we were being transported, the doors to the trailer were closed once again, and the trailer was then transported on a seven to eight-hour trip to the *Ciudad Deportiva* in Havana.

It is extremely difficult for me to describe the sounds made by our dying comrades during the course of that road trip to Havana. The unbearable heat and the lack of oxygen left deep scars in the minds of those who survived the trek. Much has been written about this single act of brutality committed by the Cuban government against unarmed prisoners; however, nothing can describe the sense of abandonment we all felt in our predicament. Upon arrival at Havana's *Ciudad Deportiva,* when the doors to the trailer were finally opened, nine of the initial group of 144 expedition members had asphyxiated. Another would die upon arrival. The deaths of those young men can only be attributed to the callous will of our captors, who were emboldened by their victory and given free reign by their superiors to let loose their vengeance upon us.

Cuidad Deportiva was a modern sports facility, and at the time, was being utilized as a holding facility for all prisoners. Subsequently, all prisoners, including myself, were herded across the street to the Naval Hospital for treatment. Once at the Naval Hospital, a medic cleaned up my facial wound without the use of anesthetics. For days, maggots crawled in an out of the wound and I did the best I could to cure myself since the assistance provided was extremely poor. Seven to eight days after our arrival at Havana, we were all transported to El Principe fortress. A total of 1,183 of us would remain at that fortress for months as we awaited our fate. From the onset of our arrival at El Principe, some of us began to plan our escape. As derisive and coarse as our captors were, we felt nothing but pity and contempt for them. Here was a group of disorganized individuals drunk over their newly minted "revolution," arguing for a government that enslaved its own citizens, destroyed families, and turned upside down a Cuban society that had been forged over four centuries. Rather than thank us for attempting to liberate them, our captors utilized every opportunity they could to strike us or drive their bayonets into our bodies. The following months at El Principe fortress would be extremely difficult.

As the Cuban government prepared for its latest spectacle, we were all playing for time. The prosecution was planning to argue for the death penalty and 30-year prison sentences; however, international pressure was mounting, and it became evident that the Cuban government (as drastic and oppressive as it was) could not execute 1,183 prisoners of war. During the course of the trial, the Cuban government insisted that all of us declare that we had committed "crimes against Cuba." We, on the other hand, chose to state, *"Me abstengo de declarer,"* meaning, we would not provide any incriminating statement.

There were many examples of valor expressed by our men throughout the course of our incarceration. Chief among them is the well-documented and nationally televised argument between Felipe Rivero and Cuban government official Carlos Rafael Rodriguez. While Rodriguez tried to present valid arguments for the actions of the Revolution, Rivero debunked each and every one of Rodriguez's arguments by retorting that Cuba was "much better off before the coming of Castro."

Another prominent incident involved an Afro Cuban named Tomas Cruz, who was told at a hearing at *Ciudad Deportiva* whether he was aware that the Revolution was "permitting Afro Cubans to swim in its former white only beaches." Cruz retorted to his captors that he "had not parachuted into Cuba to swim at a beach for whites." With that statement, Cruz made clear his conviction that he had traveled to liberate Cuba from oppression. Such strength, in the face of danger, fills me with pride to this day.

Our fate would eventually be sealed when famed attorney James Donovan negotiated our release from prison and the migration of over 9,000 family members from Cuba in exchange for tractors and cash. Just prior to my release, I was debriefed by the Assistant Warden at El Principe fortress and I was shown copies of the letters I had written home. The letters were highly critical of the treatment we had received during the course of our incarceration. The Assistant Warden started to rattle off the "accomplishments of the Revolution" and I was quick to inform him that their Revolution had not "accomplished" a single thing. The Assistant Warden was clearly shaken and sternly told me I would never be permitted to return to Cuba.

The Unhealed Wounds

Upon returning to the U.S., I commenced a new life, and along with my wife, I set out to raise a family. Though I have always felt the sting of our military loss, I have never held negative feelings for the U.S. for its failure to support us in our effort to bring about freedom to Cuba in that ill-fated mission of 1961. I am of the opinion that the entire affair was hampered by grave political errors, and the inability of the U.S. government to help us remove the Castro regime in 1961 eventually brought us to the brink of nuclear extermination in 1963. When the U.S. agreed to the Kennedy-Khrushchev pact, the final nail was hammered on Cuba's coffin, and it became perfectly clear to me and most

Top: Brigade 2506 Memorial, Little Havana, Miami, Florida. *Bottom:* Remembrance plaques containing the names of the 114 Bay of Pigs martyrs (photograph provided by Jesus Delgado).

Cuban exiles, that Fidel Castro had been given free rein to drive Cuba into the abyss.

As the years have slowly gone by, I often wonder about what would have been Cuba's fate had we succeeded in our effort to reclaim its democracy. There would not have been the massive migration of Cubans to all parts of the globe as they attempted to escape political oppression and hunger. There would not have been Cuban government armed support to Latin American guerrillas, or the deaths of thousands of Cubans in foreign wars, such as those Cuban soldiers who perished in Angola. There would not have been firing squads, political incarcerations, the sinking of the tugboat *13 de Marzo,* the shoot down of *Brothers to the Rescue* airplanes, or the thousands of drownings of fleeing refugees in makeshift rafts in the Gulf straits. The number of tragedies prevented would have been well worth our sacrifice. As for the 114 who perished in the mission, they are martyrs, and the blood they spilled on those beaches was not in vain.

Though time has managed to heal most of the wounds of my Cuban exile experience and the memories of my involvement in the Bay of Pigs invasion, I still feel a sense of loss for the distant times and experiences spent with family and friends in my native Havana before those happy times were all taken away by the Cuban Revolution. As far as my participation in that distant mission to liberate Cuba in the Spring of 1961 is concerned, I consider it an honor to have served with valiant Cuban young men whose patriotic sense and bravery elevated my spirit. We may not have accomplished our military objective on the beaches of Playa Larga and Playa Girón, but it is now written as a historical fact that at the time our nation came calling for us, a generation of young Cuban men stood up firmly and gave their all for their native country. For the most part, the world may never recognize that effort, but for me, and those who were there, we answered in unison and we became better men for it.

Jesus Delgado (right) and his son Dennis in the Florida Keys (photograph provided by Jesus Delgado).

Of Cuban Concentration Camps and the Struggle for Freedom

The Stories of Noel S. Varela, Henry Choren and Jorge Luis Brito

Luis O. Rodriguez

These are the stories of three Cuban boys and their respective families who found their way to a new life in Miami and became good friends. None of them knew each other in Cuba, but their stories are strikingly similar. All three children had parents who sacrificed their own lives in order to save them from the ravages of communism and from Fidel Castro's dictatorial government.

A commonality among all three families is the fact that each of their fathers were victimized by Castro's plan to remove undesirables, homosexuals, and those deemed as anti-revolutionaries from city centers. All men of working age who filed documents to migrate to the U.S. were also included in the plan, and most were forced to spend years in labor camps, under very difficult conditions, as they awaited a visa that would permit them to travel to the U.S. Refusal to work at such camps was an immediate rejection for travel to the U.S. and a sentence to live the rest of their days under tyranny.

The plan that became known as Military Units to Help Production (UMAP) was concocted by Raul Castro after his 1965 visit to the Soviet Union and getting a first-hand look at its gulags. The plan, originally named "Plan Fidel," was changed to plan UMAP to remove Fidel Castro's sense of responsibility. Though commonly believed to have been implemented only in the Camagüey Province, the plan was implemented in every province and resulted in the internment of hundreds of thousands of Cuban citizens.

The following stories detail how each of the three boys and their families were impacted by a callous government intent on destroying social order and interested only in promoting its communist dogma.

Noel's Story

My name is Noel Varela. I was born in March of 1958, in the city of Camagüey, just nine months prior to the coming of Fidel Castro's communist revolution. My two younger brothers were born in 1961 and 1965. The following is but one account of the many difficulties we faced while living under a totalitarian regime in Cuba throughout the 1960s and early 1970s.

My father had been employed as an inspector with the Cuban national railroad company since the early 1950s. His job consisted of collecting payroll and inspecting railroad offices in the provinces of Las Villas, Camagüey and Oriente. By 1967, my father had become totally disillusioned with the Cuban political process and the trappings placed on civil liberties by the Castro regime. As a result, he informed his supervisor at his place of employment he had initiated the process to migrate to the United States. As a standard policy at the time, the Cuban government looked very unfavorably on any citizen who pronounced a desire to migrate to the United States. In the eyes of Castro's communist lackeys, any citizen who expressed such desire was a "traitor to the motherland" and unworthy of any civil rights. As was the norm, my father was fired from his job and was told by a government official that in order to travel to the United States, he would have to perform "volunteer work" for the state. Of course, by "volunteer," the government official truly meant slave labor at locations that had all the trimmings of concentration camps.

My father was reassigned to work in a menial job at a pig farm. He toiled at that location for almost three years and he was forced to

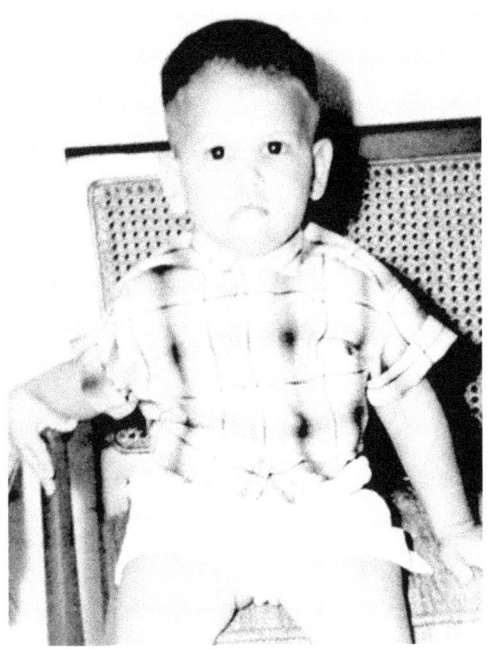

Three-year old Noel (photograph provided by Noel S. Varela).

perform those tasks considered as too demeaning for "proper revolutionaries." I vividly remember that the last two years we spent in Cuba, my father was forced to perform hard labor in sugarcane fields at a time when Fidel Castro bragged about Cuba's effort to reach production of 10 million pounds of sugar. There were times when I would not see my father for periods of up to three months. The government heavily restricted employee leave to visit family as it attempted to increase sugar production and reach the goal set by Fidel Castro. Needless to say, the goal of 10 million pounds of sugar per year failed, as did every other harebrained scheme concocted by the Castro brothers in their attempt to subjugate Cuban citizens.

As a young boy in Cuba, I knew of all the troubles my family was facing on a daily basis. Even though that was the reality of the time, I carried on with my daily routine which included attending school and of course, playing baseball with my neighborhood friends. We lived in a large home, which had been subdivided to include our family of five and a rear section which was occupied by my grandparents. The residence where we lived had once been the childhood home of Cuban composer and flute player Luis Casas Romero, known for the famed recording of *El Mambí* and many other classic Cuban music.

I remember the wonderful fruit trees in my back yard. I distinctively remember heading out the rear of my residence, crossing a river that flowed adjacent to the property by means of a fallen log, and walking approximately one street block to Cándido González Stadium, where my favorite baseball teams, Camagüey and Granjeros played. I spent much time in that stadium. It was a refreshing escape from the daily barrage of government propaganda we were being fed at our schools.

When I finished the sixth grade, I was assigned to a summer program known as *Cara al Campo,* which literally translates as "face the country," but what it actually meant, was working for the extent of 45 days on the fields for 12 hours a day, harvesting tomatoes, potatoes or any other produce that was in season. Neither I or my friends realized it at the time since we viewed the assignment as an adventure, but the program was nothing less than forced labor imposed on children as young as 11 years of age. I participated in the program in 1970 and 1971.

The *Cara al Campo* program consisted of taking children away from their families in order to indoctrinate them with communist propaganda in fields located many miles away from the protection of parents. Boys and girls would be picked up in buses driven away to the country and forced to remain at those locations throughout the extent of the program without the possibility of returning home.

During the course of my assignment in the *Cara al Campo* program, we were housed in barracks that were separate from the girls. Our days commenced at 6:30 a.m., when a bell was rung, and we toiled in the fields until late in the afternoon picking produce. Failure to participate or complete the program meant you were automatically identified as a non-conformist and you could not aspire to a professional career in a university or place of higher learning.

It was at a *Cara al Campo* camp in Central Lugareño, a sugar refinery, where one day in June of 1971, my parents arrived to find me ill with a high fever. I was not feeling well on that day, but my parents were bearing good news. The government had finally provided our family an exit visa and we would be able to travel to the United States. I was just 14 years old at the time.

While we celebrated the news, we were approached by the camp director, an obese Afro-Cuban man known as "Giron," who sported a long white beard. Giron was a strict communist sympathizer who felt he "owed much" to the Cuban revolution, and as camp overseer, he saw to it that we worked long days and that we obeyed the daily indoctrination classes and all of his draconian camp rules.

Giron was taken aback by the news of our newly found happiness, and in a bout of jealousy, he was quick to point out to my parents I would not be able to depart from the camp with them for several days until all administrative protocols had been fulfilled. My parents pleaded with Giron for quite some time, but he would not have any of it. His decision was made; I would remain in the camp and my parents would have to return for me at a later date. As the conversation turned louder and became an argument, my father told Giron he was taking me from the camp *"por sus cojones,"* a derogatory term meaning on his own will. No sooner did my father say that phrase, he proceeded to carry me out of the camp and into an awaiting truck that would take us home. Until this day, I rejoice every time I remember Giron's face when my father, who had obviously had enough of the dictatorship's lunacy, finally put Giron in his place.

I remember arriving home just in time to see government officials as they conducted their dreaded "inventory." As they went about cataloging all of our personal property, one of the officials attempted to enter the rear of our residence and he was stopped on his tracks by my grandfather. My grandfather sternly informed the official, he could not enter the rear of the residence since that was the area where both he and my grandmother resided, and they were staying behind in Cuba. For some unknown reason, the government official accepted my grandfather's explanation and he refrained from searching further.

On the day of departure from our home, I observed government officials as they arrived at what was now my former place of residence and hauled away our belongings, including my bicycle and everything else we once possessed. As we walked out of our house with our small suitcases, we were greeted by a chorus of insults uttered at us by radical neighbors who considered us traitors for "abandoning" our country. We then began a long trip to Varadero Beach where we spent the night at a small hotel and the next day, June 24th, 1971, we flew to Miami, Florida in search of the freedom we were not able to attain in Cuba.

I remember boarding an Eastern Airlines airplane and flying over to the United States. Once our flight arrived, we were transported to an airplane hangar where we were permitted to fill bags with used clothing and shoes. We were then picked up by our relatives and we made our way into our newly adopted country, not speaking the language, without jobs or any means to sustain ourselves.

It would not take long though. One week after our arrival in the United States, my father was already working, doing odds and ends to support our family. My parents would work for many years, sometimes working two or three different jobs per day to help us improve our quality of life. In the end, it was a great trade off. The terrible experiences we suffered as a family at the hands of the Castro regime were worth the price of our newly attained freedom in a country where individual rights are sacred and where dissenting from a political philosophy is not viewed as an affront to our nation.

Noel (center) on his 13th birthday, just three months prior to his departure from Cuba (photograph provided by Noel S. Varela).

We are now Americans, and though at times we feel nostalgic about the place where we were born, we will never forget the crimes committed by the Cuban government. Though at times it is difficult to grasp the thought, those crimes were committed by Cubans upon Cubans. The legacy of Fidel Castro's dictatorship is one of hate and hunger. Our story is just a footnote in a long list of suffering that continues until this day.

Henry's Story

My name is Henry Choren. I am 62 years of age, and this is a story about my memories as a 10-year old boy, living under Fidel Castro's communist dictatorship on the island of Cuba. I was born and raised in the small neighborhood of Lawton, in the province of Havana. I attended elementary school in that neighborhood and I spent my days playing baseball at a park that is located only one street block away from my old place of residence.

At the tender age of 10, I could not see the reality and the hard times my parents were facing in a communist country absent of any kind of freedom, or respect for civil rights. Due to the repression my parents were experiencing, we decided to migrate and commence a new life in the United States. It was just about that time that I began to realize how bad things were in Cuba.

As was required at the time, my father set our departure in motion by informing government authorities of our intention to migrate to the United States. As a result of his declaration, my father was fired from the Public Works department where he worked as a mechanic and he was assigned to a labor camp where he was forced to harvest sugar cane in fields located near Havana. His internment in those camps lasted approximately two years. My father's firing and the subsequent swift assignment to a labor camp was a punishment imposed on him by a callous government. His "crime" was simply disagreeing with Fidel Castro's communist dogma and aspiring to move his family to a country where freedom and the promise of a prosperous future were guaranteed rights afforded to every citizen.

My most ardent memory of the daily abuses committed against our family in those years occurred just prior to our departure from Cuba. As our travel date neared, a government official was dispatched to our residence for the purpose of inspecting and cataloging our every possession. The official position of the government was that those types of inspections served to ensure that personal assets would not be passed on to friends and family. The reality of the matter is that the "inventory," as it was commonly known, was a final insult against helpless citizens just prior to their departure from

Cuba. The inventory was also a time of much stress for families since household members would be held accountable for any "missing" item at the time of departure and your travel plans would be cancelled unless all cataloged items were accountable.

I remember vividly how the inventory transaction was conducted at my residence. The day of that event, my mother, younger brother, and I were present at home. The individual charged with conducting the inventory was fully dressed in the olive colored military uniform of the day. As he set out to conduct his task, I observed the individual jump feet first on top of my mother's bed as he pretended to check the wall closets. As if this despicable act was not insulting enough, I noticed the individual's government issued boots were very muddy and he prided himself as he walked from one side of my mother's bed to the other while muddying her bed sheets and the mattress. From there, the government official proceeded to walk to our kitchen where he counted our silverware, cataloged our coffee maker, appliances and all other items. The official then moved to our bedrooms where he continued to catalog all of our property as though we were common inmates in a prison. This memory of abuse of power has remained engrained in my mind throughout all these years and is living proof of the crimes incurred by citizens under a communist regime.

Finally, on September 6, 1967, our family was provided with an assigned date of departure from Cuba. The notice of departure came with a caveat. We were forced to evacuate our home on the day prior to departure and we were herded by government officials into an airport hangar until our time of departure. Our family was joined at that location by over 100 other Cuban citizens who were also destined to travel to the United States. The hangar was not outfitted with sleeping quarters other than the hard concrete floor and was serviced by two

Henry Choren (left) and his brother Eddie in Cuba (photograph provided by Henry Choren).

small restrooms. I remember that day to be very stressful, since we were restrained in that hangar without anything to eat, as though we were common criminals.

The following morning at approximately 10:00 a.m., we were led away from the hangar on our way to board our flight. We were then surprised to find a large group of government supporters that had been staged along our path by the government to give us our final "farewell." From the moment we walked out of the hangar, we were met with a barrage of insults and mockery that I distinctly remember until this day. The group of government sympathizers screamed madly at us as we walked past them, and their most common insults were those of "traitors" and *gusanos*, a Spanish word meaning "worms" that was utilized as an epithet by the government to describe those individuals that did not agree with its political philosophy. I remember boarding our flight after that incident and arriving at Miami International Airport where we were welcomed with open arms by U.S. government officials. We were provided with food and shelter and subsequently reunited with awaiting family members.

Henry Choren (left) and his brother Eddie in Miami (photograph provided by Henry Choren).

One week after our arrival in the United States, my brother and I started attending elementary school and we began to learn to speak English. At first, the experience was hard, but soon both of us learned to read and speak the language as we began our new life in a country known for its cherished appreciation of freedom and the opportunities afforded to the common citizen.

This anecdote is a simple account of a family of four whose only desire was to live a modest life in its place of origin and was forced by Castro's revolution to migrate to a foreign country in order to attain a brighter and better life. Sadly, our story is shared by hundreds of thousands of other Cuban families that were similarly forced into exile by a ruthless communist dictatorship that oppressed us and has continued to oppress Cuban citizens for the extent of six decades.

Jorge's Story

My name is Jorge Brito and this is the story of my family. It is a typical story of Cuban exiles, filled with moments of extreme pain and suffering in our native home and moments of happiness as we weaved a new life in our adopted country.

My father Eulalio Brito was born in 1925 in a small town named Los Palacios, in Pinar del Río Province. He was adopted at a young age by an aunt and he grew up in a farm near Melena del Sur, Havana, where he helped raise cattle and plant rice crops. Life at the farm was tedious, but happy as he shared his home with nine cousins of various ages. The farm where my father grew up was very productive and it supplied milk to many area dairies and to nearby markets.

By the time my father was 18 years of age, he was very interested in joining the military, and one day in 1943 by sheer luck he came across a Cuban Army commander whose Jeep vehicle had gotten stuck in a mud pit near the farm. According to my father, he lent his help to the commander right away and was able to free the vehicle. The commander was impressed with my father's work ethic and he offered to help my father enter Columbia, a prestigious army garrison in the city of Havana. My father accepted the offer and he attended Columbia where he received military training.

After graduation, my father was assigned to work in the Rural Guard, in Güines, Havana. My father became an auxiliary to Commander Perez-Clausel, an assignment he would fulfill until the coming of the Cuban Revolution in 1959. My father's tasks were those of restoring order and enforcing local laws. He conducted himself in a professional manner throughout his career and never took part in any of the abuses the Castro regime would later blame on the Rural Guard. He would eventually meet my mother, Caridad Martinez, marry, and father three children, including myself, (born in 1957) an older brother and a younger sister.

As the 1950s came to an end, Cuba became a hotbed for anti-government activity. Anyone associated with the government of Fulgencio Batista, and specifically those officials in the Cuban Army, became frequent targets of guerrilla warfare and unwarranted assassination attempts. As a life-long military man, my father was targeted for assassination on numerous occasions and in 1958 our family survived a bombing attack at our home that could have resulted in multiple deaths. The incident occurred when I was only a few months old. An unknown assailant placed a dynamite bundle under the basement of our home and only the quick actions of my father saved us from becoming casualties.

The Cuban Revolution and the hostile government takeover by Fidel Castro's forces in 1959 was a catastrophic event in the life of my father and the rest of our family. Castro's rise to power and his eventual defeat of the Batista government brought about a sense of hysteria that tore families apart and targeted members of the previous government. My maternal grandfather, Esteban Martinez-Arocha, suffered a premature death as a result of a heart attack at the age of 62, brought about by the theft of his land under the ruse of the new Agrarian Reform and the constant harassment of government officials who saw it fit to demean anyone termed as a *latifundista* (land baron).

Immediately upon seizing power, Castro's forces began the process of holding public events where former military officers would be brought up on charges in front of military tribunals and subsequently tried in summary trials. Most often, the intended purpose of the tribunals was to send innocent men to the firing squad or to lengthy prison sentences. My father's supervising officer, Commander Perez-Clausel, was arrested and brought to trial. The judges assigned to his case where only interested in seeing him executed. Perez-Clausel was victimized with daily beatings and torture and eventually became paralyzed as a result of the injuries he sustained. Only the pleas from Perez-Clausel's daughter to Fidel Castro saved Perez-Clausel from the firing squad. Perez-Clausel was a broken man by the time he was released.

The total number of Cuban citizens executed by firing squad from 1959 through 1962 may never be known; however, some have estimated it at least at 5,000 victims. During the course of those years, late at night, in every one of Cuba's six provinces, citizens could hear the barrage of rifles as firing squads silenced the lives of young Cuban men. For the large part, the names of many of those murdered by firing squad will remain anonymous, yet other Cubans such as Virgilio Campeneria Angel, Alberto Tapia Ruano, Rogelio Gonzalez Corzo, and many others, are well known as a result of their posthumous letters written just prior to their executions. Others, such as Pedro Luis Boitel, would die anonymously in Cuba's prisons as a result of their lengthy hunger strikes in protest of the inhumane treatment received from those under Castro's orders.

Having been employed as Perez-Clausel's assistant for a period of many years proved to be detrimental to my father. The authorities falsely accused my father of crimes he had not committed and subsequently arrested him and held him captive in the draconian La Cabaña fortress as he awaited trial. Throughout the course of my father's trial, the military tribunal brought up three false witnesses against him. One witness, a pregnant woman, falsely claimed to have been beaten by my father. Her account was staged by the government and her testimony was found to be so full of inconsistencies that the judges had no choice but to dismiss her statement. My father believed he would be executed at any time throughout his incarceration. He often told the story of seeing men being carried away from their jail cells at La Cabaña and then hearing a barrage of rifles indicating death by firing squad.

The treatment of family members by Cuban government authorities in those days was criminal in nature. According to my mother, every time she traveled to La Cabaña fortress to visit my father, she would be forced to remove all articles of clothing while women guards forcefully searched her for hidden items. My mother vividly remembers the insults uttered against her and the pleasure displayed by female Cuban guards throughout the course of the visits. Only the timely intervention of an uncle who had partaken in the July 26 Movement organization saved my father from execution or a lengthy prison sentence. My father was freed from La Cabaña after serving eight months and living in a hellish environment. His only crime was having held a job in the military. There were no governmental apologies, nor redress for such an inconvenience. The way government officials viewed those types of affairs was that the innocent prisoners were to consider themselves fortunate for walking away with their lives.

My father returned to his hometown of Güines upon his release from La Cabaña and soon realized he could no longer reside in that area. Harassment of former government officials had become a favorite sport in communist Cuba and he was accosted every time he left his home. According to my father, an uncle advised him to leave Güines for his own safety and that of his family. Left with no recourse, my family moved back to my father's old farm. Since we could not reside in the main residence, we were moved to an old shack deep in the country. Our new home was referred to as a *batey*, a location more suited for barn animals than human beings. There, in that small shack with dirt floors, our family found refuge from its communist tormentors.

By 1960 my parents realized our family had no other choice but to migrate to the U.S. Though some may ask "why not stay and fight?" the question is far from our reality. The Cuban revolution caught the majority of Cuban citizens by surprise. Nothing of that sort had even been attempted in Latin America. Normally, presidents came and went, and our way of life would remain constant. Nothing prepared us for that level of communist savagery, and though Fidel Castro was initially welcomed as the new "savior," he soon mobilized the entire country and neutralized most of his enemies. With no weapons and in constant fear of being turned in to the authorities by your next-door neighbor, it became impossible to conspire and plan to overthrow the government. To save their families, Cuban parents did the next best thing and began the massive exodus that continues to this day. Luckily, my uncle had migrated from Cuba to the U.S. in 1958 and he agreed to sponsor our family's travel here as well.

Though our travel documents were filed in 1960, we were horrified to find out over a year later that the documents had been mysteriously lost and the entire travel application process would have to be repeated. By the time we realized the documents were lost, the Cuban government was engaged in an anti–U.S. Government propaganda exchange that would eventually lead to the Bay of Pigs invasion of 1961, and the missile crisis of 1963. All migration to the U.S. was halted and we were left without options.

Our family eventually moved back to the outskirts of Güines. We lived in a small house and we would limit our trips to town to avoid confrontations. I remember a very violent episode I witnessed. I was only five years of age at the time and as we walked to the grocery store, we were approached by unknown individuals who told my father, "You are Brito, the son of a bitch who beat up my mother." Being a moral person and knowing that the individuals were government agents, intent on sending him back to prison, my father attempted to avoid the scene. The individuals continued their obscenity laced tirade against us until the grocery attendant exited his shop and helped chase away the culprits. My father would stay away from Güines for a period of three years to avoid similar events. In the 1960s, such chaos was part of the daily life of any citizen who dared to peacefully oppose the Cuban revolution.

By 1967, I was 10 years old and I attended a local school in Güines. A Cuban grade school at the time was more of an indoctrination center than a learning facility and I tried to put aside the communist dogma we were fed on a daily basis and concentrated on learning about interesting subjects such as geography and history. On one occasion, while in history class at school, the topic of Cuban patriot José Martí was brought up by the teacher. To those unfamiliar with Castro's government, they may have difficulties understanding that at that time and until this day, the regime is not only interested in influencing future events but also very much involved in portraying Cuban history as the catalyst for their Revolution.

José Martí is the Cuban government's favorite historical figure. The Cuban government obsessively views José Martí as the "intellectual figure of the assault on the Moncada barracks." The reference is an attempt to associate Marti to a raid conducted by Castro's 26th of July Movement against a Batista garrison. The Cuban government also portrays José Martí as an anti-imperialist and anti U.S. figure in its absurd attempt to provide legitimacy to its own agenda. The government correlates a specific phrase uttered by Martí that loosely translates to "I have lived in the monster and I know its entrails" to mean the "monster," the U.S., is a beast that cannot be trusted.

As my history teacher went on and on that day about Martí's involvement with the Revolution, I resorted to raise my hand, and when asked to speak by the teacher, I frankly told him that I did not see a correlation between a Spanish War figure of the 1800s and the current Cuban government of the 1960s. The debate placed the teacher in a precarious position with the class and he summoned my parents to school that same day.

My history teacher informed my father that I was an insolent child and he made it known that he had to teach class topics according to the views of the government. The teacher further told my father that my defiance to his statements about José Martí could place him in a predicament with government officials and he asked my father to ensure I did not let my subversive thoughts be known in class ever again. How a discussion in class could turn into a political event and lead to the firing or possible incarceration of a school teacher was beyond the grasp of a 10-year-old boy but such were the days we were living at the time.

Just prior to entering the 6th grade, I was informed I would no longer be permitted to attend the same school where all my friends would be attending. Instead I would be interned at Integrado Militar Osvaldo Sanchez, a faraway boarding school intended for "troubled children." I believe to this day that my debate with my history teacher was the cause for my reassignment. I would pay dearly for that transgression.

My new school, if it can be referred to as a school, was nothing more than a boot camp intended to correct our "anti–Revolutionary attitudes." The school consisted of four barracks, with outdoor *letrines* and an assortment of bunk beds. There were 300–400 children of many ages at the school and I was one of the youngest members. We were only permitted to go home every 15 days and our parents could only visit us on the weekend. We were not permitted to travel.

Our school was headed by a heavy-set and imposing individual referred to as Commander Gilberto Girón. Girón ruled the school with an iron fist and he imposed all kinds of rules. While at that school, your activities would be controlled from the moment you rose out of bed until the time you went to sleep late at night.

Our activities at school consisted of preparing for an upcoming "Yankee invasion." We would be woken up sometimes at 3:00 a.m. and be forced to march to adjoining sugar cane fields with our hands on top of our heads as we attempted to run away from fictional "imperialist attacks." We were instructed on military drills on a daily basis. We were taught to assemble and disassemble rifles and crawl through prearranged obstacle courses under barbed wire while holding bamboo sticks that imitated rifles. By the end of the day we would be forced to listen to long lectures regarding the benefits brought about by the Revolution.

If there is anything positive I remember from that period, it was the effort made by my father to try to secretly visit me and bring me a bit of milk or a piece of bread as often as he could. To do so, he would have to travel 10 kilometers on horseback and meet me by a sugarcane field. The saddest part of the story was that my father would travel from a concentration camp where he himself was now interned. All in all, it was an unrealistic experience that left a deep impression on a boy my age and until this day, I can't help but wonder about the fate of all those poor boys from that camp.

In May of 1968, after years of constant harassment by the Cuban government, we were permitted to migrate to the U.S. We departed Cuba for Miami International Airport (MIA) on a Pan Am flight from Varadero Beach, but not before being stripped of every possession we had by Cuban authorities. I truly believe the Cuban authorities were permitting us to travel to the U.S. but would not have cared if the aircraft made it safely to its destination. In the eyes of Cuban government officials, we were all expendable.

We were met by our uncle at MIA and my father was hired at a construction site just three days later. We lived near Miami's Orange Bowl and my sister and I attended Citrus Elementary School. I remember we would frequently travel to the Freedom Tower in Downtown Miami and the Refugee Center for cans of peanut butter and cheese bars. My father would toil in many different menial factory jobs for the following decades and by 1971, he had saved enough money to purchase a small home in the city of Hialeah, Florida. My father has always been a hard-working and religious man, and the actions he took in life fill me with pride and a sense of honor.

My next few years in South Florida would go by in a blur. As a teenager I worked many menial jobs in order to help my parents pay for our home expenses. I attended Booker T. Washington School, Miami Senior High School and later Miami-Dade College. In 1984, I joined the Miami-Dade Police Department and I had a very rewarding 30-year career. Through the years, I managed to take the time and become involved in various local charity organizations such the Kiwanis of Little Havana, where I continue to volunteer until this day. I believe that volunteering to help those in need is a form of paying back our gratitude to this great nation that opened its arms to my family and has given us so much hope.

I often think back about our past lives in Cuba and I draw strength from the stories told by my parents. With the passing of dictator Fidel Castro, I wonder if true freedom will ever come to Cuba again. I real-

Jorge Brito, at 7 years of age in Güines, Cuba, and at 17 years of age in Miami, FL (courtesy Jorge Luis Brito).

ize now that only a mad man such as Castro could have implemented a malevolent government intent on destroying the lives of its own people. Often, when asked by citizens of other nationalities about the experience of living under a totalitarian system, I paraphrase my father and I tell them that communism is the "perfect lie." I know from experience that my father's brief phrase encompasses all those dark days we survived long ago.

The previous stories are just three of the hundreds to thousands of similar stories. In all of the years I lived in Cuba and

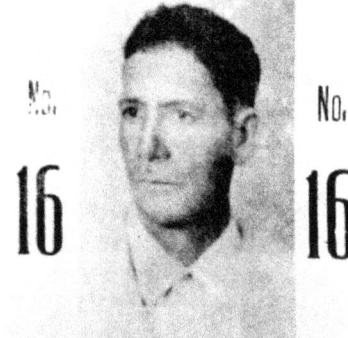

Jorge's maternal grandfather, a victim of Castro's Agrarian Reform (courtesy Jorge Luis-Brito).

Jorge (left) with his parents, Eulalio and Caridad, and his older brother Jose Gabriel (courtesy Jorge Luis Brito).

later in exile, I have not met a Cuban citizen whose family has been spared from the execution, incarceration, immigration, or drowning of a family member due to the actions of the Cuban government. Yet, while these crimes against humanity continued to occur, the majority of the international community remained silent and for the most part, many left-leaning governments supported Fidel Castro and created a cult following around a brutal and sadistic assassin named Ernesto "Che" Guevara.

As the Cuban government fast approaches its 60th year of existence, Cuban citizens share little hope that their destructive form of government will change in the near future. As far as archival records of the crimes committed against its own citizens by the Cuban government, and even structures of those concentration camps listed in the stories, very little trace remains, and most of those individuals responsible for such actions have already passed on or are older than 80 years of age.

As an elderly Cuban exile once said to me, "we were left alone, in an island prison and at the behest of a mad man, and they threw away the key."

Memories

Corina Fernández-Máscaró

My Family

I was born in Santiago de Cuba, Cuba's second largest city, to a German mother, Waltraud Heisinger and a Cuban father, Raul Fernandez-Máscaró. Our house was located in a suburb of Santiago called Vista Alegre where my parents, my brother and I lived until the Castro revolution forced us to seek political asylum in the United States. My father was an attorney and one of six children of a very prominent man, Dr. Guillermo Fernandez-Máscaró. My mother was a housewife in Cuba and the daughter of a German diplomat stationed in Havana at the time my parents met.

My mother had attended a German school in Havana and spoke fluent Spanish, German and English. At the outbreak of World War II, the German government recalled all civil servants outside of Germany and my grandparents left Cuba and spent the war years in Dresden. They were able to return to Cuba in the 1950s and by that time, my mother had married and moved to Santiago de Cuba where part of my father's family lived.

As a young child, I did not know much about my maternal or paternal grandparents. I now look at their history with great pride. Dr. Guillermo Fernandez-Máscaró was a brilliant man in his own right. He was a chemist and physicist, medical doctor and educator, who decided, at a point in his life, to enter politics. He became Minister of Education during the presidency of Gerardo Machado, who commissioned my grandfather to turn Cuba's education system into "the Athens of the Americas." My grandfather Guillermo was one of the founders of Cuba's Republican Party and was twice elected to the House of Representatives. He also became governor of the Oriente province, where Santiago is located, and Ambassador to Mexico during his political years.

I was particularly close to my maternal grandparents, Anton and Freda

Heisinger, and loved them dearly. I believe they tolerated my more mischievous behavior as a child. I remember the day I spilled tomato juice on what seemed to be a white linen suit of a visiting German diplomat. I don't think my grandparents ever forgot that incident and neither did I. They lived with us for a time after returning from Germany. Both lived with us in the U.S. and passed away in Kansas City, Missouri.

Childhood Memories in Cuba

We were a social bunch. I don't think we sat still for a minute. I cannot remember ever wanting to sit and watch TV. I always wanted to be outside socializing with neighborhood friends who also were schoolmates at a catholic school in Vista Alegre, Colegio del Sagrado Corazon. Santiago de Cuba was smaller than Havana and Cuba's second largest city. In the suburb of Vista Alegre, practically everyone knew each other. It was a close-knit society, totally safe for children to play outside and socialize and no one dared hurt you. When I now meet with friends that I knew from early childhood, we comment about those early worry-free days. We reminisce about the innocent fun times we had and sometimes compare the differences we find in children growing up today, children that are less innocent, who socialize less and perhaps grow up too fast.

Grandfather Antonio Heisinger (Corina Fernandez-Máscaró).

Sometimes on weekends, my father would visit my grandfather at his ranch outside of Santiago. My grandfather Guillermo loved horses, and at his ranch he had many beautiful ones which had won prizes at one time or another. As a child, I liked to go into the storage place where all the saddles were kept and inspected. I remember the great smell of Italian leather and today, when I smell that fine leather in a store, the scent takes me back, in a sort of *Proustian* way, to my grandfather's ranch and the Italian leather smell of his saddles.

The beautiful beach of Siboney, outside of Santiago, was my favorite place to go on weekends with my parents and friends. We were great swimmers and divers at an early age and swimming was one of Cuba's favorite and competitive sports. I remember my friends and I used to go out into deeper waters to a high and large wooden raft to dive. A thought never crossed our minds that a shark or barracuda might be lurking around for a tasty lunch and we were very lucky then to never have experienced an incident of that kind. We were in the sun most of the day. There were no sun protection creams available in those days, and no one thought about it. I always tell my friends that moving to Kansas City saved my skin.

Corina at Siboney Beach with maternal grandmother (Corina Fernandez-Máscaró).

The beautiful Siboney beach is also the name of a famous song by Cuba's most famous and prolific composer, Ernesto Lecuona. Lecuona wrote the song while away from Cuba and the words reflect his homesickness and longing to return.

Pre-Exile Days

I don't believe most people ever conceived or expected that such radical changes would one day come to Cuba. In hindsight, Cuba had no experience with a democratic system of government as we know today. It was a very divided country along racial and economic lines. People of color did not socialize with whites or attend the same

Grandfather Antonio and Corina (Corina Fernandez-Máscaró).

schools, clubs or churches. The wealthy and strong middle-class of Cuba before Castro lived extremely well. The poor and colored people lived badly, many in abject poverty.

Cuban support for Castro spread in the 1950s, not only due to his charisma and nationalistic rhetoric, but mainly because of an increasingly corrupt and inefficient Batista government. Many Cubans knew of Castro's communist tendencies, but many did not. After his ascent to power, Fidel declared himself a Communist-Leninist and began to make radical changes such as changing the monetary system and confiscating businesses and private property. He began the process of communist indoctrination in schools, instituted a military age for male children and forced labor in cane fields. Cuban children who fell into the military age requirement were not allowed to leave Cuba.

As a young child, I did not know exactly what was happening. What did it really mean to leave for the United States? Was it going to be a temporary journey or a permanent one? I heard friends say their family was leaving for Mexico, others for Spain or Puerto Rico, many for the U.S. Families with male children close to military age hurried to send them out of Cuba. My very good friends and neighbors Nilda and Luis López Grillé left for Miami

First communion: Sagrado Corazon, father and mother to my left and Grandmother in black (Corina Fernandez-Máscaró).

184   Escape from Cuba

At a school recital, first from left (Corina Fernandez-Máscaró).

as part of the *Pedro Pan* program. Eventually they left for New York to live with friends of their father and then to Vigo, Spain where they still live. I never saw these great friends until I vacationed in Spain during my university years and visited them. What an amazing reunion that was! Sadly, Nilda and Luis never saw their father again after leaving Cuba. He became ill and died rather young. It took their mother 10 years to be allowed to leave for Spain and reunite with her children, and such as this one, there are many stories.

I saw my parents making many trips to Havana to prepare papers for leaving Cuba. This must have been one of the most stressful and agonizing time of their lives. My mother had seen her parents leave at the beginning of World War II when the German government recalled civil personnel back to Germany. I am sure she did not know if she would ever see them again. My mother saw her parents again, but my parents never saw Cuba again.

Leaving Cuba

What are these people doing here? Why are they looking at everything in the house? Why are they looking at and touching my bicycle? I did not understand what was going on, but something strange was happening. In the three months prior to departure, the Castro government sent officials or militia people to our home to take a detailed inventory of all items inside the house. The officials came back before our authorized departure day to make sure all items were present, and nothing had been removed. Failure to comply meant cancellation of departure, or worse consequences. Days before leaving Cuba, my father handed over his car and home to the government. We left for Havana to wait for departure day.

The day of departure arrived and all the belongings we could take were meticulously searched at Havana's airport. Some persons were even stripped down to make sure no valuable items were hidden. I remember crying during the search. My grandparents had given me a small pearl bracelet that I treasured. The militiaman asked me to take it off and leave it. This is how cruel some people had become. They now felt empowered by the revolution and entitled to those things that did not belong to them. The so-called oppressors were leaving the country and the "Fidelistas" believed they now had a savior. Little did they know then that they would live a life of hunger and suppression, a daily battle in search of food, clothing items or medicine. The revolution brought equality to all at a heavy cost.

A New Life in Independence, Missouri

My parents decided to settle in Independence, Missouri, where my maternal grandmother had a German niece who had settled there with her husband many years earlier. They lived on West Maple Street in a kind of Victorian looking home very close to where President Harry Truman had his home on Delaware Avenue. We stayed with our German relatives for a few months until my parents leased a house near a Catholic school where my mother would eventually teach, and I would go to school.

We were one of the first Cuban families to settle in the Kansas City or surrounding areas, such as Independence. Most Cubans opted for settling in Miami with their families. Eventually, many Cubans arrived in Kansas City, helped by the Catholic Church or relocated by the government. The Cuban community grew and most remain there to this day. I developed a large group of friends within that Cuban community with whom I even shared a few undergraduate university classes.

I remember Americans to be so generous and welcoming to newly arrived Cubans. Several American families helped my parents in many ways. During all my years in the Kansas City area, I never heard a derogatory comment expressed against Cubans either in school or in public. My classmates were curious and having the first foreign student in their school was surely a novelty. Initially, classmates would surround me and ask me questions and I understood little of what they were asking me. I knew some words or phrases in English, but certainly not enough to carry on a conversation. I sat in classes without understanding much. But young people learn languages quickly, it seems almost by osmosis, so that within a period of four or five months, I could understand and get along quite well. At school, with classmates, I never felt like a foreigner. I became part of the family, so-to-speak.

Corina with mother and brother Raul, Kansas (Corina Fernandez-Máscaró).

St. Mary's was a coed Catholic school where I completed elementary and high school years. My high school education was excellent. Many of the teachers were nuns, but there were also lay instructors. The nuns, or sisters, as we used to call them, were highly educated. The principal during my high school years was Sister Mary Paula. She was a native Czechoslovakian and spoke several languages fluently. She taught English literature and Latin, and no one dared to ever go to her classes unprepared. It was in high school that I developed a love for literature, history and languages. Sister Mary Karlanne was a fabulous French instructor. She always thought I should become a linguist. At that time, I did not know exactly what that meant or where being a linguist would take me in my future career.

Parents and Grandparents

I look back at my parents' journey with awe and great admiration. They left a country they loved, with many losses along the way, including very close friends they would never see again. Adapting to a new way of life, in a new country, with new customs and language was not easy for them. They were always there for my brother and I and always insisted on the importance of education.

Though my mother was not born in Cuba, she loved Cuba and always had tales to tell and memories to share. She became a Spanish instructor at

St. Mary's and began to pursue an MA Degree at the University of Missouri. She left St Mary's when she was hired to teach Spanish and German undergraduate classes at the university and studied for her MA in the evenings. My father struggled with English and eventually became proficient. The transition from being an attorney in Cuba to one in the U.S. essentially meant a new law degree. Cuba, as well as most Latin and European countries, followed a legal system based on the Napoleonic Code. My father eventually found employment at a Kansas City Bank, the name of which I do not remember.

The years 1978 and 1979 were sad years for all of us. My father and both maternal grandparents passed away. In Cuba, the land of tobacco, coffee and sugar, most men smoked. This was a habit my father never overcame, and it finally took its toll. He passed away from a massive heart attack while visiting family in Miami. My mother remarried some years later and passed away in Kansas City in 2006. I believe she lived a good life in Kansas City, but she never forgot Cuba. My brother still lives and works in Kansas City.

University and Beyond

My interest in Literature and Languages led me to pursue a BA and MA in Spanish and French Literature. My long-term goal at the time, was to teach literature at the college or university level and attain a Ph.D. I taught secondary school Spanish and French while I studied for my MA degree. During that period, I saw evolving changes in the field of education, particularly affecting the liberal arts. Languages became electives rather than required subjects. I had friends with doctorates in German or Spanish teaching in secondary schools. Teacher salaries, as it is evident today, are one of the main reasons talented individuals opt for different careers and the liberal arts particularly, have suffered along the way. Over time, these changes have affected the essence of education itself.

After completion of my MA degree in Languages and Literature, I began studies for an MBA with emphasis in Finance. I started my business career in banking in the city of Minneapolis. There were not many Cubans in Minneapolis when I arrived. Later, a few did settle in Minneapolis and perhaps always wished to move to a warmer place. My career took me to Los Angeles where I lived for many years.

It was not until the year 2000 that I came to Miami as a co-founder, with Celeste De Armas, of a Latin Foods company by the name of Nueva Cocina. Celeste had spent a great part of her career with Nestle USA. She held positions in Marketing, Strategic Planning, and was the Executive VP for the Chilled Foods Division of Nestle.

The Nueva Cocina project evolved from an idea to the market place with

188 Escape from Cuba

several rounds of capital procurement along the way. Nueva Cocina was an all-natural line of packaged Latin foods that brought flavors of the Latin world to the home kitchen with easy to follow preparations. It was the first company of its kind. By the time of the financial crisis in 2008–2010, Nueva Cocina products were available in close to 2,000 food markets, schools and restaurants. As many others during those years, we were greatly affected by the lack of growth capital available.

For growing businesses, access to capital is a never-ending necessity. The market had no appetite for risk. We barely survived those years, but the company lost a lot of its value by the time a U.S. multinational acquired it in 2013. I now remember the years of Nueva Cocina with great pride and all the achievements that two entrepreneurial Cuban women were able to accomplish.

Currently, I am a Consultant for CSMB International Inc., a risk management and banking consultancy with offices in Miami, Mexico and Panama. My love for literature and history continues. I reside in Fort Lauderdale, Florida.

Final Thoughts

Many persons have asked me if I believe the Castro government would not have lasted as long if the first wave of Cubans exiles had stayed in Cuba. I believe that probably many would have been killed had they remained or

Nueva Cocina founders Corina Fernandez-Máscaró (left) and Celeste De Armas (Corina Fernandez-Máscaró).

would have been imprisoned for many years. Fidel Castro became a ruthless, repressive totalitarian dictator. He assassinated and jailed many who withstood horrible prison conditions for even insignificant things such as having a one dollar bill in their pocket.

Castro silenced the press. There was no way to dissent or even express contrary opinions. The consequences were severe. In a kind of Orwellian manner, Castro set up neighborhood watches with persons who listened and monitored a person's movements. The lives of those people that Castro spoke about improving became worse. Scarcity of foods and other essentials have been pervasive to this day. Food staples were rationed and people stood in long lines for hours to be able to obtain monthly allotments.

Castro, such as many dictators, was ill prepared and unfit to manage a country. It was all about power and control and total abdication of moral principles. History has proven as much. While it is very sad and painful what happened to Cuba in 1959, I consider that my family and others who were welcomed to this great and free nation, were very fortunate. I hope that Americans never take for granted their freedoms or disregard the democratic principles that are the foundation of this great nation. That would be very sad indeed and a loss that may never be regained.

A Long Road to Freedom

Francisco Pérez Sabatier

Life in Cuba

I was born on October of 1957 in Las Martinas, Pinar del Río to Omar Perez Gonzalez and Nelida Victoria Sabatier Suarez. Las Martinas is a small town on the western tip of Cuba. My father ran the family business with his two older brothers and we lived a comfortable, healthy life typical of a small town anywhere in a free world. I was only two years old when Castro's communist regime took over the country. I don't remember much of those early years and unfortunately my father passed away in 1992, at age 59. I wanted so much to sit down with him and talk about those early years of the revolution. My mother is 85 years old and suffering from dementia and unfortunately, I cannot ask her. Opportunities such as this book makes me wish that I had interviewed my parents many years ago. My recollection of those early years is based on stories I heard from my older brother and family members. My mother and father were married in 1955. My brother, Omar Eduardo Perez, was born a year later in 1956.

I remember growing up and hearing my parents and family members whispering about the Castro government. My father had installed an extremely large TV antenna that could pick up channels from the United States in South Florida, and I would watch cartoons every Saturday morning. I could not understand the words, but it was my favorite day of the week. At the time, I did not know what was going on, but I do remember the secret meetings and conversations, people coming to my house to watch TV channels from South Florida, the crying, the fights, and the arguments. My mother wanted to leave Cuba and migrate to the United States of America, but my father felt that things were going to get better and kept waiting to make a decision.

During those days, non-communists were afraid of the *comité* (committee), a system of spies that Fidel Castro had installed through out all the neighborhoods in Cuba. My paternal grandfather, Ildelfonzo Perez, was an immigrant from the Canary Islands and migrated to Cuba with no material possessions. He worked hard and by the 1930s, owned a good size farm and was raising his 10 children; 5 girls and 5 boys. His oldest son, Arsenio Perez, became a traveling salesman and later a successful businessman.

My parents' wedding (Francisco Pérez Sabatier).

My uncle, Arsenio Perez, took over the family business and brought one of his brothers, Herminio Perez, and my father into the family business. By 1959, my family owned a thriving tobacco growing business, which was all appropriated during Castro's agrarian reform of 1961. My grandfather was left with a few acres of land around his home and from that point on, he could only sell to the government. It was at that time that my oldest uncle, Arsenio Perez, decided that Cuba was no longer a place he wanted to live and left the country for Santo Domingo; he became a successful businessman there. My family was never sympathetic to the communist regime, but at that point in our history, my family had turned totally anti-communist.

The family also owned several stores, a movie theater, and a bakery, all of which were confiscated. By 1967, the only thing left was a trucking company that my father was still running. His older brother, Herminio Perez, had given up, moved to Havana, and started the process to leave Cuba. I remember that my father had two International trucks, one silver and one red. The third one was a black Fargo, which was his favorite and the one he usually drove. Also, by this time, a large percentage of my close relatives had left for the USA, but my father kept waiting and hoping "things" would change.

Sometime in 1967, I am

My brother and I (Francisco Pérez Sabatier).

My dad's two brothers on a business trip to North Carolina in 1953 (Francisco Pérez Sabatier).

not sure of the date and no one remembers, I had my first face-to-face encounter with ruthless people; an immoral experience that I remember with the communist regime. I was only 10 years old and was home with my brother. Our aunt was caring for us, since my parents were not home. There was a knock at the door and when my aunt opened the door, there were three military men, dressed in all green garb with long and unkempt beards, displaying guns. They asked to speak with my parents and when my aunt told them that they were not home, they told her that they were there to take my dad's trucks. They asked for the keys to the trucks, but my aunt refused and an argument ensued. I don't remember the exact details (a young boy usually suppresses these horrible experiences), but I do remember screaming at the military guys and kicking at them. They left but came back later with a mechanic that apparently "hot-wired" the trucks and seized them.

I think that it was at that moment, at the tender age of 10 years old, that I became a diehard anti-communist. I developed a total hatred for anything communist, which is prevalent today. I remember seeing my mother and father crying, knowing that everything they ever owned and worked hard for was gone. At that moment, I realized for the first time the horrifying situation we were in. I stopped being a child that day and the miserable experience robbed me of my happy childhood. Even after that incident, my father did not leave the country. He foolishly thought that he could start a new business.

He purchased a 1940s Chevy car and had a mechanic, a friend, cut the car from the front seats back to convert it into a homemade pickup truck.

Using the Chevy, my dad would buy Cuban bread from the same bakery that used to be owned by my family and deliver the bread to small stores in the countryside. I remember helping him when I was off from school and, as a reward, he would let me drive the car while sitting on his lap. There was not much of a profit, and my dad had to work extremely long hours to make ends meet. Well, that did not last long. Soon we had another visit from the "menfolk in green" and, as anticipated, they took the pickup truck from my father. Finally, after this incident, my dad realized that we had no future in Cuba and made the decision to leave. I think he knew things would get worse, but he did not know how bad things would get; I believe this occurred sometime in 1968.

My father had dual citizenship, Cuban and Spaniard, so he applied to leave the country through Spain hoping that the process would be quicker. The communists immediately came and did an inventory of the house and its contents. As part of a punishment plan, they ordered my father to a forced labor camp to cut sugar cane from sun-up to sun-down. My mother was left with two small children without any means to support the family. In the eyes of the Cuban regime, anyone leaving the country was an anti-communist and a traitor. Sadly, I don't remember seeing my dad much during those years. I remember visiting him with my mother and brother, but the deplorable conditions that he worked under is the only reminder that haunts me.

A forced labor camp cutting sugar cane is an extremely hard life, especially when you have never done anything like that before. Since everyone at these forced labor camps were dissidents, they were treated extremely harshly in what amounted to state-sponsored slavery. These men were offered little food, and I remember my dad telling stories of eating dogs and cats to supplement their meals. They were mistreated, abused physically and mentally, and constantly called despicable names. While at the labor camp, my father had a serious accident during which he almost lost his arm. While working in the fields, a truck loaded with sugar cane drove by and a sugar cane that had been cut at an angle and was sticking out in the open, struck my father in his left elbow and virtually ripped his arm off. My father was in the hospital for a while but was sent back to the forced labor camp before he was totally recovered. For a while, he was responsible for the cooking chores until he got better. But, he was never released until a few days before we left Cuba for Spain. Regrettably, that injury haunted him physically and psychologically for the rest of his life.

My father was not the only one going through hell. My mother, my brother, and I, in many ways, had it worse than my dad. My mother was a stay-at-home mom and suddenly she found herself alone with two small children without means to support them. My mother was a seamstress by trade before meeting my dad, so she started making children's clothing and trading them for food and other items we needed to survive. I remember that she would spend all week creating clothing from scraps of cloth or old dresses and then we would go with her on the weekends to the countryside where we could trade them to the farmers for food. I remember on one occasion that my brother and I went alone to visit a farmer, my father's friend, to see if we could find something to eat. I was 10 years old and my brother was 11 years old. We took a bus to this place in the middle of nowhere. We got off the bus and walked on this dirt road for a couple of miles to get to the farm. The farmer told us that we could take whatever we could dig out of the ground. Thus, my brother and I started digging *boniatos* (sweet potatoes) and *yucas* (cassava) until we filled up a large bag. The bag was too heavy for us to carry and we had to drag it all the way to the bus stop by the main paved road. Luckily, from there, we made it home safe.

Since we lived in a small town, everyone knew each other, and we were never impacted much by the current political turmoil. My father was never sympathetic to the government, but out of fear he kept a neutral attitude. The town's people that were with the Castro government knew that we were not sympathetic to the current regime, but as a local rule left us alone. Immediately after we applied to leave the country, things changed for the worse. Moreover, it did not help that I became a rebel with a cause, which resulted in more headaches for my family. People stopped talking or associating with us, they would call us despicable names, and spit towards us. My mother, now alone with us, would only get help from close family, and dejectedly, some of those stopped talking to us too. We became second-class citizens in our own country, and the target of *"el comité"* (the committee). From that point on, we lived in fear until the day we left Cuba.

If you were in school, you were required to be a *Pionero*, something similar to a communist boy scout and wear a uniform with the famous red scarf. I refused to wear the uniform or to participate in any of the Pionero activities. Once a year, on the anniversary of Camilo Cienfuego's death, all kids had to go to the closest ocean and throw flowers at the waves, but I refused to do it. Every morning we had to stand in formation outside the school and sing the national anthem *"La Internationale."* However, I refused to do it. We then had to march by the Cuban flag and salute it, but I refused to do it and never did. As a result, I was sent to the principal's office daily. They would call my mother, and she would tell me not to do it out of fear that they were going to be arrested or worse. But, the next day I would do it again. To this day, I cannot explain why I acted that way, but I believe that it all started the day they barged into my house and seized the trucks from my father. I hated anything that had to do with communism!

At 11 years old in sixth grade, my brother and I were forced to attend La Escuela al Campo (School at the Farm) for 45 days during the summer break. I remember like it was yesterday, crying my heart out when I had to leave my mom behind; those were the worst 45 days of my life. It was difficult enough that you had to go away to school at 11 years old, but because we were *gusanos* (Worms/Non-Communists) and we were attempting to leave the country, they made our life a living-hell. They considered our family traitors for leaving Cuba. The physical and mental abuse that we suffered is too painful to describe. Mostly, it was psychological. But, there was plenty of physical abuse, which was condoned by the people in authority. Not a day went by that I did not get into a fight with another kid, usually a lot bigger than me. They were particularly abusive to my brother because he did not fight back like I did.

The facilities at the camp were worse than a concentration encampment. The girls' facilities were a "five star" hotel compared with the boys. We stayed in the small barracks made out of Royal Palm boards. There were large cracks all around. The wind would seep-in and it would get really cold at night. We slept in bunk beds made out of rebar with a very thin mattress. The bathrooms were 100 yards away with no roof in either the showers or the restrooms; there was no hot water, only cold water. We had to get up at 5:00 a.m. and be on the fields digging grass around orange trees by 7:00 a.m. Breakfast consisted of Russian powdered milk with a small piece of hard bread. Lunch and dinner typically consisted of a scoop of rice (full of maggots), pea soup, and some type of meat or fried fish. I remember working in the kitchen and seeing the fish covered with maggots which would disappear after they deep fried the fish.

The next year when I went to 7th grade at the age of 12, the Escuela al Campo became *Escuela en el Campo* and it was all year around. You had to wear a uniform and we had formation every morning. We also had to practice marching around like a military boot camp. We would work all morning in the fields until noon. The work mostly consisted of digging around the orange trees to clear the grass and other manual intensive labor. We would then come back to the barracks, take a shower, and go to school all afternoon. I remember the school principal walking around in his green uniform with a big gun attached to his hip.

The psychological and physical abuse continued, but now it was all year around instead of 45 days. Unfortunately, kids can be crueler than any adults, and without supervision, there is no limit to their cruelty. We worked and went to school 6 days a week and most Sundays you had to work in the kitchen. We were allowed to visit our family every other weekend and they could visit us on Sunday. My mother was by herself and oftentimes could not find the means to visit the school, so most of the time we would see her every other week. There are so many things that happened during that time that I could write a book on that alone. Besides the verbal abuse and the fights, there is one thing that I always remember. My uncle, Berto Sabatier, built me a wooden suitcase with a lock so I could keep my possessions locked and secure; mostly food that my mom would bring my brother and me. Other kids knew what was in the case and they would threaten us in an attempt to take it from us. When that did not work, they broke into the case by smashing it with a large rock. From that point on we would eat everything the same day because it was the only way to keep it away from the other kids.

In January of 1971, my brother and I were expelled from the Escuela en el Campo after undergoing a military style tribunal. A few days before, on a Sunday, I was picked to work the kitchen all morning. At about noon, they released me, and on my way back to the barracks, I heard a commotion coming from the side of the road leading to the barracks. I approached to see what was going on, and I found my older brother, Omar surrounded by a dozen kids. They were punching and kicking him, spitting on him, and calling him all kinds of verbally abusive anti-communist rhetoric. I became really angry, picked up a tree branch and proceeded to strike several of the kids until they ran away. I badly injured some of them, so they somehow blamed my brother and me for the incident. The judge in the trial was the school's principal who was dressed in his full military uniform, including the gun. They found us guilty and the punishment was expulsion from the school. At the end of the trial, the judge asked me if I had anything to say, to which I responded, "No, but you are a dirty communist son of a whore." The trial ended late at night and we were supposed to be officially expelled from the school during the next morning's formation. That night I told my brother that I was not going to give them the satisfaction of expelling me, and that I was going to leave in the middle of the night. I asked my brother to come with me, but he refused, so I left alone. I made it home at about noon the next day.

At the time, the communists instituted a condition to authorize an exit visa: you had to be working or in school for them to officially approve your exit visa. My mother was very worried that we were not going to be approved to leave, so she tried to get us enrolled in another school, but no one was willing to take us. Approximately two months later, we got our exit visas and left for Spain on April 18, 1971. We were fortunate to leave as a family because my father was the only one with the Spanish citizenship and I know of many families that were separated.

There are a few things that I remember from those last days in Cuba. We had a really large house and they had tried to convince my dad to exchange the house for a smaller one, but my father refused. I think that's one of the reasons they allowed us to leave as quickly as they did without any concerns; they wanted our house. Surprisingly, within a few days, our house

Current picture of my house in Cuba that was turned into a funeral home (Francisco Pérez Sabatier).

was converted to a funeral home and to this day it's still the town's funeral home. When they kicked us out of the house, we took the few things we could and moved for a few days to my aunt's house across the street, while waiting to travel to Havana. That same day, the communists trespassed into our home's back yard and cut down two old cedar trees that had been planted by my grandfather. That incident still hurts to this day and I am not sure why; maybe it's because of the sentimental value of the trees.

On Our Way to Spain

On April 18, 1971, we traveled to José Martí International Airport and boarded an old Turboprop airplane from Cubana airlines. I will always remember that trip, not only for the length of it (23 hours) but for an incident that happened during the flight. We made a refueling stop on Miguel Island in the Portuguese archipelago of the Azores. While the plane was attempting to take off for the last leg of the trip to Spain, it had some mechanical problems and had to abort the takeoff. We taxied back to the terminal, and they took us out of the plane while they did maintenance. They gave us breakfast, a slice of ham, scrambled eggs, toast, and orange juice. It was the first time in my life, at the age of 12, that I had tasted ham. I always remember that day, walking through the airport and seeing all the stores full of merchandise. It is something that we all take for granted today, but for me, that day was a miracle. Both ends of the runway at the Azores airport end on a cliff to the sea. Taking off on that runway, in an old turboprop airplane that had just had mechanical problems, was a terrifying experience.

Life in Spain

We arrived in Madrid, Spain's Barajas Airport on April 19, 1971. We were happy to finally be out of communist Cuba, but we were extremely apprehensive about what the future would hold. We were in a new country without money and without any tangible family support. We stayed with my mother's cousin, Ismael Sabatier, while my parents looked for work. He lived in a small one-bedroom apartment in Madrid, and we were sleeping on the living room floor. It was difficult to find employment in Spain in 1971. Spain was still under the dictatorship of Generalissimo Francisco Franco and was not part of the European Union. There was still a lot of animosity towards Spain from the rest of Europe because of Franco's support of Nazi Germany. The economy was not good, and the few jobs available were for Spaniards only. My father was a Spanish citizen, but he was considered a Cuban immigrant by all Spaniards.

After two days, my mother's cousin gave us 200 *pesetas* and took us to a *Casa de Huéspedes* (Guesthouse) located at Calle Fundadores #5 in the area of Goya, Madrid for a place for us to live. The only good thing I remember about this place is that it was close to El Parque del Retiro, a large park similar to Central park in New York City. I remember going there with my brother just to take in a slight piece of nature. My father could not find a permanent job; he worked several odd jobs trying to put food on the table and pay the rent. This guesthouse consisted of a room for all four of us with a little kitchenette and the bathrooms were down the hallway, shared with all the other guests. It was still cold in Madrid and the temperature would drop dramatically at night. I remember grabbing whatever clothing I had, clean or dirty, and pulling it on top of me to stay warm. During those days, we did not have any jackets and I would wear five and six shirts, one on top of the other to stay warm because we could not afford to pay for heating. We did not have enough money to buy food, so my mom would take us to a nearby church that had a soup kitchen to eat a decent meal.

After several months of this hell guesthouse, my parents finally were able to save enough money to rent a two-bedroom apartment and share the cost with another Cuban family. We were all still sleeping in the same room, but we had a bathroom inside the apartment and we had a full kitchen, dining room, and living room. We even had a TV, and we were able to see the two black and white channels they had in Spain at the time. Still, it was better than Cuba, since at least we were free of the communist oppression. The apartment was located at Avenida Manzanares 162, 7D in the area of Comillas, Madrid. Next to the main entrance to the apartment building, there was a small *bodega* (store) that we used to visit to buy drinks and snacks.

Even though we shared the same heritage, names, and physical appearance, I did not find it easy to assimilate into the Spanish culture. We spoke the same language, but not really. The accent gave us away. They could tell immediately that I was not a Spaniard, and they treated you differently. I found Spaniards of that time to be extremely prejudiced against immigrants and probably it had to do with the fact that at the time, the economy in Spain was not doing well. Like everything in life, you have good and bad in every race, country or society, and a perfect example of the good was a young man my father met soon after we moved to the new apartment.

After months of unsuccessfully looking for a job, my dad was in this *bodega* buying a drink and he ran into a young man that had stopped to get a drink. My father struck up a conversation with him and told him his story and the difficulties he was having getting a permanent job. This young man's father owned a large taxi company in Madrid and his mother owned a chain of Camy ice cream stands all over Madrid. I am talking about permanent structures, not the temporary street vendors you see today. This young man was a godsend to our family. He told my father that he was sure his mother or father could get him a job, and thus he put my father in contact with his mother, Josefina Martin. She hired him on the spot, and he ended up working for her until the day we came to the USA.

It is not only fitting, but with a sense of gratitude, that I make this Spanish family part of my family story. Not only did they give us hope in our darkest hour, but they continued to help my family for all three years that we lived in Spain. More about that later. My brother had turned 14 and got a full-time job at a warehouse called Demi Plas to help pay the bills. He would then go to school at night to keep up with his studies. My mom worked at home making wood ornaments, and I would help her after school. I remember helping her carry bags full of these ornaments, and she would sell them to a factory that re-sold them.

Josefina Martin, after hearing our story and all the hardships we had gone through, decided to do something special for me, since I was the youngest one. She somehow was able to get me free admission to the most prestigious Catholic School in Madrid, El Instituto San Isidro located in La Calle de Toledo, near the Plaza Mayor. So, while I lived in Madrid, I was able to get the best education money could buy, for free. El Instituto San Isidro is the same school that the king of Spain, Don Juan Carlos de Borbón had attended. I cannot say that my time attending school was totally enjoyable, but I did get a good education. Like anything else I have good and bad memories. I remember how strict the nuns and priests were, and the beatings that I received. I learned how to play soccer, and later was a starter for my high school team. I also remember how difficult it was for me to assimilate and blend in with the other kids. They always looked down at me because not only was I an immigrant, but I was not of their same social class.

Life after my dad got a permanent job was unadventurous, and we lolled into a routine waiting for our U.S. visas, and our final destination. El Estadio Vicente Calderón, home of the Atletico Madrid, was just down the street from us. My brother and I would walk there to try to see the players and try to find a way to sneak into the stadium, since we could not afford it. We lived across from the Manzanares River and on the other side, between the Toledo Bridge and the Praga Bridge was a park. I would go there with other Cuban kids that I had met in church to play baseball. I remember people would line up on the Praga Bridge to watch us play baseball. I am sure that in Spain during the early 1970s, there was little knowledge of baseball, and people were curious about what we were doing.

In October of 1973, after almost three years living in Spain, my family was granted entrance visas to the USA. On October 31, 1973, we arrived in Miami, Florida, finally to realize our American Dream of living in a democratic society. I remember all the families that came to see us, people that I had not seen for years and some that I did not remember at all. I remember getting into my aunt's car, Hilda Sabatier, and driving out of the Miami International Airport and

Instituto San Isidro de Madrid. The school I attended while in Spain (Francisco Pérez Sabatier).

Four of my Cuban friends and I in Spain. I am the one on the right (Francisco Pérez Sabatier).

taking State Road 836 west. I had never seen a road like it, and I asked my aunt about it. She said to me: *"Es un Expressway"* (it is an expressway). That was the first English word I learned in the United States. We arrived on October 31, Halloween night. I remember driving to my aunt's house and seeing all the kids dressed in costumes "trick-or-treating" through the neighborhood and thinking that they all had lost their minds.

Life in the USA

We lived with my aunt for a few months in the area of South Miami in Dade County; we later rented a house near her house. My father started working construction the next day, and my mother found a job at a factory a few days later. By the end of the week, my brother and I were both working at a Kentucky Fried Chicken washing dishes.

We had arrived at the "Promised-Land," but things were not easy for me. Arriving here was a bigger culture shock than in Spain. I was 16 years old in a new country with a totally different culture. I did not speak a word of English, and starting school was interesting to say the least. I remember getting on the school bus with my brother for the first time and sitting quietly because I did not know if anyone spoke Spanish on the bus. In school, I would sit in the back of the class and would stay quiet just trying to make it through the day. With time, things got better, and I started to make friends and to learn and understand the English language, so things improved.

For almost two years, my brother and I would give our parents our complete paychecks until they were able to save enough money to buy a house. I graduated from Killian Senior High School in 1976 and was offered a job as an Assistant Manager at the Kentucky Fried Chicken store in Homestead. I took the job, but knew that it was not what I wanted to do with my life. My parents were doing well and enjoying their new home in the USA. I always felt that I owed this country something and wanted to give back. After much consideration, I decided to join the United States Marines. I knew all along that I wanted to serve in the military, but I was not sure which branch. I read about the different branches of the military and the phrase, "the few, the proud" caught my eye. I felt that if I was going to do it, I was going to enlist in the military branch that would test my limits and capabilities.

Life in the Marines

In August of 1977, I volunteered and joined the United States Marines. This was a big step in my life and one that gave me purpose and a sense of "pay-back." I started training on August 24, 1977, and graduated from basic training on November 7, 1977. Marine boot camp is the hardest of all the branches and extremely challenging for anyone, but when you add the lack of proficiency with the English language, it becomes much more difficult. But, I was committed to work harder than anyone else and graduated. Not only did I graduate, but I was promoted meritoriously to Private First Class for outstanding performance at the rifle range.

After graduation from Marine Corps Boot Camp, I was given 10 days leave to see my family and then I had to report to Fleet Marine Force 2nd Marine Division Camp LeJeune, North Carolina for assignment. I was assigned to Weapons Platoon, Delta Company, 1st Battalion, 8th Marines. I enjoyed the Marine Corps life; it gave me purpose and structure in my everyday life. For the next two months we were busy training for a deployment to Europe. I was really looking forward to the deployment and my first time leaving the country as an American Marine.

In January of 1978 we deployed to the Mediterranean Sea with the 6th Fleet as part of the 24th Marine Expeditionary Force. At the time, Castro had sent Cuban troops to Angola, Ethiopia, and Somalia. There was a lot of talk about American troops being sent to fight against the Cubans. Since I was the only Marine of Cuban descent, I used to get a lot of questions about what

I would do. I remember always saying, "I am an American Marine and that's my only allegiance." I have to admit that, secretly, I was hoping for a confrontation with Cuban troops, so I could make then pay for what they had done to my family and me. I harbored a lot of animosity against communism, and especially Cuban communists. Fortunately, or unfortunately, we were never deployed to Somalia; however, years later Marine units were deployed there. During this deployment, I came face to face with death for the first time. In our first military exercise off the coast of Sardegna, Italy, I was involved in a helicopter crash that killed three Marines and injured several others. We returned to the USA six months later on June of 1978.

We spent the next six months training and getting ready for another deployment. During that time, I was meritoriously promoted to E-3, Lance Corporal. An interesting story that I always like to tell occurred during this time. It is a perfect example of doing your job the best you can and sooner or later someone will notice, even if you are being discriminated against. I was an E-2, Private First Class, and the picture of a perfect Marine. Since I was in Weapons Platoon, my Platoon Sergeant was a Gunnery Sergeant. I was the only Hispanic in the unit, and it was pretty obvious that he did not like Hispanics. He would always give me the worst details and made my life difficult at every turn. I remember him walking by me singing Harry Belafonte's "Banana Boat Song." I have to admit that I came close to physically attacking him in moments of anger, but I contained myself. One day I was leaving the barracks for lunch and the First Sergeant, an old crusty Korean and Viet Nam vet, called me into his office. He said to me, "Frank I have been observing you and you are an outstanding Marine. I looked through your record and it is as clean as it can be. Why are you still a Private?" I was not going to rat out the "Gunny," so I just said, "I don't know, ask the Gunny." He just looked at me and said, "OK, I will look into it." The next day in the morning formation, the First Sergeant called my name out. I was surprised and had no idea what was going on, especially when the

Marine graduation picture (Francisco Pérez Sabatier).

First Sergeant never attended morning formation. Next thing I know, I am being presented with a hand-written document promoting me to E-3, Lance Corporal. I remember the First Sergeant whispering to me, "You will get the real one in a few days." Years later, when I was already a Miami-Dade Police officer, I was walking into the Youth Fair Grounds and I heard someone calling my name and it was that "Gunny." He had been a Marine Corp recruiter in Miami, met a Cuban American woman, and married her. He wanted to get together and be friends, but it was too much for me and I told him to go and "pound-sand."

In December of 1978, we were deployed again to the Mediterranean Sea with the 6th Fleet as part of the 24th Marine Expeditionary Force for another 6 months. This deployment was uneventful. By now, I was a 20-year old salty Marine and had a lot more fun than before. We stopped in Barcelona, Spain for 30 days, and I took the opportunity to go and visit our family's friend and benefactor, Josefa Martin. I had a great time meeting her and her family again. I stayed with them for a couple of weeks and would never forget how gracious they were to me, especially considering that I was just a former employee's son. I was able to visit many cities in Spain, France, Italy, and Greece. We returned to the USA in June of 1978.

Soon after, in September of 1979, we were deployed again with a Naval Fleet to be part of a NATO training operation for about 3 months. Our first stop was Southampton, England. I was always interested in visiting new places, and always took whatever opportunity I had to travel and see as much as I could. We were there for a couple of weeks and I took the opportunity to visit several places in England, including London. During this cruise, I was meritoriously promoted to E-4, Corporal. Soon after, we visited the Netherlands and then Norway. In Norway, we were part of a large NATO military exercise, and there I received my first of two Marine Corp Exceptional Service Awards. I was in charge of a small unit that was playing the part of a Guerrilla Unit fighting against the NATO forces. We were in the field for 30 days and were never captured. I was actually ordered to set up a defensive position and to allow the NATO units to find me because the exercise was ending. These 30 days were probably the toughest time I had in the Marine Corp. I always remember it because it was my birthday and I was cold, wet, and miserable averaging a couple hours of sleep a day. We returned to the USA soon after in November of 1979.

Between December 1979 and January of 1980, we were deployed to a 30-day "cruise" to the Caribbean. We visited the American Virgin Islands and then Puerto Rico. In Puerto Rico, we were part of a live ammunition training exercise at the Island of Vieques. I always remember that time because there were demonstrations about us training on the island. I believe that the military closed the base, and it is a national park now. We returned to Camp

Lejeune, North Carolina, and I requested leave to go home and see my family. After I returned to Camp LeJeune, my unit was placed on active reserve, which means that you must be ready to go at a minute's notice.

The Mariel Boatlift

On or about April 20, 1980, my unit was activated and within hours I was in a C130 cargo plane traveling to Key West. The Mariel boatlift had just started and they needed us there for security. We arrived in Key West without a place for our unit to "stay." We had to clear-up and clean some old naval barracks that had been closed since World War II, so we could have a place to sleep and store our gear. I remember working for over 48 hours nonstop and without any sleep trying to get things in order. Since I was one of the few Spanish speakers and a Cuban American, I was tasked with receiving everyone and explaining to them what was going to happen.

Dozens of watercrafts would arrive in Key West with refugees. They would be removed from the boats and put into buses, which then transported them to some old naval hangers where I was stationed. I would enter every bus and explain to them what we were doing and what was going to happen. Generally, everyone understood, but we encountered a few incidents. From April to May, almost all Mariel refugees that arrived in Key West were processed by me. We would divide all refugees into three categories, single males, single females, and families. There have been many things said about the Mariel boatlift refugees, and generally it is said that they were all criminals. I can say from personal experience that there were a lot of criminals and people with mental disorders, especially the single males and females, but the vast majority were no different than us. Just people trying to get away from an oppressive tyrannical communist regime. During those days, we had no cell phones and I personally spent hundreds of dollars, that I really could not afford to spend, calling their family members from a payphone trying to help them connect with relatives and family. During my time in Key West, I was interviewed by CNN about the Mariel boatlift as the only Cuban-American in that part of the Marine Corps Unit. Sometime in May of 1980, we were relieved by the Army 503rd Police Battalion from Fort Bragg, North Carolina. We were all awarded the Humanitarian Service Medal and a Certificate of Appreciation for exemplary service. We returned to Camp LeJeune, North Carolina.

Soon after returning to Camp LeJeune, North Carolina, my unit was deployed again with the 6th fleet, but this time we crossed the Suez Canal and were sent into the Persian Gulf because of the ongoing Iran Hostage Crisis. Besides doing a lot of waiting for President Carter to grow the "*cojones*" to do something, we spent most of our time training and followed-up with more training. I was also promoted meritoriously to E-5, Sergeant. We were in the Persian Gulf until late January of 1981. One of the things I remember about this deployment is when we crossed the Suez Canal. I was stationed on the USS Tarawa, a helicopter carrier that they had secured from flight deck operations. When the flight deck was secure, you could go up to the flight deck and we usually either did our daily 5-mile run or just went up to look around. I was surprised how narrow the canal was, and every mile or so they had artillery emplacements pointing towards the Sinai Peninsula. You could also see hundreds of military vehicles scattered on the sand rusting away. I assumed they were left over from the 1973 Yom Kippur war between Israel and Egypt. It was impressive and disheartening to see all those military vehicles in such a degrading state.

The 6th Fleet consists of 40 to 50 ships and they have to move tactically, so it took us weeks to move from the Persian Gulf, Arabian Sea, the Red Sea, Suez Canal, and then the Mediterranean Sea to Rota, Spain, where we met the new Fleet relieving us. Upon arrival at Rota, Spain, we were met there by the newly elected Vice President, George H. W. Bush, to thank us for a job well done. I always thought it was a great gesture (allowing the Vice President to visit us in the field) from the newly elected president, Ronald Regan. I always remember to this day that Jimmy Carter made me a Republican, and Ronald Regan made sure that I stayed one. The one thing I always took from my experience in the Persian Gulf is that we, as a nation, and the President, as our duly elected representative, cannot allow our nation to be "dragged through the mud" by anyone. President Carter looked like a weak and ineffectual leader, and when he finally attempted to do something, he completely failed. He launched Operation Eagle Claw too late and over the objection of his military advisers, costing eight American servicemen their lives. Ronald Regan, on the other hand, came across like a strong leader willing to do whatever it took to bring our people home. On January 21, 1981, just a few hours after Ronald Reagan delivered his inaugural address, the remaining hostages were released. They had been in captivity for 444 days.

In January of 1981, after I came back from the long deployment to the Persian Gulf, I was given a 30 day leave to go home. While at home, I reconnected with a high school female friend, who would become my wife and soul mate. I loved the Marine Corps and my plans were to re-enlist after my original 4 years were over, and I never thought of getting married and having a family that soon. A family was in my plans for the future, but not then. During my last year in the Marines, I started dating my wife Ofelia and the more serious our relationship got, the more I realized that the Marine Corps was not a place for a married man. I knew she was the "one" and I did not want anything to jeopardize our relationship and our future together. At that moment I made the decision that I would leave the Marines and seek employment with the Miami Dade Police Department, which was called the Public Safety Department at the time. I was honorably discharged from the Marine Corp in July of 1981.

During my time in the Marines, I was awarded many medals and commendations, including Good Conduct Medal, Humanitarian Medal, and two Marine Corps Exceptional Service Award Medals signed by the Secretary of the Navy for outstanding performance during NATO operations and the Key West Humanitarian Mission. I served in several deployments, including one to the Persian Gulf during the Iran Crisis. I was promoted meritoriously to every rank I obtained in the Marine Corp up to E-5 Sergeant. I was also recommended for Officer Candidate School, but declined when I made the decision to leave the Marines.

Life at MDPD and Beyond

On January 23, 1982, I married my wife Ofelia Alicia, my soul mate and mother of our three children Kristina Marie, Kristopher Michael and Katrina Marie. I applied for the Miami-Dade Police Department, and in March of 1982 I was accepted. I started the Academy on March 31, 1982; Basic Law Enforcement class, BLE 73. I graduated in October of 1982 and was assigned to the Kendall District where I went through riding assignments. At this juncture, I truly felt that I had achieved the "American Dream." I was living in the best country in the whole world, I had a job that I loved, and a beautiful and loving wife. For the next 34 years, I worked at the Miami-Dade Police Department in many duties and assignments. I retired in May 31, 2016, and I am enjoying my retirement.

I could write a full chapter just on my career at the Miami-Dade Police Department, but I don't think this is what this book is about. It is about the struggles the Cuban exiles have gone through

My wedding picture (Francisco Pérez Sabatier).

to get to a point in their life where they felt not only free, but that they had accomplished something meaningful in their life, worth all the hardship, adversity, and suffering that they and their family went through. I would be remiss if I didn't bring up a few incidents that happened at the beginning of my career with MDPD that illustrate the struggles that Cubans, and Hispanics in general, were still going through in the early 1980s.

The first incident occurred on my first day at the Kendall District station. It was a Monday and I was to report for the 3:00 p.m. to 11:00 p.m. shift. Like a good "Rookie," I was there almost an hour early. I was waiting by the mailboxes before it was time to walk into roll call. I am assuming it was really easy to tell that I was a Rookie; I am sure my age (24), my pressed uniform, and crew cut gave me away. An older Anglo gentleman (at that age everyone looked older) walked in and was going through his mail. He suddenly looked at me and said with a hostile and questioning voice: "Perez?" I responded: "Yes Sir." He looked at me up and down and said, "I know why you are here." I really did not know what he was talking about and I asked him, "What do you mean by that?" He responded, "You got to be a Police Officer because you are Hispanic, not because you are really qualified for the job." I took extreme offense to what he said, but I am not a fool, so I did not respond as I would today. I just said, "I was number one shooter in my class, was second in the physical fitness test, top ten academically (overall number one in my class), so I am sure you are correct." He did not say a word and walked away.

Another incident worth mentioning occurred on my second riding assignment. My Field Training Officer (FTO) took a day off and they assigned me to ride with a different FTO for the day. He was an Anglo Senior Officer, and extremely unfriendly and abrasive. We left the station and were driving south on SW 117 avenue, just north of SW 112 St along a neighborhood called Sabal Chase. There was a lawn service crew working on a yard and they all consisted of African Americans and Hispanics. He looked at me and said, "Look at all those "N word" and Spicks, that's all they are good for." Again, I had to play it smart and just ignored him. A good Hispanic friend from the academy, who was also assigned to Kendall District, quit the Police Department because he could not deal with all the harassment coming from his Anglo Field Training Office. Harassment directed to him only because he was Hispanic.

I always felt, and still do to this day, that those types of people are a minority. Good people always come forward to mitigate those bad ones. A perfect example of that was what happened to me while assigned to the Midnight Relief Squad. I was working for an extremely prejudiced Sergeant, one that on a daily basis would make fun of Hispanics. I was the hardest working officer in the squad and, not because I say so. The statistics backed me up. While working on that squad between 1984 and 1986, I was the Latin Officer of the Year and twice runner up for Officer of the Year. No matter what I did, he would not acknowledge it and he would not recommend me for any awards or commendations. It became so obvious that two Anglo Officers in the squad had a word with him and suggested for him to change his ways or else. He got his a few years later when he was kicked out of the Miami-Dade Police Department. Things steadily improved, and the more Hispanics got into command positions, the better it got.

I like to think that I served my country and my community honorably and I thank my parents every day for taking me out of the hellhole called Cuba. I truly believe that I would be dead today if they had not done so. I still have a lot of animosity towards the Cuban government and the Castro brothers for what they put my family through and I don't think that will ever change. I would love to visit Cuba one day with my family and show them where I spent the first 12 years of my life, but not until Cuba is free. I made an oath to never return as long as it was a communist country, and I am not breaking that oath. But, I do hope that I get to visit before "my time is up."

Miami-Dade graduation picture (Francisco Pérez Sabatier).

The one thing I hate the most about my life is that at times I feel like a man without a country. I can't go back to Cuba and I don't want to, but sometimes I feel like I don't belong here. I love this country more than life itself, and I have done everything that I could to belong and to make my adopted country proud of me. But still, at times, I feel like a man without a country. I don't know if it is just me feeling this way, but I've been here 45 years, I served my country, I served my community, I worked all my life and have been a model citizen, and still, at times, people make you feel like a second-rate citizen. I know that I should not let these people bother me, but they do.

Now, I am just enjoying my retirement, enjoying my three beautiful grandchildren Katalina Marie Gutierrez, Liam Konrad Lledo, and Viktor Xavier Gutierrez, and working on my golf game. I am also doing all the traveling that we can to enjoy the fruits of my labor. *Semper Fi!*

Epilogue

Ernest G. Vendrell

The idea for this book was first discussed between the editors in August of 2016. Initially, it was the dream of finding an avenue for sharing the personal stories of our families' trials and tribulations of leaving Cuba after Castro assumed power in 1959, taking the once prosperous island country on the road to communism and despair, and how our families acclimated to new lives in the United States. However, living in South Florida and being a part of the Cuban Exile Community also afforded us the opportunity to hear many accounts of the ordeals encountered by ordinary Cubans under Castro. Although there were many common threads to these stories, there was also a richness to the individual reports that deserved to be told. Each was different in its own way, primarily because of the adverse impact that it had on so many individuals and families. In effect, Cubans leaving the island were forced to leave everything behind, and in many cases, families were torn apart. Sadly, some exiles were never able to once again see family members that stayed behind for a variety of reasons. However, the Cuban Exile Community is also quite resilient, and the accounts that we heard chronicling various trials and challenges were often accompanied by inspiring stories of success in all facets of life in our new country. Thus, from its inception, the aim of this book was to provide a powerful account of the struggles, perseverance, and triumphs of the Cuban Exile Community, and how these factors combine to provide an enduring legacy for Cuban Americans everywhere.

Therefore, we began the process of assembling a group of authors willing to share the accounts of their families' Cuban Exile experience. Admittedly, this was not difficult to do. Before long, we had an excellent group of writers eager to share their families' stories, and each embarked on the journey as a labor of love, knowing full well the potential impact that this project could have on the Cuban Exile Community, both now and in the future. The authors were comprised of an artist, a housewife, retired law enforcement officers, retired military personnel, university professors, a screenwriter, and a business professional currently working in the banking industry. There were also survivors of the Cuban Resistance Movement and the Bay of Pigs Invasion. Additionally, there were those whose families who endured harsh treatment in forced labor camps or were imprisoned under false pretenses and bore torturous treatment at the hands of their captors. As many of the stories painfully detail, there was a heavy price to pay for those who did not support the Castro Revolution, and the various accounts provide a glimpse of the abuses encountered by so many ordinary Cubans who found themselves under the oppressive authority of the Castro government.

However, as mentioned at the start of this book, the various stories do not constitute a historical account of Cuba, nor is this a book about Fidel Castro. There are other books that cover these topics. The backdrop of the abuses and executions suffered by so many Cubans on the island once Castro assumed power, as well as the resulting exodus of refugees over a prolonged period, only serve as historical context for these stories. Instead, these are stories about real people, how they overcame a myriad of obstacles under very difficult circumstances, and how they continue to thrive in a welcoming country.

Unfortunately, to this day, there are many Cubans who continue to suffer at the hands of the Castro government, imprisoned or harassed for simply disagreeing with the communist ideology and failing to toe the line, so-to-speak. Oftentimes, their predicament is not reported in the international media, and many languish in confinement or isolation with little hope for the future. Their accounts are part of the overall story of the Cuban Exile experience, and it is hoped that one day, they too will be able to make the journey to freedom. As Cuban Americans, we can offer them hope in how we live our lives as contributing members of society, making the most of our cherished freedoms. In the meantime, we cannot forget those that are oppressed, providing our brothers and sisters assistance and support whenever and wherever possible.

In closing, through stories detailing a multitude of struggles, and the sacrifices that were needed to overcome various challenges, this book has illustrated how the human spirit cannot be broken. To the Cuban American Community, freedom is not an abstract concept. Instead, it is a valuable reality that so many sacrificed to attain once again after it was abruptly taken from their midst by a repressive communist government. Viewed from this perspective, it is the sincere hope of all those who contributed to this effort, that the book provides a lasting legacy to the Cuban Exile Community, while serving as an inspiration to future generations of Cuban Americans.

About the Contributors

Corina **Fernandez-Máscaró** was born in Santiago de Cuba. In 1962, she left Cuba with her family and settled in Independence, Missouri, where she obtained BA and MA degrees in French and Spanish literature and taught both languages while working on her MA. She later pursued an MBA with an emphasis in finance. She is a consultant for CSMB International, Inc.

Diego Luis **Mella** was born in Guantánamo, Cuba, in 1949. He fled Cuba by swimming across Guantánamo Bay and entered the U.S. Naval base in 1969. After processing, he moved to Miami to be reunited with relatives. He served with distinction in the Army Air Defense Center, was later a police officer and was recruited into the U.S. Army Management Staff College. In 2009, he accepted a position as Professional Mentor to the Chief of Operations of the Afghan Police, in Afghanistan. He is semi-retired and working on his memoirs while providing consulting services.

Eloy L. **Nuñez** is an associate professor at Saint Leo University. Born in Havana, he immigrated to the United States with his family in 1960. He obtained a Ph.D. in global leadership from Lynn University. His research focuses on the unintended consequences of corporate social responsibility and how it pertains to anti-globalization protest groups that target specific corporations. He has over 26 years of law enforcement leadership experience; his career has included stints in organized crime investigations, robbery and burglary suppression, and uniformed road patrol and field training.

Mirta Solis **Nuñez** was born in Santa Clara, Las Villas, Cuba, in 1946. In 1958 she attended Lestonnac School in Havana but in 1960 was exiled to South Florida. She graduated in 1963 from Immaculata Academy in Miami and later attained an Associate in Arts from Miami Dade College. For 46 years, she worked in several organizations in the Miami-Dade County area, doing secretarial and administrative assistant work before retiring in 2014.

Ramón Luis **Núñez** was born in 1939 in Marianao, Cuba. In 1960, he left Cuba with his father and settled in Miami, where both were granted political asylum. In 1963 he enlisted in the U.S. Army, where he served until 1969 as member of the U.S. Army Reserves. In 1977, he received a BS in electrical engineering from the University of Miami and later a degree in fine arts, suma cum laude, from Florida International University. He worked for Florida Power & Light Company for 26 years and joined Miami-Dade County Public Schools as a Construction Project Manager. In 2002, he retired from the engineering world and pursued a new dream in the fine arts world.

Luis O. **Rodriguez** retired from Miami-Dade Police Department after a distinguished 29-year career. During those years, he was assigned to several investigative bureaus. His area of expertise focused on international and domestic terrorism, specifically related to the activities of the Cuban government and also Cuban exiles in the U.S., Latin America and the Caribbean. He attained a BS in management and public administration degree from Barry University. He is part owner of Moonstone Investigations and Security.

Francisco Pérez **Sabatier** was born in Pinar del Río, Cuba. He left Cuba with his parents and brother in 1971 and settled in Madrid, Spain. In 1973, he settled in Miami and after graduating from high school in 1976, joined the U.S. Marine Corps, where he served with distinction for 4 years, receiving numerous decorations. In 1982 he joined the Miami-Dade Police Department. During his 34 years at the MDPD, he worked in a number of positions and assignments, including homicide, major fraud investigations and computer forensics. He retired from the MDPD in 2016.

Ernest G. **Vendrell** is a professor as well as the associate director for the Department of Public Safety Administration at Saint Leo University. He has been teaching at the college level since 1995, primarily in the areas of emergency and disaster management, public administration, and criminal justice. He earned a Ph.D. in public administration and policy and was awarded a Fulbright Scholarship in police studies and was a visiting fellow at the University of Leicester, Scarman Centre for the Study of Public Order. He retired from the Miami-Dade Police Department after serving 27 years in a variety of patrol, investigative, administrative, and supervisory assignments. He lives with his wife, Gemma, and his son, Christopher Nicolas, in Weston, Florida. His son David Ernesto lives in Los Angeles, California.

David Ernesto **Vendrell** graduated from Biola University in 2015 with a Bachelor's degree in Cinema and Media Arts and a minor in Biblical Studies. He is currently attending Southern New Hampshire University, where he is pursuing a Master's degree in English Literature. David has spent the past four years working in development around Hollywood at companies such as Paramount Pictures, Heyday Films, and OddLot Entertainment. Now a professional screenwriter based out of Los Angeles, California, he has written content in features, television, and digital entertainment. David is always looking for ways to share adventures through storytelling.

Oscar **Vigoa** is a professor in the Criminal Justice Department at Florida International University. He teaches undergraduate and graduate level criminal justice courses along with classes in leadership and global and international terrorism and homeland security. Born in Havana in 1955, he immigrated to the U.S. at age 7 (under the Pedro Pan Project). He obtained an associate degree in criminology and psychology from Miami-Dade Community College in 1978 and graduated from the Public Safety Department Police Academy later that year. In 2010 he finished his Ph.D. in global leadership at Lynn University. He has over 33 years of law enforcement leadership experience.

Glossary

"Abajo Batista!"—"Down with (Fulgencio) Batista."
Abuela—Grandmother.
Abuelo—Grandfather.
Academia Torrado—Private preparatory school in Morón, Cuba, pre–Castro.
Acción Católica—Catholic Youth Group at the time of Fidel Castro's rise to power.
Agrarian Reform—1961 agrarian reform led to the confiscation of land by the Castro government.
Alfabetización—1961 Castro government literacy campaign that was really intended to recruit government support and spread communist propaganda.
Almendares River—River in the western part of Cuba. A part of the river flows through the city of Havana.
Apátridas—One lacking a nationality. A derogatory term for Cubans seeking to leave the island.
Artime, Manuel Francisco—Mission Commander for the Centro Frente Cubano Democratico, a CIA-sponsored Cuban Exile Organization dedicated to the overthrow of Fidel Castro.
Azores Islands—Portuguese archipelago in the Atlanta Ocean.
Bahia de Cochinos—The Bay of Pigs was the site of the failed 1961 invasion of Cuba.
Bahía Honda—An island situated in the lower part of the Florida Keys.
Balsero—Rafter. Refers to Cubans who fled the island on makeshift rafts and boats.
Baracoa, Cuba—A city in Guantánamo Province on the eastern end of Cuba.
Barajas Airport—The main international airport serving Madrid, Spain.
Barrio—Neighborhood.
Batabanó, Cuba—Municipality situated along the southern coast of Cuba in Mayabeque Province.
Batista, Fulgencio—Former President of Cuba (1940–45, 1952–59).

Battle, Jose Miguel—Cuban-American organized crime figure known as "El Padrino." Battle died in prison in 2007.

Battle of Ceja del Negro—Bloody battle for Cuban independence fought on October 4, 1896, near Viñales, Pinar del Río, wherein Mambí Cuban General Antonio Maceo defeated Spanish forces.

Bay of Pigs (Bahía de Cochinos)—Site of the ill-fated military invasion of Cuba in 1961 by the CIA-sponsored Brigade 2506.

Bay of Pigs Invasion—Ill-fated invasion of Cuba on April 16, 1961, by approximately 1,400 CIA-sponsored Cuban exiles at the Bay of Pigs on the south coast of Cuba.

Bodega—Small food store.

Bolita—Illegal lottery originating in Cuba and popular in some Hispanic neighborhoods in the United States.

Boniato Prison—A prison in Santiago de Cuba where many political prisoners were held in deplorable conditions.

Borbón, Don Juan Carlos de—Former King of Spain (1975–2014).

Border Battalion—Military group surrounding the U.S. Naval Base in Guantanamo Bay in 1969.

Boza-Masvidal, Msgr. Eduardo—Auxiliary Bishop of the Archdioceses of Havana in 1960.

Brigade 2506 (Brigada Asalto 2506)—Brigade 2506 was a CIA-sponsored group of Cuban freedom fighters that was formed to overthrow the Castro government. Many lost their lives or were imprisoned in the ill-fated Bay of Pigs Invasion. There is a monument to their bravery and perseverance in Miami.

Brothers to the Rescue (BTTR)—Anti-Castro, Cuban exile organization dedicated to rescuing rafters fleeing the island.

Caballería—Latin American measure of land. One caballería equals approximately 33 acres.

Caballero-Brunet, Juan—Attorney, former Congressman, and Director of the Interior Ministry under the Batista government. He later became a university professor in the United States.

La Cabaña Prison (Cabana Fortress)—Stone fortress located in Havana, Cuba, that was used as a military headquarters and prison. Ernesto "Che" Guevara oversaw the tribunals and executions of many political prisoners there.

Cafecito—Strong Cuban coffee served in a small cup.

Calle Ocho (S.W. 8th Street)—The main thoroughfare in Little Havana known for authentic Cuban food, good Cuban coffee, etc.

Camagüey, Cuba—City in central Cuba. It is the capital of Camagüey Province.

Camagüey Province, Cuba—Cuba's largest province. The capital city is Camagüey.

Camp Lejeune—U.S. Marine Corps base located in North Carolina.

Camy Ice Cream—Popular ice cream in Madrid, Spain, in the early 1970s.

218 Glossary

Canary Islands—Spanish archipelago consisting of seven main islands situated in the Atlantic Ocean approximately 60 miles from the country of Morocco.

Cándido González Stadium—Multi-use stadium in Camagüey, Cuba.

Casa de Huéspedes—A guesthouse.

Casas-Romero, Luis—Cuban composer and flute player known for his recording of "El Mambi" and much other classic Cuban music.

Castillo de San Marcos—Located on the shores of Matanzas Bay in the City of St. Augustine, Florida. It is considered the oldest masonry fort in the U.S.

Castro's Agrarian Reform—Castro's Agrarian Reform Law in 1959 led to land distribution.

Cayo Carenas (El Cayo)—Small key in the Bay of Cienfuegos.

Celda Tapiada ("Tapiada" Cell)—A dark punishment jail cell used in Cuba. Typically, it has a solid steel door instead of bars and no windows.

Celia Cruz—Popular Cuban singer known as the "Queen of Salsa" who passed away in the United States in 2003 as a Cuban exile.

Central Hershey, Cuba—Cuban town approximately 34 miles east of Havana that was originally built by the Hershey Chocolate Company.

Central Lugareño—Sugar refinery in Camagüey Province.

Centro Frente Cubano Democratico—CIA-sponsored Cuban exile organization dedicated to the overthrow of Fidel Castro.

Cienfuegos, Cuba—City situated along the Bay of Cienfuegos on Cuba's south coast.

El Cobre, Cuba—Town in what was once known as Oriente Province (present-day Homonym Province).

Cochino—Pig (pork).

Colegio de Belén—Prestigious Jesuit school in Havana, Cuba until 1961 when the school was closed by the Castro government. The school was re-established in Miami, Florida, the same year.

Columbia Military Headquarters—A prestigious army garrison in the City of Havana pre–Castro.

Comillas, Madrid—A neighborhood in Madrid, Spain.

Comité—Comites de Defensa de la Revolucion (CDR) was a Castro government program that selected one residence and its occupants on every city block to act as the "eyes and ears" of the government. In essence, it was a system of spies in all of the neighborhoods in Cuba that identified and kept track of potential dissidents.

Compañero—Comrade.

Company of Mary—Order of nuns active in Cuba at the time of the Castro Revolution.

La Coubre—French freighter that exploded in Havana Harbor on March 4, 1960, while it was unloading 76 tons of munitions.

Cuartel Loma de los Coches—Military headquarters in Pinar del Río where men and boys were executed by firing squad.

Cuban Dominoes—Considered the national game of Cuba. Two teams of two partners sit around a table, typically outdoors, to play the game.

Cuban Missile Crisis (October Missile Crisis, 1962)—Confrontation between the United States and the Soviet Union over nuclear missiles in Cuba.

Cubana Airlines—Cuba's largest airline.

Dictator Machado—President Gerardo Machado y Morales (1925–1933).

DIER—Military police of the Departamento de Inteligencia Ejército Revolucionario.

Dominicanas Francesas Catholic School—Catholic school for girls in Havana, Cuba, pre–Castro.

El Encanto—Luxury department store in Havana in pre–Castro Cuba.

"Un enemigo de la revolución"—"An enemy of the revolution."

Esbirro—Refers to government henchman or minion.

Escambray Mountains—Mountain range in the central region of Cuba.

Escolapios de Guanabacoa—Catholic boarding school near the City of Havana pre–Castro.

Escoria—Human waste or scum. Name given by the Castro government to those wishing to leave the Island of Cuba.

Escuela al Campo—Initial school at the farm for students was implemented in the 1960s. Attendance was mandatory for 45 days during the summer break. It took children away from their families to work long hours in the fields. Children were thus indoctrinated with communist propaganda while far away from the protection of their families.

Escuela en el Campo—The mandatory Escuela al Campo during the summer break later became mandatory year-round school at the farm.

El Estadio Vicente Calderón—Home stadium of the soccer club Atlético Madrid until it was closed in 2017.

Estrada Palma, Tomas—Became the 1st President of the Cuban Republic in 1902.

Fernandez-Máscaró, Dr. Guillermo—Medical doctor who was one of the founders of Cuba's Republican Party. During his political career he was twice elected to Cuba's House of Representatives, was Governor of Oriente Province, and was an Ambassador to Mexico.

"Fidel, esta es tu casa!"—"Fidel, this is your house." Phrase often heard repeated by supporters of the revolution once Castro assumed power.

Fidelista—A supporter of Fidel Castro.

Florida City—Community in southern Miami-Dade County, Florida.

El Floridita—Famous bar that Ernest Hemingway used to frequent when visiting Havana, Cuba.

Fountain of Youth—A spring that is supposed to restore the youth of those who drink from its waters. The Fountain of Youth Archaeological Park is located in St. Augustine, Florida.

Franco, Generalíssimo Francisco—Francisco Franco-Bahamonde was a Spanish general who ruled Spain from 1939 to 1975 under a military dictatorship.

Fuerza Aérea Rebelde—Known as the Cuban Air Force Headquarters in Havana prior to Fidel Castro seizing power.

Garcia Line—Shipping line used to transport members of Brigade 2506 from Guatemala to Nicaragua.

Gonzalez, Eduardo "Eddie"—Former Deputy Director of the Miami-Dade Police Department, Chief of the Tampa Police Department, and Director of the U.S. Marshals Service.

González, Elián—Young Cuban boy found stranded at sea with 2 other survivors after fleeing Cuba for the United States in 2000. Among those losing their lives was the boy's mother. An ensuing international custody and immigration battle resulted in the boy being returned to his father in Cuba by the Clinton Administration.

Goya, Madrid—A neighborhood in Madrid, Spain.

Granma—Yacht used to transport the 82 members of the 26th of July Movement, including Fidel Castro, from Mexico to Cuba in 1956.

Guajiro—Country person.

Guanabacoa, Cuba—Town in the Province of La Habana.

Guanito—Government hospital where electric shocks were used to "correct" the political leanings of dissidents.

Guantánamo, Cuba—City in southeast Cuba within close proximity to Guantanamo Bay.

Guaso River—River in the City of Guantánamo.

Guayabera—A traditional Latin American shirt originating in Cuba.

Guevara, Ernesto "Che"—Argentine Marxist revolutionary who assisted Fidel Castro in overturning the Batista government in the late 1950s. Guevara is responsible for the death of many political prisoners.

Güines, Cuba—Municipality approximately 31 miles southeast of the City of Havana.

Gusanos—Worms. Derogatory term given to Cubans seeking to leave the island for the United States.

La Habana Vieja—Old Havana.

Hialeah, Florida—City situated in Miami-Dade County, Florida.

Hispanic American Police Command Officers Association—National organization consisting of Hispanic police executives from across the United States.

Hispanic Police Officers Association—Association dedicated to advancing the careers of Hispanics at the Miami Dade Police Department.

Holguin, Cuba—City in eastern Cuba, and the capital of present day Holquin Province.

Hombrecito—Little Man

Homestead, Florida—A city in southern Miami-Dade County.

Hotel Leamington—Hotel in downtown Miami in 1960.

Hotel Nacional—Historic hotel located along the Malecón in Havana, Cuba.

"Houston" (Vessel)—Vessel used to transport members of Brigade 2506 to Cuba.

Huelga—A worker's strike.

Immaculata Academy—Catholic school in Miami, Florida, which would later change its name to Immaculata-LaSalle.

Instituto #1 de la Segunda Enseñanza—High school in Havana, Cuba, pre-Castro.

El Instituto San Isidro—Prestigious Catholic school in Madrid, Spain, in the early 1970s.

Integrado Militar Osvaldo Sanchez—A boarding school for children with anti-Castro attitudes.

La Internationale—Communist anthem.

Inventory (Inventoria)—Consisted of inspecting and cataloging a home's possessions once the resident(s) notified the government of their intention to leave the island. It was a time of stress for families, since household members would be held accountable for any "missing" items at the time of departure and travel plans would be cancelled.

Isla de Pinos—Known today as Isla de la Juventud, this island is situated south of the Cuban mainland near Havana and Pinar del Río. The island has been used to detain many political prisoners.

JM Trax Base—CIA-sponsored training base in Guatemala.

José Martí International Airport—International airport located near Havana, Cuba.

Jovellanos, Cuba—Town in the Matanzas Province of Cuba.

Juicio de los Pilotos—The 1959 trial of a group of Cuban air force pilots, gunners, and mechanics that had served under the Batista government. The men were falsely accused of inciting revolution and committing genocide.

Kangaroo Court—A court that disregards recognized standards of law and justice.

Kennedy-Khrushchev Pact—Agreement reached between President John F. Kennedy and Soviet leader Nikita Khrushchev in 1962. The Soviets would remove nuclear missiles in exchange for the U.S. agreeing not to invade Cuba in the future.

LaSalle Catholic School, Havana—Catholic school in Havana pre-Castro.

222   Glossary

LaSalle Catholic School, Santiago de Cuba—Catholic school in Santiago de Cuba in the early 1960s.

Latifundistas—Term used by Castro government to describe wealthy landowners who exploited workers.

Lawton, Cuba—Neighborhood in Havana, Cuba.

Lestonnac Academy—Elementary school in the Biltmore Section of Havana.

Little Havana (La Pequeña Habana)—Neighborhood in Miami known as the center of social, cultural, and political activity for Cuban exiles.

Los Palacios, Cuba—Municipality in the Province of Pinar del Río.

Luyanó, Cuba—Neighborhood in the City of Havana.

Machado y Morales, Gerardo—President of Cuba from 1925–33. He was also a former general during the Cuban War of Independence (1895–98).

Malecón, Havana—Long esplanade and seawall that stretches for approximately 5 miles along the City of Havana coastline.

Malena del Sur, Cuba—Municipality in what is now the Province of Mayabeque.

Manzanares River—A river in central Spain which passes through Madrid.

Mariano Beach, Cuba—A suburb of Havana, Cuba.

Mariel Boatlift—Mass emigration of approximately 125,000 Cuban refugees from the Port of Mariel in Cuba to the United States.

Marielitos—Name given to those who departed Cuba in 1980 from the port city of Mariel.

Martí, José—Cuban national hero who became a symbol for Cuba's struggle for independence from Spain in the 19th Century.

Las Martinas, Cuba—Region in Pinar del Río Province, Cuba.

Mary Immaculate Catholic School—Catholic school in Key West, Florida in the early 1960s.

Masferrer, Rolando "El Tigre"—Anti-Castro Cuban exile leader killed by a car bomb in Miami in 1975.

"Me abstengo a declarer"—Declarative statement that the accused will not provide any incriminating statement.

Melrose—Neighborhood in Miami-Dade County, Florida.

Miami-Dade Police Department—Largest police agency in Miami-Dade County, Florida. Previously known as the Dade County Public Safety Department.

Mid-day Siesta—Custom in Cuba, as in many Latin American countries, to close at 12 noon and then re-open at 2:00 pm.

Miami Lakes, Florida—Town in northern Miami-Dade County, Florida.

Miami Freedom Tower—Designated as a U.S. National Historic Landmark in 2008 for its role in processing thousands of Cuban exiles.

Miami Springs, Florida—Municipality in Miami-Dade County, Florida.

Milian, Emilio—News Director of radio station WQBA who spoke up about anti-Castro violence. He narrowly survived a car bombing in 1976.

Miliciano—Member of Castro's militia.

Minas de Matahambre—Town in Pinar del Río Province.

Mojito—Traditional Cuban cocktail.

Moré, Benny—Famous Cuban singer, songwriter, and bandleader. He died in 1963.

Morón, Cuba—City in the Province of Camagüey (present-day Ciego de Ávila Province).

Naval Blockade of Cuba—U.S. naval blockade of Cuba that was imposed on October 22, 1962, to prevent further Soviet nuclear missiles from reaching Cuba.

Nochebuena—Christmas Eve.

"Nos Jodimos"—"We are done for" or "We are screwed," etc.

Nueva Cocina—Miami-based Latin foods company founded in 2010 by Corina Fernandez-Mascaro and Celeste de Armas.

Nueva Gerona, Isla de Pinos—Capital city of the Isle of Pines (known today as Isla de la Juventud).

The Old Man and the Sea—Ernest Hemingway's classic story about an old fisherman that struggles with a giant marlin.

Oliva, Erneido—2nd in command of the Centro Frente Cubano Democratico, a CIA-sponsored Cuban exile organization dedicated to the overthrow of Fidel Castro.

Operation Pedro Pan—Freedom flights from Cuba to the United States from 1960–1962. Created by Father Bryan O. Walsh, Director of the Catholic Welfare Bureau.

Oriente Province—One of the six provinces of Cuba until 1976; situated in the eastern part of the country.

Palenque, Cuba—A municipality in the Oriente Province of Cuba (present-day Guantanamo Province).

Paredón—The infamous execution wall, where many Cubans faced the firing squad.

Paris Treaty—Officially ended the Spanish American War of 1898.

El Parque del Retiro—Large public park in the center of Madrid.

Party Line—Telephone lines in the 1960s used by multiple households.

The Patana (small pier)—American bunker in Guantanamo Bay in 1969.

Pearl of the Antilles—Cuba is often referred to as the Pearl of the Antilles because of its beauty and abundant natural resources.

Perez-Clausel, Comandante—Commander of the Rural Guard in Güines, Cuba, pre-Castro.

Picadillo—Traditional Cuban dish made with ground beef and other ingredients, and typically served with rice.

224   Glossary

Las Piedras, Puerto Rico—Small city near San Juan, Puerto Rico.

Pina, Cuba—Town in the Province of Camagüey (present-day Ciego de Ávila Province).

Pinar del Río—City and the capital of Pinar del Río Province in Western Cuba.

Pionero—Focused on teaching the principles of communism. Membership was required of all school-aged children. Members were required to wear a uniform with a red scarf.

Platt Amendment—Led to 1903 treaty between the U.S. and Cuba that gave the U.S. the right to intervene in Cuban affairs.

Playa Girón—Landing site for the ill-fated 1961 Bay of Pigs invasion.

Playa Larga—Landing site for the ill-fated 1961 Bay of Pigs invasion.

Plaza de Armas—The oldest square in the City of Havana.

Plaza de San Francisco—Plaza facing Havana Harbor.

Previsora Latino America—Bank specializing in real estate development in Havana, Cuba, pre–Castro.

El Principe Fortress—Military fort in Havana, Cuba.

Quinceañera or Quince—Right of Passage for every Cuban girl.

Radio Morón—Radio station in Morón, Cuba, in 1960.

Rancho-Boyeros Airport—Airport in Havana, Cuba, that is known today as José Martí International Airport.

Rebeldes—Rebels.

Retouleo Air Base—CIA-sponsored training base in Guatemala.

La Revolución (the revolution)—Refers to the communist revolution in Cuba.

Río Piedras, Puerto Rico—A former municipality of Puerto Rico, it became a part of the capital city of San Juan in 1951.

Rota, Spain—Municipality in southern Spain where the U.S. maintains an important military installation.

Sabal Chase, Miami—Neighborhood in Miami-Dade County, Florida.

Sam DeCavalcante—Former head of Northern New Jersey organized crime, who is also known as "Sam the Plumber."

San Basilio el Magno Seminary—Seminary in the City of El Cobre in Oriente Province in the mid 1960s.

Sandino, Cuba—Town in Pinar del Río Province.

Santa Clara, Cuba—City in the central region of Cuba. It is the capital city of the Province of Villa Clara (formerly the Province of Las Villas).

Santa Fe, Cuba—Coastal neighborhood in Havana.

Santa Teresita—Name of farm owned by the Solis-Mazzaredo Family.

Santiago de Cuba—Cuba's second largest city situated in the southeast part of the island. Previously situated in Oriente Province (present-day Santiago de Cuba Province).

São Miguel—The largest island in the Portuguese archipelago of the Azores Islands.

Servitec—Aerial photography, mapping, and surveying company in business in Cuba prior to Fidel Castro seizing control of the government in 1959.

Siboney Beach—Beach located near Santiago de Cuba.

Sierra de los Órganos—Mountain range in the Province of Pinar del Río in Western Cuba.

Sierra Maestra—Mountain range that runs westward across the south of the old Oriente Province of Cuba (now mainly in Santiago de Cuba and Granma Provinces).

Society of Jesus—Jesuit Order that was expelled from Cuba in 1961.

Sosa-Blanco, Jesús—Batista government Colonel who was falsely accused and tried in 1959 at the Havana Sports Palace in front of approximately 17,000 spectators. He was found guilty and executed.

South Beach—Neighborhood in Miami Beach, Florida.

Southeast Florida Institute of Criminal Justice—Known today as the School of Justice, Public Safety and Law Studies at Miami Dade College, North Campus.

Spanish "Concentración" of the 1890s—Spanish policy of moving civilians into concentration camps during the Cuban War of Independence.

Tomeguin—A type of Cuban finch.

13 de Marzo—The July 13, 1994, sinking of the tugboat "13 de Marzo." Forty-one Cubans attempting to flee the island lost their lives at the hands of the Cuban Coast Guard.

Trompos—Refers to a spinning top.

23 de Noviembre—Anti-Castro dissident group on the island of Cuba in 1959.

26th of July Movement—Revolutionary organization led by Fidel Castro that overthrew the government of Fulgencio Batista in 1959. The basis behind the name of the organization is the Moncada Barracks attack led by Fidel Castro that took place on July 26, 1953, in Santiago de Cuba.

UMAP—"Military Units to Aid Production" were "rehabilitating" centers for individuals that the Cuban government labeled as deviant or "politically immoral."

Union City, New Jersey—City in northern New Jersey where a large number of Cuban exiles settled following Fidel Castro's rise to power.

University of Havana—Oldest university in Cuba, established in 1728. The university was the site of anti-government protests prior to Fidel Castro seizing power in 1958.

University of Villanueva—Universidad Catolica de Santo Tomas de Villanueva (St. Thomas of Villanueva Catholic University) was a private Catholic university in Havana, Cuba, founded by American Augustinians. The Augustinians were expelled from Cuba in 1961 and the university was confiscated by the Castro government. Former faculty members established what is now St. Thomas University in Miami Gardens, Florida.

Valladares, Armando—A Cuban political prisoner who endured much hardship at the hands of the Castro government. He authored the book "Against All Hope."

Varadero Beach, Cuba—Popular beach resort town in the Province of Matanzas.

Vedado—Business district and urban neighborhood in the City of Havana.

Velocipedo—Small tricycle.

Las Villas Province—One of the 6 provinces of Cuba until 1976.

Vista Alegre—Suburb of Santiago de Cuba.

"Viva Cristo Rey!"—"Long live Christ the King."

"!Viva Cuba Libre!"—"Long live a free Cuba."

Walker Park—Neighborhood park in Hialeah, Florida.

Walsh, Monsignor Bryan O.—Played a crucial role in Operation Pedro Pan, which brought thousands of Cuban children to the United States from 1960–1962. At the time, he was the Director of the Catholic Welfare Bureau.

Westchester—A neighborhood in Miami-Dade County, Florida.

Yo-Yo Fishing Line—A Cuban hand-fishing system that does not use a rod or reel.

Index

A B Malone Company 137
Abajo Batista! 140
abuelos 114
Academia Torrado 95
Acción Catolica 143
Afghanistan 59, 88, 89, 213
Agrarian Reform 9, 142, 173, 178, 191
Aguado, Primitivo 159, 160
Air International 28, 30, 31, 33
alfabetisación 9
Almejeiras, Efigenio 159
Almendares River 26
Alonso, Manrique 28
Alvarez, Miguel 157
American Legion 60
American Red Cross 105
Angola 17, 18, 163, 202
apátridas 11
Apex Photography 31, 56
Apple, Art 56
Arabian Sea 206
Artime, Manuel Francisco 156
Associated Photographers 31, 56, 67, 70
el avispón verde 30
Azores Islands 197, 198

B-26 Aircraft 49, 67, 158
Bacardi 98
Bahamas 106
Bahía de Cochinos 15; *see also* Bay of Pigs
Bahía Honda, Florida Keys 45
balseros 11
Baracoa, Cuba 81
Barajas Airport, Madrid 198
Barcelona, Spain 204
barrio 8, 135
Batabanó, Cuba 26
Batista, Fulgencio 1, 5, 116, 139, 153, 172
Battle, Jose Miguel 83, 84
Bay of Pigs 15, 31, 55, 58, 75, 121, 148, 162, 163, 175, 211; *see also* Bahia de Cochinos
Blanco, Manolo 57, 59, 60, 62

Blanco-Navarro, Carmen 57
Blanco-Navarro, Mercedes 57
Blanco-Navarro, Renaldo 51, *63*
BLE 73 207
bodega 47, 120, 199
Boitel, Pedro Luis 173
bolita 17
Boniato Prison 75
Booker T. Washington High School, Miami 177
Border Battalion 77
Boza-Masvidal, Msgr. Eduardo 29, 30
Brigade 2506 (Brigada 2506) 58, 75, 153, 157, ***162***
Brito, Eulalio 172, ***178***
Brito, Jorge 172, ***177***, ***178***
Brito, Jose Gabriel ***178***
Brothers to the Rescue 17, 163
Broward County, Florida 60
Buria, Luis Delfin 25
Bush, President George W. 206

caballería 138
Caballero, Juan 101, 103
Cabaña (La Cabaña) 15, 51, 52, 155, 156, 173, 174
Cabrera, Eudaldo 108
Cabrera, Josefina 108
Cadena Azul 106
cafecitos 112
Calle Ocho (S.W. 8th Street) 56
Camagüey 90, 92, 94, 98, 164, 165, 166
Camp Lejeune, North Carolina 202, 205
Campeneria Angel, Virgilio 173
Camy Ice Cream 199
Canada 62, 103, 149, 151
Canada Dry 98
Canary Islands 8, 97, 191
Cándido González Stadium 166
Carter, Pres. Jimmy 206
Casas Romero, Luis 166
Case de Huéspedes 198

Castillo de San Marcos 64
Castro, Raul 17, 139, 164
Catholic Charities 136
Catholic Church 33, 55, 76, 119, 123, 124, 132, 136, 185
Cayo Carenas (El Cayo) 145
Ceja del Negro 15
Celda Tapiada ("Tapiada" Cell) 17
Celia Cruz 16
Central Hershey, Cuba 134
Central Intelligence Agency (CIA) 31, 156, 157
Central Lugareño 167
Centro Frente Cubano Democratico 156
Charron Williams Commercial School, Miami 150
Cherry Hill, New Jersey 105
Choren, Eddie **170**, **171**
Choren, Henry 169, **170**, **171**
Cienfuegos, Cuba 99, 145
Cinfuegos, Osmani 160
Citrus Elementary School 177
City of Miami Police 63
Ciudad Deportiva 155, 160, 161
CNN 205
Cochino Pig (pork) 117
Colegio de Belén 93
Colegio del Sagrado Corazon Vista Alegre, Cuba 181
Colgate/Palmolive Company 74
Collingswood, New Jersey 105
The Colonial (El Colonial) 31, 54, 55, 56
Columbia Military Headquarters 154
Comillas, Madrid 199
Comité 118, 120, 121, 134, 190, 194; see also Committees for the Defense of the Revolution
Committees for the Defense of the Revolution (CDR) 9, 11; see also comité
compañero 77
Company of Mary 140
Concentración 5
Congo, Africa 17, 32
Coral Park High School, Miami 61
Cosa Nostra 17
La Coubre 26
Cruz, Tomas 161
CSMB International, Inc. 188, 213
Cuartel Loma de los Coches 15
Cuban Air Force 23, 24, 67, 158
Cuban Mafia 18
Cuban Missile Crisis (October Missile Crisis, 1962) 31, 54, 175
Cubana Airlines 16, 197

Daytona Beach, Florida 106
De Armas, Celeste 187, **188**
De Borbón, Don Juan Carlos, 199
DeCavalcante, Sam 84
De la Torre, Diego 89
De la Torre, Nilda 89

Delgado, Dennis **163**
Delgado, Jesus 153, ***163***
Delta Airlines 32
Delta Company 202
Del Vecchio, Joseph 124, 125, 126, 136
Del Vecchio, Josephine 125, 126, 136
Del Vecchio, Marianne 124, 136
Del Vecchio, Matthew 124, 125, 136
Diaz, Benigno 29
Diaz, Daniel 108
Diaz, Delvin 108
Diaz, Jessica 108
Diaz, Ofelia 108
Diaz, Velentin 27
Díaz-Balart, Rafael 104
DIER (Departamento de Inteligencia Ejercito Revolucionario) 25, 26
Dominican Republic 106
Dominicanas Francesas Catholic School 93
dominoes 16
Don Tomás Estrada Palma 5
Donovan, James 161
Dresden, Germany 180

Eastern Airlines 168
Eisenhower, Dwight D. 31
El Cobre, Cuba 76
El Paso, Texas 82
El Encanto 141
"Un enemigo de la revolución" 143
esbirro 154
Escambray Mountains 10, 155, 159
Escolapios de Guanabacoa 92
escoria 11
Escuela al Campo 195; see also Escuela en el Campo
Escuela en el Campo 195, 196; see also Escuela al Campo
El Estadio Vicente Calderón 200
Estrada Palma, Tomás 5
Ethiopia 202
European Union 198

Fairfax, Virginia 103
Federal Bureau of Investigation (FBI) 16, 17, 18
Fernandez-Máscaró, Corina 180, **186**, **188**, 213
Fernandez-Máscaró, Dr. Guillermo 180
Fernandez-Máscaró, Raul 180, **186**
"Fidel, esta es tu casa" 41
Fidelista 25, 117, 185
Finca Betia 157
Flagami Elementary School 31, 60, 61
The Flintstones 44
Florida Capitol Rotunda 35
Florida City 7, 123
Florida Governor's Mansion 35
Florida Hispanic Artist of the Year 35
Florida International University (FIU) 34, 136, 214

Florida Power and Light Company (FPL) 33, 34,
El Floridita 110
Fort Bliss, Texas 81
Fort Jackson, South Carolina 81
Fort Knox, Kentucky 32
Fountain of Youth 65, 66
Franco, Generalisimo Francisco 198
free-hand calligraphy 68
Freedom Flights 12
Freedom Tower, Miami 177
Fuerza Aérea Rebelde 24

Garcia Line 158
Girón, Gilberto 176
Glidden Paints 98
Gonzalez, Eduardo "Eddie" 86
Gonzalez, Elian 17
Gonzalez, Fr. Pastor 76
Gonzalez Corzo, Rogelio 173
Gonzalez Vigoa, Carmen 114
Goodyear Blimp 56
Goya, Madrid 198
Granma 139
Grau, Polita 132
guajiro 8
Guanabacoa, Cuba 92, 93
Guanito 10
Guantánamo, Cuba 73, 74, 75, 76, 77, 81, 84, 213
Guantánamo Bay (U.S. Naval Base) 77, 78, 86, 213
Guatemala 157, 158
Guaso River 78
Guayabera 16, 108
Guevara, Ernesto "Che" 15, 75, 120, 140, 155, 179
Güines, Cuba 172, 174, *175*
Guirado, Nicky 84
gusanos 11, 121, 171, 195
Gutierrez, Katalina Marie 209
Gutierrez, Viktor Xavier 209

Habana Vieja 25, 109
Harris, Eddy 15
Havana Harbor 26, *50*
Heisinger, Antonio 180–*181*
Heisinger, Freda 180–181
Heisinger, Waltraub 180
Hialeah, Florida 14, 15, 19, 60, 134, 136, 177
Hispanic American Family of the Year Foundation 107
Hispanic American Police Command Officers Association 86
Hispanic Police Officers Association 86
Holguín, Cuba 74, 75
Homerlein, Rodolfo 115, 116, *118*
Homerlein, Rudy 115, *118*, *128*, 130, 131
Homestead, Florida *72*, 202
The Honeymooners 44
Hotel Leamington 146

Hotel Nacional 19
USS *Houston* 158
Huelga 140

Immaculata Academy 148, 213
Independence, Missouri 185, 213
Instituto #1 de la Segunda Enseñanza 93
El Instituto San Isidro 199, *200*
Integrado Militar Osvaldo Sanchez 176
La Internacional 122, 194
Inventory (Inventoria) 167, 169, 170, 185, 193
Iraq 59
Isla de Pinos (Isla de Juventud) 25, 49, 52; see also Isle of Pines
Isle of Pines 15, 49

Jai Alai, Miami 129, 132
JMTrax Base 157
José Martí International Airport 153, 197
Jovellanos, Cuba 160
Juicio de los Pilotos 23

Kangaroo Court 44, 132
Kansas City, Missouri 181, 182, 185, 187
Kennedy, John F. 31, 32, 55, 58, 59, 62, 75
Kennedy-Krushchev Pact 162
Key West, Florida 5, 14, 27, 106, 144, 146, 147, 148, 205, 207
Killian Senior High School 202
Kiwanis of Little Havana 177

Las Piedras, Puerto Rico 149
Las Villas Province 138, 139, 165, 213
LaSalle Catholic School 116, 119, 148
Latifundistas 142
Lawrence Welk Show 44
Lawton, Cuba 169
Lecuona, Ernesto 182
Lestonnac Academy 140, 213
Little Havana (La Pequeña Havana) 56, 57, 58, 60, *162*, 177
Lledo, Liam Konrad 209
Lopez Grille, Luis 183
Lopez Grille, Nilda 183
Los Angeles, California 42, 187
Los Palacios, Cuba 172
Lutgerio Pena, Felix 23
Luyanó, Cuba 114, *119*
Lynn University *136*, 213, 215

Machadato 5
Machado, Gerardo 180
Madrid, Spain 12, *13*, 198, 199, *200*, 214
Malecón 110
mambí 9
El Mambí 166
Manzanares River 200
Mariel Boatlift 205
Marielitos 11
Marist Brothers Catholic School 74
Martí, Josée 175, 176, 197

Martin, Josefina 199
Martinez-Arocha, Esteban 173
Martinez-Brito, Caridad 172, *178*
Mary Immaculate Catholic School 144
Mary Karlanne, Sister 186
Mary Paula, Sister 186
Máscaró, Raul *186*
Masferrer, Rolando "El Tigre" 16
"Me abstengo a declarer" 161
Medina, Daniel 63
Medina, Gladys 37, 62, *70, 71, 72*
Medina, Onuence 63
Mediterranean Sea 202, 204, 206
Mella, Diego, Jr. 88
Mella, Diego Luis 52, 73, *77, 87, 89*, 213
Mella, Lourdes 88
Mella, Monica 88
Mella Barrios, Jose 89
Mella Monterroso, Jose 89
Melrose 132
Merrill Lynch, Pierce, Fenner and Smith 82
Meurice, Fr. Pedro 76
Miami, Florida *61, 71*, 85, *87*, 128, *162*, 168, 200
Miami-Dade College 33, 87, 177
Miami-Dade Police Department 17, 38, 43, 48, 85, 86, *135*, 136, 137, 177, 204, 207, 209, 214
Miami Herald 156
Miami High School 81
Miami International Airport 14, 28, 62, 123, 157, 171, 177, 200
Miami Lakes, Florida 42, 43
Miami Springs, Florida 131, 132
Miami Springs Senior High School 136
Michel Yabor, Antonio 23
Milián, Emilio 16
miliciano 55, 122
Minas de Matahambre 11
Ministry of the Interior Secret Police (G-2) 77
Minneapolis, Minnesota 187
Mitchell, Mitch (colonel, U.S. Army, Ret.) 88
mojito 19
Montura Ranch 51
More, Benny 19
Morón, Cuba 90, 92, 95, *96*, 97, *98*, 101, *102*, 103

Napoleonic Code 187
National Association of Counties 86
National Defense University 87
National Strategic Gaming Center 87
Nestle USA 187
New Jersey State Police Academy at Sea Girt 83
New York City 62, 82, 103, 104, *106*, 148, 198
Newark, New Jersey 83
Niagara Falls 62
Nochebuena 138
"Nos Jodimos" 29

Nueva Cocina 187, *188*
Nuñez, Beatriz (Betty Marsenison) 33, 63, *70*
Nuñez, Cristina (Crissy Ravelo) 33, 63, *70*
Nuñez, Eloy, Jr. *37, 47, 48, 61, 70*
Nuñez, Eloy, Sr. *70, 72*
Nuñez, Gladys (Gladys Medina) 37, 62 *70, 71, 72*
Nuñez, Luis 22, *70*
Nuñez, Maria Elena *70, 72*
Nuñez (Solis), Mirta 33, 38, 63, *70, 138, 150, 151, 152*, 213; *see also* Solis, Mirta
Nuñez, Pilar "Pili" 39, 42, *50*, 51, 54, 55, 59, 62, *63, 70, 72*
Nuñez, Susana (Suzy Fryman) *29*, 63, *70*
Nuñez-Pinacho, Pilar *35, 37*, 38, *41*, 45, *50, 53, 70, 72, 150*

Ocean City, New Jersey 106
O'Farrill, Albertina 132, 133
O'Farrill, Luis "El Nene" 24
The Old Man and the Sea 52
Oliva, Erneido 157
Operation Eagle Claw 206
Operation Pedro Pan 132; *see also* Pedro Pan
Orange Bowl Stadium, Miami 31, 53, 55, 58, 177
Oriente Province 74, 76, 100, 139, 165, 180

Palenque, Cuba 97
Pan American World Airways 139
paredón 23
Paris Treaty 5
El Parque del Retiro 198
party line 57
The Patana 223
Pearl of the Antilles 90
Pecuch, Barbara 104
Pecuch, John 104
Pecuch, Mary Beth 104
Pecuch, Rita 104
Pedro Pan 7, 119, 123, 124, 132, 184, 215
Perez, Arsenio 191
Perez, Herminio 191
Perez, Ildelfonzo 191
Perez, Katrina, Marie 207
Perez, Kristopher Michael 207
Perez, Ofelia 206, *207*
Perez, Omar Eduardo 190, 196
Perez-Clausel, Commandante 172, 173
Perez-Sabatier, Francisco (Frank) 190, *191, 201, 203, 207*
Persian Gulf 205, 206, 207
Philadelphia, Pennsylvania 84, 105
Picolo's Club 73
Pina, Cuba 92, 93, 95
Pinacho, Carmina
Pinacho, Elizabeth
Pinacho, Luis
Pinar del Rio 6, 10, *15*, 114, 172, 190, 214
Pionero 194
Plan Fidel 164

Platt Amendment 5
Playa Girón 157, 158, 159, 160, 163
Playa Larga 157, 158, 159, 163
Plaza de Armas 110
Plaza de San Francisco 109
Polk County, Florida 137
Popeye the Sailorman 48
Preciado, Jose 28, 30
Previsora Latino Americana **94**, **95**
El Principe Fortress 161
Puerto Cabezas, Nicaragua 158
Puerto Rico Police Department 88
El Pura 145

Queens, New York 62
El Quemado 95, 96
quinces 7

Radio Mambi 106
Radio Morón 102
Ramos-Ramos, Maria 97, 105
Rancho Bolleros Airport 153
Raritan, New Jersey 105
ration booklet 111
Reagan, Pres. Ronald 206
rebeldes 74
Red Sea 206
Red Skelton Show 44
Retouleo Air Base 157
Rio Piedras, Puerto Rico 149
Rivero, Felipe 161
Rodriguez, Carlos Rafael 161
Rodriguez, Kathy 17
Rodriguez, Orquidea 17, **20**
Rodriguez, Ryan 17
Rodriguez-San Gil, Bonifacio 97, **98**, **99**, 101, 102, **105**
Rosemarie, Sister 147
Rota, Spain 206
Royal Caribbean Cruises 109

Sabatier, Berto 196
Sabatier, Hilda 200
Sabatier, Ismael 198
Sabatier-Suarez, Nelida 190
St. Augustine, Florida 64, 65
St. Brendan's Church
Saint Dominic Catholic Church 33
St. Mary's Catholic School 186, 187
San Basilio El Magno Seminary 76
San Roman, Jose "Pepe" 159
Sandino, Cuba 10
Santa Clara, Cuba 138, 139, 140, 141, 142, 144, 145, 147, 213
Santa Fe, Cuba 156
Santa Teresita 138, 142
Santana Estevez, Carlos 158
Santiago de Cuba 74, 75, 180, 181, 213
Seminary San Basilio el Magno 76
Servitec 22
Siboney Beach **182**

Sierra de los Órganos 155
Sierra Madre 157
Sierra Maestra 116, 139, 140
siesta 101, 102
Sinai Peninsula 206
Society of Jesus 76
Solis, Fernando 138, **150**
Solis, Maria Luisa 138, **150**
Solis-Mazarredo, Mirta Susana 138; *see also* Mirta Nuñez
Solis-Mazarredo, Raquel 138, 139, 147
Somalia 202
Somerville, New Jersey 82, 83, 84, 85, **104**, 105, 106
Sosa-Blanco, Jesus 155
South Beach 14
South Miami High School 61
South Miami Hospital 38
Southeast Florida Institute of Criminal Justice 85
Southampton, England 204
Spanish Civil War 74
Spanish "Concentración" 5
Statue of Liberty 62
Suarez, Ricky **135**
Suerio, Hugo 157
Suez Canal 205, 206
Superior School of Physical Education in Havana, Cuba 76
Survivors of Guantanamo Bay 86

Tapia Ruano, Alberto 173
tapiada cells 17
USS *Tarawa* 206
Terrorism Task Force 17
Theresa Cecilia, Sister 147
Tomequin 225
Toronto, Canada 62
Trece de Marzo (tugboat) 17
La Trinidad Primary School 92
Trompos 225
Turks and Caicos Islands 106
26th of July Movement 175
23 de Noviembre 74

UMAP 10, 11, 164, 225
Union City, New Jersey 82, 83
Union City Police Department 83, 84
U.S. Army 32, 36, 51, 62, 82, 81, 88, 157, 213
U.S. Army Air Corps Reconnaissance Squadron 67
U.S. Army 503rd Police Battalion, Fort Bragg, North Carolina 205
U.S. Army, Management Staff College 87, 213
U.S. Department of Defense 87, 88
U.S. 4th Army Judo Championship 82
U.S. Marines 51, 62, 80, 202, 203, 206, 207
U.S. Naval Intelligence 80
U.S. State Department 88
U.S. Virgin Islands 204

University of Havana 23, 26
University of Miami (UM) 34, 55, 87
University of Missouri 187
University of Villanueva 140

Valladares, Armando 49, 51
Varadero Beach, Cuba 18, *97*, 168, 177
Vazquez, Ofelia 133, *134*
Vazquez, Santiago "Neno" 133
Vazquez, Santiago "Sam" 133
Vazquez Vigoa, Maria Esperanza 133
Vedado 140
Velocipedo 115
Vendrell, Ann *91*, *97*, *102*, 103, *104*, *106*
Vendrell, Christopher Nicolas *112*, 214
Vendrell, David Ernesto 90, 91, 92, 108, 109, 110, 111, 112
Vendrell, Ernest G. 90, 92, *112*
Vendrell, Gemma *112*, 214
Vendrell, Joaquin *97*, 103, *104*, *105*
Vendrell, Lourdes *97*, 103, *104*, *105*
Vendrell (Rodriguez-Ramos) Oneida 95, *96*, *97*, *98*, *100*, 101, *102*, 103, *104*, *105*, *106*, *107*, 108
Vendrell-Pelegrin, Carmen 93, 103
Vendrell-Pelegrin, Ernesto Antonio *91*, *92*, *95*

Vendromax 99, *100*
Vero Beach, Florida 106
Vieques Island, Puerto Rico 204
Vietnam 17, 59, 83
Vietnam War 59
Vigo, Spain 184
Vigoa, Betty 118, 128
Vigoa, Jesus 114, 115, 116, 118, 119
Vigoa, Jesus "Jay" *118*, 119, *129*, 136, 137
Vigoa, Maria Esperanza (Vazquez) 133
Vigoa, Oscar, Sr. 134
Vigoa, William *129*, *135*
Vigoa Suarez, Michelle 127, *133*, 134, *135*
Vista Alegre 180, 181
"Viva Cristo Rey!" 15, 155
"Viva Cuba Libre!" 15, 155

Walker Park 14, 15
Walsh, Monsignor Bryan O. 123, 136
Warshaw and Associates 88
West Miami Junior High School 61, 66
Westchester 43, 56, 60, *61*, *63*, *70*, 139, 147
White House Blue Room Christmas Tree 35
White House Hotel 14

yo-yo fishing Line 45
Yom Kippur War 206

www.ingramcontent.com/pod-product-compliance
Ingram Content Group UK Ltd.
Pitfield, Milton Keynes, MK11 3LW, UK
UKHW032219260325
456756UK00013B/127